INCORRECT THOUGHTS

INCORRECT THOUGHTS

THOUGHTS

Notes on Our Wayward Culture

John Leo

Transaction Publishers
New Brunswick (U.S.A.) and London (U.K.)

For Alexandra

Library of Congress Catalog Number: 00-059926
ISBN: 0-7658-0038-1
Printed in the United States of America

Library of Congress Cataloging-in-Publication Data

Leo, John.
    Incorrect thoughts : notes on our wayward culture / John Leo.
        p. cm.
    "The essays in this book originally appeared in U.S. News and World Report"—T.p. verso.
    ISBN 0-7658-0038-1 (alk. paper)
        1. United States—Civilization—1970– 2. United States—Social conditions—1980– 3. United States—Politics and government—1989– 4. Political correctness—United States. 5. Political culture—United States. 6. Popular culture—United States.

E169.12 .L444 2000
973.92—dc21   00-059926

CONTENTS

Introduction

Like many people and most columnists, I keep a dignified, one-page biography on file and send it along when anyone in the media asks for it. I also have a slightly skewed, not-so-dignified version that goes to friends, and it includes a brief explanation of how I got to be a columnist.

The relevant section goes like this:

> Mr. Leo left Time magazine at the insistence of Mortimer B. Zuckerman, owner of *U.S. News & World Report* and a fellow player on Mr. Leo's summer softball team of aging and vaguely coordinated would-be athletes in Sag Harbor, Long Island.
>
> "Mr. Zuckerman explained at the time that he was tired of hearing Mr. Leo burst forth with interesting arguments at the dinner table, and then go back to *Time* and write stories which he woundingly characterized as "often unexciting." Mr. Zuckerman said he would prefer to reverse the process, with the interesting arguments appearing in *U.S. News*, even if it meant listening to lifeless stories over dinner at Mr. Leo's.
>
> This sounded right to Mr. Leo, who has striven ever since to be as excitement-free as possible in table conversation with Mr. Zuckerman, thereby to increase the likelihood that his columns would seem riveting by contrast. He has been at *U.S. News* 12 years now, and is under the impression that he likes it.

I do indeed like it, and I am grateful to Mort Zuckerman for his wisdom or cronyism or whatever it was that got me the job.

Once installed at *U.S. News*, I decided to write primarily about the culture and popular trends. In the column-writing business, prestige and money generally flow toward those who write from Washington about national politics. The obvious result is that two-thirds of journalists want to be Washington-based pundits and talking heads. But when I started my column, there wasn't a lot of generally available commentary about the trends that were shaping—and sometimes convulsing—the country. So I decided to take a weekly look at what was going on in education, law, advertising, television, the news media, language, and the various liberation movements. This was an extension of what I had been doing as a reporter, covering ideas and the behavioral sciences for *Time* magazine and the *New York Times*.

As the nineties wore on, more and more of my commentary concentrated on political correctness. Most of the media treated the rise of PC as if it were a collection of unimportant oddball anectlotes—the woman at Penn State was felt sexually harassed by a Goya painting, the Sarah Lawrence student brought up on charges of inappropriate laughter, the *Boston Globe* columnist who was suspended and fined for uttering a crude synonyrm for "henpecked" in a private newsroom conversation with another male. But PC was actually a coherent social movement sweeping steadily through the colleges, the courts, the media, the feminist movement, and the arts world.

The goals of the movement were traditional goals of the left—equality, inclusion, liberation, racial justice—but the tactics were often less noble and the contempt for tradition, standards, and Western culture grew by the year. The movement developed a taste for censorship and coercion. Speech codes and anti-harassment policies were used as weapons to silence and intimidate opponents. Speakers were shouted down and whole editions of college newpapers were stolen to keep students from reading the arguments of conservatives and moderates.

The rise of the PC movement—what humorist Fran Liebowitz calls "the religious left"—helped give the nineties their odd character. Politically, the country was becoming ever more conservative, but culturally, it was heaving just as hard to the left, so conflict was likely to erupt at any time.

Some other stray thoughts about the pieces collected here. Columnists have to decide how they want to sound. Various famous ones have chosen to come across as erudite, polemical, debonair, or incredibly well-connected. I've tried to sound conversational, as if I were talking to a friend about a subject that interests us both. And if something funny occurs to me, I throw that in too, just as most of us would in ordinary conversation. People are allergic to pomposity these days, so it's best to avoid fancy effects and all words not used in the spoken language (Goodbye to "moreover," nonetheless," and "mutatis mutandis.")

Though syndicated to newspapers by Universal Press Syndicate, these columns mostly show that they were originally created for a magazine. If you opine for a newspaper, you are usually writing very quickly, in direct reaction to a breaking story, and you are usually limited to 500 or 600 words, Most magazine columns are longer and denser, and since they usually come in later than most other media commentary, they are likely to take a broader, long-term view. The good news about broader, long-term views is that they tend to have a longer shelf life than columns reacting to quickly forgotten breaking news. This means you can collect them in books two or three years later and still interest a lot of readers. At least my publisher says this is so. I hope it is.

PART ONE

MEDIA

THIS COLUMN ALMOST MATTERS

A familiar nonsense phrase—"it almost doesn't matter"—seems to be making a comeback. News stories say the budget deficit is so low that "it almost doesn't matter" whether it is eliminated. The phrase shows up in crime stories too, mostly to indicate that we shouldn't care whether or not a defendant is guilty. In the Melissa Drexler case, after a high school girl gave birth during a prom and was accused of killing the baby, an editorial in *USA Today* said that the girl's predicament was so wrenching that "it almost doesn't matter whether Drexler's baby was stillborn or murdered." Whatever.

As a rule, use of the "almost" phrase indicates that someone is in the process of selling you snake oil, so it is best to turn off your hearing aid quickly and check to see if your wallet is still there. In the budget case, the "almost" phrase translates as this: "we think the deficit doesn't count, and we wish to say so emphatically, but don't hold us to it." In the Drexler case it means: "don't bother us with facts; we are busy having some important emotions."

The two most famous perpetrations of things that allegedly don't seem to matter occurred in the 1980s. *Newsweek* made the mistake of paying big money for newly discovered diaries of Adolf Hitler, but the diaries turned out to be fake. The magazine ran long excerpts anyway, telling readers "Genuine or not, it almost doesn't matter in the end." This is believed to be the first time that any news organization announced that fake news is just about as good as real news.

The other triumph of the Eighties involved another hoax, Tawana Brawley's claim that she was kidnapped and raped by white law enforcement officers. Unwilling to give up on the story, the *Nation* ran an article claiming that "this faked crime" was useful in calling attention to the suffering of blacks, so "in cultural perspective, if not in fact, it doesn't matter whether the crime occurred or not." Though morally and intellectually bankrupt, this sort of nonthinking hovered around the Brawley case for years. People who knew very well she was lying invited her up on stage at rallies and university events as a major celebrity.

A computer search shows that the strategic use of the phrase is quite common. In New York, an official says "it almost doesn't matter" whether a controversial study of aircraft noise levels is correct because noise is obviously a problem anyway. In the *Washington Post*, an opinion piece about alleged injuries from indoor air pollution says: "In some respects, it doesn't matter whether the injuries are faked or not." In a sexual harassment case, a male executive is charged with sexist comments, but a plaintiff's lawyer says, "it almost doesn't matter what he really said because whatever it was...became the culture of the firm." A *Frontline* television report on the unearthing of repressed memories didn't use the magic words, but caught the "almost doesn't matter" mentality. A California therapist helped convince a patient that her parents had abused her. The patient sued her parents and the therapist told *Frontline*, "I don't care if it's true....What actually happened is irrelevant to me."

The recent case involving alleged racial slurs by Texaco executives displays the "almost" mentality in action. The *New York Times* reported that a secret tape recording showed the executives using a nasty racial epithet and referring to black employees as "black jelly beans at the bottom of the jar." The uproar and the damage to Texaco were so great that the company settled a long-standing racial discrimination suit for $176 million. But the *Times* was wrong. The nasty N-word in the transcript turned out to be a holiday reference to "St. Nicholas." The "black jelly bean" comment was innocent too. It referred to words and images supplied by a diversity trainer who was working with Texaco executives. The *Times* reporter who mishandled the story wrote a Sunday piece saying that the corrections "made little difference" to civil rights groups. They almost didn't matter to some news organizations too. Several kept on reporting the nonexistent Texaco slurs as real. Author Walter Olson wrote in the *American Spectator* that after plaintiffs dismissed the corrected transcript as much ado about nothing, "it didn't matter after all" whether the slurs had really been made. The story line—a racist company brought to heel—was so strong that the actual facts never penetrated the consciousness of the media or the public.

The report from the *San Jose Mercury News* about CIA involvement in the inner-city drug trade had similar results. Three prominent newspapers, the *New York Times*, the *Los Angeles Times* and the *Washington Post*, all investigated this report and concluded, as the *Times* said, that "scant proof" supports the allegations. The *Mercury News* backed off on the story too. But many black leaders believe "it almost doesn't matter" whether the conspiracy actually existed, according to the *New York Daily News*, because the story has already achieved wide acceptance in the black community.

The outcome was almost identical to the more celebrated Texaco case. When the accurate transcript revealed the nonexistence of the racial slurs reported by the *Times* the media was slow to acknowledge that a serious injustice had been done to Texaco and its executives. To make things worse, Assistant Attorney General Deval Patrick said, "it didn't matter in the end what words were on the tape." It did, of course.

"Almost doesn't matter" is a woeful appeal to feelings and story line over facts. It almost doesn't belong in almost anyone's vocabulary.

SCOTCH THE ADS? ABSOLUT-LY

It could be a put on, but *Adweek* magazine says liquor ads on television may be good for society. The magazine noted that the first booze ad shown on American TV in nearly fifty years celebrated fundamental American values. It was a Seagram commercial, placed on a station in Corpus Christi, Texas, and it featured two dogs.

One dog, labeled "obedience school graduate," carried a newspaper in its mouth. The other, carrying a bottle of Crown Royal, was labeled "valedictorian." *Adweek* said this positioned liquor as a reward for achievement and delayed gratification in a world sadly governed by instant gratification. Liquor ads flourished in the pre-60s culture of self-restraint, said *Adweek*, and the impact of televised liquor ads "could well be salutary."

Maybe. But it's possible to doubt that the rapid spread of self-restraint is what the distillers have in mind. The more likely long-term result is a set of psychologically clever ads aimed at young people and resulting in another upward tick or two each year in the death rate from drunk driving.

Adweek's odd commentary contains a germ of truth—one genre of liquor and beer advertising does indeed stress authority, hard work, and sons following the lead of fathers. Many scotch ads are filled with dogs, castles, and other emblems of tradition, the central message being "We know Scotch tastes like iodine, but your dad drank it and you should too." This lives on in Dewar's current "let's grow up and drink

Scotch" campaign, and a Chivas Regal ad in which a grown man actually wishes his father would tell him what to do more often.

But these are upscale magazine ads aimed at the well-off. Do not expect many dog and daddy ads once the booze industry gets revved up for the TV youth market and spots on *Seinfeld*. Instead we will see a lot of MTV imagery, Orwellian fantasies about sex and power, and Joe Camel-like appeals to the young.

The ad industry is very good at generating commercials that break down restraint and promote impulse. It's also important to know that the legal drug business (tobacco and alcohol) accumulates a lot of private psychological research, the better to know which of our buttons to push. The generic stuff appears in marketing magazines, but the really potent findings, which result in all those manipulative and coded ads, aren't made public. No psychologist on the take has yet come forward to blow the whistle, à la Jeffrey Weigand. But now that the Federal Trade Commission is issuing subpoenas in connection with TV alcohol advertising, it surely should try to get the closely guarded research behind many beer and liquor ads.

The general rule of thumb is: the more dangerous the product, the more coded the ads are likely to be. Newport cigarettes "Alive with pleasure" ads, for example, which seem much cleaned up nowadays, depended for years on coded themes of sexual hostility and violence running beneath all those merry scenes of outdoorsy couples at play. Among the egregious magazine ads for liquor, my favorite is the Bacardi Black "Taste of the Night" campaign with its unmissable theme of night and liquor as liberators of the real you (and your darker side) from the bonds of civilized society. Just what we need in this troubled culture—more promotion of everyone's darker side. The booze industry as Darth Vader.

When they dropped their self-imposed ban on TV ads, the distillers said they wouldn't target the young. We should be dubious. The liquor executives fear they won't be able to sell their brown drinks any more— bourbon, scotch, and brandy have not caught on among boomers or post-boomers. The trend is toward white drinks—vodka and gin—and sweet-tasting or healthy-looking drinks that disguise alcoholic content. That's why Miller Brewing is testing "alcopops," a malt-based drink that looks and tastes like lemonade. Anheuser-Busch isn't far behind. Alcopops have been successfully marketed in Britain and Australia with ads featuring lovable cartoon characters—a way of conceding that the young are indeed being targeted.

The distillers' argument about beer ads has more merit. They say a can of beer has about as much alcohol as a mixed drink, so either ban beer from TV or let liquor ads on. In fact, some conspiracy theorists think the distillers' real goal is to drive beer off TV. That's extremely unlikely. Beer is so entrenched in TV economics that it's hard to imagine the sort of social upheaval necessary to drive it away. But if beer and liquor ads are going to be on TV, the ads should be regulated in the public interest. Alcohol is a drug and we have a long tradition of regulating drug ads to protect the public. The makers of Rogaine or Prozac aren't permitted to say whatever they wish in ads. Why should the good-tasting narcotics be exempted?

The regulation might cover TV only—our most emotional medium and the one watched most closely by children. The regulating could curb appeals to children as well as devious psychological manipulation of adults along the lines of Bacardi's Darth Vader print ad.

We know that that the televising of liquor ads will promote accelerated consumption, with predictable increases in addiction and drunk driving. If we can't stop it, let's at least set some sensible rules that reflect the true social costs involved.

PRIME-TIME "GOTCHA" JOURNALISM

NBC's *Dateline* began a recent segment with this teasing, taunting introduction by Jane Pauley: "Good evening. Do you feel that everyone is after your job, and they just might have an unfair advantage? That people can criticize you and it's OK? Are you a white American male? In California, two men have taken up the cause of the beleaguered species."

The subject, of course, was affirmative action, and alert viewers immediately knew where this segment was going. Race and gender preferences are controversial, and honorable people can be found on both sides of the issue. But maybe not in *Dateline*'s opinion. The two opponents, who are trying to get the subject on the ballot in California, were portrayed as uninformed, fumbling, and perhaps deceptive members of a "beleaguered species."

The men, Tom Wood (who has a doctorate in philosophy) and Glynn Custred (a professor of anthropology), were allowed to say that they want what Martin Luther King, Jr., wanted—an open, colorblind America. Then NBC reporter Josh Mankiewicz came on like a prosecutor: "They are portrayed as 'genial scholars,' just two 'apolitical professors,' an image Wood and Custred have worked hard to maintain." But, he charged, Wood "is actually not a professor at all." Bingo! Without actually saying so, Mankiewicz left the impression that Wood is a liar. Wood, in fact, is not a professor, but says he never pretended to be one. Last week, when I asked Mankiewicz if he had any evidence of such pretense, he said no, but "Wood doesn't seem to correct newspapers that call him a professor."

On *Dateline*, Wood denied that he and Custred "are in any sense political animals." Then Mankiewicz cut in with another McCarthyite "gotcha," saying the two are actually "key figures" in the National Association of Scholars, a group that is "hardly apolitical" since it is "very critical of many aspects of higher education, including black and women's studies (and) sexual harassment policies..."

Senator Joe himself could not have phrased this better. It artfully left the impression that NAS is a sinister anti-woman, anti-black group. Given the ideological makeover of the modern campus, NAS is indeed largely conservative, but some members are liberals, many are Democrats, and a prominent Marxist, Eugene Genovese, sits on the board of advisers. It is surely politically involved with affirmative action. But it's apolitical in this sense: it isn't partisan, and deals only with campus issues, mostly defending academic freedom and a non-ideologized curriculum.

Mankiewicz insisted on trumping everything Wood and Custred said. Wood said Tulane University has faculty quotas. Mankiewicz said some people call it a quota system but the university says "there were absolutely never any quotas." Maybe not, but Tulane's complicated and arcane system of faculty set-asides (since modified) seemed designed to achieve the effect of quotas without looking like a suspect quota plan. "Call it an unstated quota system," Tulane Professor Paul Lewis told me.

Mankiewicz was annoyed that Wood and Custred couldn't say how many white men have lost jobs due to reverse discrimination. He noted that "when it comes to hard numbers...they come up empty-handed." But nobody has good statistics on this. Since a lot of reverse discrimination is legal under Title VII, many who are hurt by it never bother to file any complaints and thus don't get counted. Demanding accurate stats is like asking how many Irishmen lost jobs when the "No Irish Need Apply" signs went up in Boston and New York.

Wood says Mankiewicz asked the same questions over and over, perhaps to get the soundbite that would make him look the most foolish. Mankiewicz said it was because Wood kept being unresponsive and was hard to pin down.

Wood and Custred may not be the most polished, camera-ready guys in the world. And we all know that NBC has reporters who can run rings around academics. But why did NBC think this was worth doing? The national upsurge against affirmative action has little to do with these two men. Race and gender preferences are wildly unpopular from coast to coast. A *Washington Post*/Kaiser/Harvard poll last October showed that 68 percent of blacks, 86 percent of whites and 78 percent of Hispanics endorsed this statement: "Hiring, promotion and college admissions should be based strictly on merit and qualifications rather than on race or ethnicity." Instead of dealing with this upsurge, NBC thought it was a good idea to spend twenty minutes shooting two of the messengers.

The unconscious assumptions of the newsroom culture are surely part of the problem. It's almost inconceivable that NBC would try to eviscerate an environmentalist or a gay activist trying to get their initiatives on the ballot. But "beleaguered species" are fair game, because everyone in the newsroom already knows they are wrong.

Bernard Goldberg, the CBS correspondent, told me: "It was a hatchet job. They set out to demolish these two guys and ended up demolishing their own credibility. This is why people don't like or trust TV reporters. We swear we have no agenda and we go out and produce something like this."

On the next fifty panel discussions of media bias, I hope someone remembers to bring up this sorry program.

WHY RUIN A GOOD STORY?

Whenever friends complain about deep bias in the media, my usual strategy is to sigh, then try to explain the difference between bias and the framing of issues in the newsroom culture.

The Ellen DeGeneres story is a good example. This was a mildly tedious story of a likeable woman in a harmless sitcom, coming out of the closet slowly for six months to get some ratings and then having her ratings-week decision vastly overplayed because the media felt they had been stuck much too long in a no-news news cycle.

Nobody should have been surprised by the way the story was played. Almost without exception, the media tend to look at stories about gays and lesbians through the familiar lens of the black struggle for civil rights. Whatever the actual news, these narratives are told in terms of bias, exclusion, tolerance, and rights. So the Ellen story was told as a social breakthrough against prejudice, often with reference to other firsts—the first black to get a TV series, the first frank references to sex, and so on.

This is certainly a valid narrative line. Bias and the denial of rights are real, and straights have a lot to answer for in their historic cruelty toward gays. But rights-and-bias is only one way of framing a broad, continuing, and confusing story.

In fact, most Americans have a live-and-let-live attitude toward gays, but they don't frame the story the way the newsroom does. They are mostly concerned with questions of substance, all centering on the question of what homosexuality is (or what homosexualities are) and what the social impact is likely to be as we glide rather casually from social tolerance to social approval.

Polls show a large majority have reservations and conflicted feelings, particularly when it comes to gay marriage and teaching in the schools that amounts to an endorsement of homosexuality. In the newsroom, of course, all this is viewed as nonsense and homophobia. The upshot is that because of newsroom framing, the real national conversation on homosexuality is not really being reported. It is off the table because of the narrow framing of the story in terms of prejudice.

Having worked in many newsrooms, I can tell you that most reporters are honest and try hard to be fair, but they are keenly aware of the conventional narrative line on most controversial and recurring stories. They know how such stories are expected to be handled and how newsroom rewards and punishments tend to follow certain kinds of treatment. In his 1990 *Los Angeles Times* series on abortion coverage, David Shaw explained how reporters could expect a challenge from colleagues when they tapped out a story that gave even indirect aid and comfort to anti-abortion forces.

"Angry white male" stories tend to lump any opposition to affirmative action to social intolerance, backlash, and personal fears. Here's the opening section of a segment last year on NBC's *Dateline* dealing with the two academics who got California's Proposition 209 on the ballot: "Do you think that everyone is after your job...that people can criticize you and it's ok? Are you a white American male...the beleaguered species." Intended to be jaunty and cute, the opening was simply snide. All it really showed is that the people at *Dateline* had difficulty imagining any principled opposition to race and gender preferences, possibly because such opposition is unknown on the *Dateline* staff.

A subset of the conventional angry-white-male story is the story linking conservatives to loony extremists, and linking every available disaster to angry-white militiamen. Here's how the Associated Press began an early and misguided story on the bombing at the Atlanta Olympics: "The bomber who brought terror to the Olympics was a white male, may not have worked alone and may have shared militia groups' hatred of international organizations." Could be. Or it might been a miffed Tibetan U.N. employee who is related to the Unabomer and several violent Weatherpeople left over from the 1960s.

The church-burning story is a classic example of media framing so strong that it can ward off even a sturdy set of actual facts. Once the story was seen as a startling new epidemic of classic racial hatred, it was very difficult for the media to drop this powerful narrative line, even though information piled up very quickly showing that the story was exaggerated to the point of being a hoax. Robert Lichter, the media critic, points to the odd fact that even after several prominent newspapers and magazines demolished the original story line, most of the media kept on reporting the debunked epidemic as if it were true.

The same thing happened with the dramatic reports of racial slurs in taped conversations of Texaco executives. Even after the *New York Times* ran a big story admitting that these "slurs" were based on a mistaken transcript, the media kept referring to the slurs as real. One network news show was still talking about Texaco "slurs" five weeks after the *Times'* clarification (i.e., retraction). Texaco, a hard company to love, has a terrible record on minority hiring. So the story line had a powerful pull, even though it wasn't true. That's the way it goes when reporters, mostly unconsciously, report their feelings about the news rather than telling us the news itself.

MORE GUESTS WHO GUESS

After the Jonesboro shootings, I gave an unsuccessful drive-time interview to a St. Louis radio talk show. The co-hosts were professional, polite, and single-minded. They seemed to think that gun control was the obvious main topic of the day. When I strayed to talk about something else, they gently steered me back to guns and the gun culture.

Well, yes, I said, gun control is important, but you can kill people a lot of ways. One of the pubescent killers had been flashing a knife the day before—he might just as well have slaughtered four or five class-mates with a machete. Would we then be talking about machete culture?

This was a "yes, but" point, and yes-buts do not play well on talk shows. The only thing worse in the modern radio interview is to ramble on about "many factors." "There are many other factors," I said, causing many mid-western drivers to grope for the dial on their car radios. For the benefit of any remaining listeners, I talked about the movement to teach adolescents impulse control so they won't go directly from anger to violence. These programs are valuable. Teaching the habit of restraint in a culture that seems overly devoted to impulse is important work. But in the middle of this argument, I realized it had almost nothing to do with Jonesboro. The killings there were clearly premeditated and cold-blooded, not the result of sudden unchecked rage.

Most of the avalanche of analysis seemed as unsatisfactory as my own. Why did the Jonesboro massacre happen? Nobody seemed to have much of a clue. Details were sketchy, but everyone jumped in anyway, offering standard responses. Guns, television violence, and the popular culture in general all drew early and predictable abuse. One of the Jonesboro boys admired gangs, rap music, and Beavis and Butthead, thus opening three other familiar lines of analysis. Some commentators seemed eager to blame parents or the Jonesboro school, but the school quickly reported that the two boys had clean records and reporters turned up no evidence of bad parenting. A reporter for a major newspaper couldn't resist applying her gender theories: the boys may have been influenced by the "many men" who stalk or kill their wives and girlfriends.

The "Southern culture" theory seemed to blanket TV coverage for an hour or two, then play itself out. Researchers report that homicides associated with a personal grievance are four times more common in the south than in the mid-west. In response, southern politicians tended to argue that violence is a product of the national culture (translation: we are tired of hearing that violence is a southern problem). Black commentators tended to point out that all peoples and regions can produce hideous violence (translation: we are tired of hearing that this is a black problem). Marion Wright Edelman was sure that the federal government needed to spend billions more on children.

Geoffrey Canada, a child expert speaking on ABC's *Good Morning America*, said that children's access to guns "turns this issue from a 13-year-old and 11-year-old who have a chip on their shoulder...into murderers." Children's access to guns makes me nervous too, but so do commentators who speak as though guns themselves turn innocents into killers. In the south and west, hundreds of thousands of children grow up hunting with rifles and never shoot anybody. The enormous media coverage of Jonesboro surely underlined how rare an event it was.

Many talking heads spoke about the phenomenon of school violence, but other analysts pointed out that school violence is rare and decreasing. Ninety percent of American schools report no serious violence at all. One said that the Los Angeles Unified School district has 600,000 students and hasn't had a homicide since 1995.

Perhaps inevitably, some of the commentary made the shooters seem like helpless victims of an irresistible popular culture. Arkansas Governor Mike Huckabee said he wasn't sure "we could expect a whole lot else in a culture where these children are exposed to tens of thousands of murders on television and in movies." No round-up of instant wisdom is complete without a bit of long-distance psychological analysis, so a University of Kentucky researcher weighed in with a syndrome known as "fledgling psychopathy," the result of hyperactivity interacting with an emotional disorder, expressing itself in fighting, cruelty, and truancy.

Does all this instant opining have redeeming social value? Alas, the modern media are set up for the rapid collection of emphatic guesses on the causes of disturbing news. Yes, it's fair to criticize the popular culture for depicting violence as cool, effective, and emotionally satisfying. But almost automatically, the media now turn tragedies into trends, individual acts into pop symbols of decline. We no longer think it's unusual for far-off commentators to explain the actions of children they never met, or even heard of a week ago. Some of us think this is social commentary. The rest of us think it's blather.

Boyz to (Marlboro) Men

Marshall Blonsky mentioned the other day that an ad agency once offered him $25,000 for two weeks work on a tobacco account. Blonsky, a professor at New York University, is an expert on semiotics, the study of signs, symbols, and other non-verbal communication. The agency wanted him to do a psychological profile of all existing American cigarette brands and their ads, "a sort of Human Genome project" of the mental world created by Big Tobacco. The idea was to find psychological space for a new brand.

Blonsky said no, but his story is a reminder of how hard the tobacco companies work on depth psychology. This extends to the ritual cues of smoking, right down to the satisfaction a smoker gets from crunching an empty cigarette pack and hearing the crinkle of cellophane.

Cigarette packs and their ads bristle with "visual rhetoric," a term used by playwright Anne Deveare Smith to express the idea that words are not nearly as persuasive these days as images that work on us without any argument at all. Many Newport ads are filled with coded images of sexual combat and attempts by females to eclipse the dominant males, all buried in happy scenes of outdoorsy horseplay. A decade or so ago, one brand experimented with ads showing a lot of white lines. They looked like lines of cocaine, apparently an attempt to link smoking with snorting and hipness.

Blonsky has written about Reagan-era ads for Merit filled with military imagery, thus associating the brand with the military build-up and Morning in America. Military imagery in smoking is an old story. The famous Marlboro chevron is a military insignia. Both Marlboro, named for a famous general, and the former best-seller, Pall Mall, carry the military mottoes of conquering Roman emperors on every pack. One analyst thinks the Marlboro chevron hard pack subconsciously functions as a medal, which the smoker "pins on" himself each time he stuffs it in his shirt pocket.

Maybe, maybe not. But don't underestimate the industry's commitment to finding powerful non-verbal hooks, particularly for young beginning smokers. A lot of psychologists are reportedly on the payroll, and rumor has it that they include child psychologists, too.

The most powerful hook so far is the Marlboro man, which the Leo Burnett agency more or less stumbled upon in the fifties while working on a series of images of blue-collar males. Philip Morris's research showed that young people in search of an identity were starting to smoke to declare their independence from their parents. The idea was to harness a yearning for freedom and rebellion without making the message too anti-social. (The early Marlboro man had tattoos, a much stronger anti-social symbol then than now.)

A lot of work has gone into aping Marlboro's success—70 percent of beginning white male smokers pick Marlboro. The pre-Joe Camel ads for Camel featured a lone rugged male, clearly a Marlboro imitator. Canada's Imperial Tobacco Limited mocked this Camel man because he "does not show feelings, excludes women and isn't concerned about society." However, Imperial agreed with the selling theme of "nobody to interfere, no boss/parents."

Rugged machismo is apparently not the key to the success of Marlboro's cowboy. The "secret" RJR report, now available on the Web, says young Marlboro smokers are actually less interested in traditional, rugged masculinity than are smokers of other brands. The Marlboro success apparently comes from the sense of quiet rebellion against constraints and rules, and from a sense of belonging (to the tribe of Marlboro smokers). The RJR reports says it could be that "as social pressures tend to isolate younger adult smokers from their nonsmoking peers, they have an increased need to identify with their smoking peers, to smoke the "belonging" brand.

Here we have arrived at the central problem of the anti-smoking campaign. The cigarette companies are selling a sense of belonging and psychological self-control in a society in which nobody seems to belong any more, except tribally by skin color or gender. The anti-smoking lobby is selling the rational health findings of an advanced technological society and the high probability of a longer lifetime, which the young translate as a chance to die at age 81 instead of 77.

Worse, the cigarette companies are selling rule-breaking and freedom from adult authority, which the anti-smoking adult world (saturated with the anti-rule message itself) thinks it can combat by exercising its authority and creating more rules and laws.

My friend Alan Brody, an anti-smoking ad executive, argues that the cigarette companies have long understood that their real role in America is to address—and exploit—the psychological struggles of teenagers. He thinks the companies have shaped smoking as a powerful adult initiation ritual in a society that doesn't have one, and taken the side of the young against the adult message of "Just say no." Brody wants to set aside some of the money from the proposed tobacco settlement to address coming-of-age problems and to match some of the tobacco industry's spending on psychological research. Good idea. If it happens, maybe the fight against the cigarette companies won't be such a terrible mismatch.

THE SELLING OF REBELLION

Most TV viewers turn off their brains when the commercials come on. But it's worth paying attention. Some of the worst cultural propaganda is jammed into those 60-second and 30-second spots.

Consider the recent ad for the Isuzu Rodeo. A grotesque giant in a business suit stomps into a beautiful field, startling a deer and jamming skyscrapers, factories, and signs into the ground. (I get it: nature is good; civilization and business are bad.) One of the giant's signs says, "Obey," but the narrator says, "The world has boundaries. Ignore them." Trying to trample the Rodeo, the hapless giant trips over his own fence. The Isuzu zips past him and topples a huge sign that says "Rules."

Presumably we are meant to react to this ad with a wink and a nudge, because the message is unusually flatfooted and self-satirical. After all, Isuzus are not manufactured in serene fields by adorable lower mammals. The maddened giant makes them in his factories. He also hires hip adwriters and stuffs them in his skyscrapers, forcing them to write drivel all day, when they really should be working on novels and frolicking with deer.

But the central message here is very serious and strongly anti-social: we should all rebel against authority, social order, propriety, and rules of any kind. "Obey" and "rules" are bad. Breaking rules, with or without your Isuzu, is good. Automakers have been pushing this idea in various ways since "The Dodge Rebellion" of the mid-1960s. Isuzu has worked the theme hard, including a TV ad showing a bald and repressive grade-school teacher barking at children to "stay within the lines" while coloring pictures, because "the lines are our friends."

A great many advertisers now routinely appeal to the so-called "postmodern" sensibility, which is heavy on irony (wink, nudge) and attuned to the message that rules, boundaries, standards, and authorities are either gone or should be gone. Foster Grant sunglasses has used the "no limits" refrain. So have Prince Matchabelli perfume ("Life without limits"), *Showtime* TV (its "No Limits" campaign) and AT&T's Olympics ads in 1996 ("Imagine a world without limits"). "No Limits" is an outdoor adventure company and "No Limit" is a successful rap record label. Even the U.S. Army used the theme in a TV recruitment ad. "When I'm in this uniform I know no limits," says a soldier—a scary thought if you remember Lieutenant Calley in Vietnam or the Serbian army today.

Among the ads that have used "no boundaries" almost as a mantra are Ralph Lauren's Safari, Johnny Walker scotch ("It's not trespassing when you cross your own boundaries"), Merrill Lynch ("To know no boundaries"), and the movie *The English Patient* ("In love there are no boundaries").

Some "no boundaries" ads are legitimate—the Internet and financial markets, after all, aim at crossing or erasing old boundaries. The anti-social message is clearer in most of the "no rules" and "anti-rules" ads, starting with Burger King's "Sometimes you gotta break the rules." These include Outback steakhouses ("No rules. Just right"), Don Q rum ("break all the rules"), the theatrical troupe De La Guarda ("no rules"), Nieman Marcus ("No rules here"), Columbia House music club ("We broke the rules"), *Comedy Central* ("See comedy that breaks the rules"), Red Kamel cigarettes ("This baby don't play by the rules"), and even Woolite (wool used to be associated with decorum, but now "All the rules have changed," an ad says under a photo of a young woman groping or being groped by two guys). "No rules" also turns up as the name of a book and a CD and a tag line for an NFL video game ("no refs, no rules, no mercy"). The message is everywhere—"the rules are for breaking," says a Spice Girls lyric.

What is this all about? Why is the ad industry working so hard to use rule-breaking as a way of selling cars, steaks, and Woolite? In his book *The Conquest of Cool*, Thomas Frank points to the sixties' counterculture. He says it has become "a more or less permanent part of the American scene, a symbolic and musical language for the endless cycles of rebellion and transgression that make up so much of our mass culture...rebellion is both the high- and mass-cultural motif of the age: order is its great bogeyman."

The pollster-analysts at Yankelovich Partners, Inc. have a different view. In their book, *Rocking the Ages: The Yankelovich Report on Generational Marketing*, J. Walker Smith and Ann Clurman say that rule-breaking is simply a hallmark of the Baby Boom generation: "Boomers have always broken the rules....The drugs, sex and rock 'n roll of the sixties and seventies only foreshadowed the really radical rule-breaking to come in the consumer marketplace of the eighties and nineties."

This may pass—Smith says the post-Boomers of Generation X are much more likely to embrace traditional standards than Boomers were at the same age. On the other hand, maybe it won't. Pop culture is dominated by in-your-face transgression now and the damage is severe. The peculiar thing is that so much of the rule-breaking propaganda is funded by businessmen who say they hate it, but can't resist promoting it in ads as a way of pushing their products. Isuzu, please come to your senses.

NOTHING BUT THE TRUTH?

The cases of Stephen Glass and Patricia Smith are being lumped together—two journalists caught lying repeatedly by their employers, the *New Republic* and the *Boston Globe*.

But each represents a different problem for American journalism, already struggling with credibility ratings somewhere between those of used car dealers and serial killers.

Glass is an example of what can happen because of the Washington buzz factor. The *New Republic* found that he had fabricated all or part of at least 23 of 41 articles he wrote for the magazine in the past two and a half years. The twenty-something Glass made a name for himself quickly, partly because of his output (huge) but mostly because of the startling stories he turned up that nobody else seemed to have. One of the most memorable was the tale of drunken young conservatives humiliating a homely woman at a Washington hotel.

Ten or fifteen years ago the pages of the *New Republic* were filled with sober reports or analyses of social problems by earnest scholars and journalists. Geraldo-ized articles were unknown. But this is the age of celebrity TV journalists who are better known than most of the politicians they cover. The *New Republic* is a serious magazine, but it's also a prime platform from which to launch a Washington celebrity career. But you have to create buzz as quickly as possible, and one way to do it is to pump up your material, or, as Glass did, just make it up.

Glass is an extreme case. He filled notebooks with phantom interviews and even created an Internet web-site to document one of his fictional stories. The major lesson is that Washington journalism has changed. In the old days, political magazines just assumed that their writers were basically honest. But they can't do that any longer. The rewards for cutting corners are just too great.

Patricia Smith, 43, who wrote a popular twice-weekly metro column for the *Boston Globe*, was asked to resign after admitting that she made up parts of four recent columns. A finalist for last year's Pulitzer Prize for commentary, Smith told dramatic and emotional stories of everyday life in the Boston area. She admitted making up almost entirely a column about "Claire," a woman dying of cancer. In addition, she created a woman named Dorothy Gibson in a column about a little girl's celebration of Easter, and a man named Jim Burke, a worker putting up barricades at the Boston Marathon.

Like Glass, Smith wanted her writing to come across as exciting. "I wanted the pieces to jolt," she wrote in her apology to readers, admitting that she sometimes quoted non-existent people "to create the desired impact or slam home a salient point."

The *Globe* ombudsman, Jack Thomas, took a sour view of this explanation. He wrote: "Although Smith's column of apology was written with her customary flair, she continued to compromise the truth. Making up an entire column of fictitious people and fictitious quotations is not, as she would have us believe, slamming home a point. It's lying."

But Smith apparently doesn't think of it as lying. She wrote: "I will survive this knowing that the heart of my columns was honest and heartfelt." This is a somewhat ambiguous sentence, but it seems to be a claim that emotional truth (the stuff of fiction) justifies or excuses fictional techniques in a column. One media critic, Tom Rosenstiel of the Project for Excellence in Journalism, read Smith's statement that way. "You get the sense reading her apology that she has the mentality of an artist who's talking about truth with a capital T," he said. " But journalism is fundamentally about nonfiction."

What makes this interesting is that much journalism today has turned away from the old ideal of objectivity in reporting. Many reporters accept the currently fashionable postmodern theory that objective knowledge of any sort is a myth. (A couple of years ago, I gave a speech at a convention of young journalists, and when I talked about the ideal of objectivity, a mildly exasperated rumble of dissent swept through the room.)

The postmodernists put quotation marks around words like "reality," and push their disciples to embrace the principle of subjectivity. One of the teachings is that there is no fixed history—history is created in the minds of historians. It is what historians choose to make of the past. Journalism often seems to come under this heading too. Since objectivity has been declared a myth, journalism is inherently a subjective exercise in which the feelings and will of the journalist function to create the truth of what has just occurred.

"Throughout our culture, the critic Michiko Kakutani writes, "the old notions of "truth" and "knowledge" are in danger of being replaced by the new ones of "opinion," "perception," and "credibility." At the least, we are living in a docudrama culture in which the techniques of fiction and nonfiction are beginning to blur. That's why Smith's defense of her emotional honesty is more alarming than the straightforward faking of Stephen Glass.

THE JOYS OF COVERING PRESS RELEASES

The new survey on abortion by the Alan Guttmacher Institute is a good example of how statistics rarely reach us these days without spin or heavy message. The press release for the survey is headlined "Abortion common among all women"; then, in slightly smaller letters, it adds, "even those thought to oppose abortion." Right below, after a bland opening item, the release says that Catholic women have an abortion rate 29 percent higher than Protestant women, while one fifth of women having abortions are born-again or evangelical Christians.

The Guttmacher Institute, which is strongly in favor of abortion rights, was clearly inviting reporters to write a "Gotcha!" story about hypocrisy among women in the religious groups most opposed to abortion. Sure enough, the story appeared that way last week in the *New York Post*("Abortion-survey Shocker") and in many other newspapers.

The actual survey, however, tells a different story. On a scale showing subgroup abortion rates (with black and Hispanic women separated out to form their own subgroups), it turns out that women who say they are Catholic have an age-adjusted abortion rate of 0.63 based on an index arbitrarily set at 1.0. In other words, they have abortions at a rate 37 percent lower than average.

Protestants at 0.49 are even lower (29 percent lower than Catholics, as the press release tells us in its backhanded way). Born-again and evangelical Christians, mentioned high up in the press release for heavy abortion use, have the lowest abortion rate of all subgroups; it stands at 0.4, meaning that their rate is 60 percent below average. These women account for 18 percent of abortions (hence, the one in five that's mentioned in the press release), but they represent 46 percent of all American women ages eighteen to forty-four.

When black and Hispanic women are factored back in by religion, rates rise, and the Catholic rate becomes 1.01, or right at the average, and the Protestant rate emerges as 0.69. But even so, the study shows that religious women have abortions at one fourth the rate of nonreligious women.

Sloppy reporting. The study itself seems fair and professional. But advocacy groups have caught on to the fact that a lot of reporters rarely go beyond the release summary to look at the actual report. So the release is often the news we get. And in this release, the Guttmacher staff couldn't resist spinning it against their antiabortion opponents. Nothing in the release is flat-out untrue, but it presents a misleading picture and it becomes another salvo in the abortion wars posing as neutral information.

The current issue of *Forbes MediaCritic* cites another example of how numbers can be massaged to exaggerate differences. Last summer, the Federal Reserve Bank of Chicago looked into charges of racial bias in granting bank mortgages. The bank released numbers showing that among applicants with good credit histories, blacks and Hispanics were approved for mortgages about as often as were whites. But blacks and Hispanics with bad credit histories got mortgages 81.19 percent of the time, compared with 89.62 percent of poor-credit whites.

The *New York Times's* story on the report led this way: "White mortgage applicants with bad credit histories were only half as likely to be rejected for loans as black or Hispanic applicants with similar credit records." How did the reporter turn this eight-point difference into a dramatic 200 percent or double rejection rate? Simple. To get rejection rates of 9 percent and 18 percent, he subtracted the approval rates from 100 (his numbers were a little off) and argued that the rejection rate for blacks was double that for whites, since 9 is half of 18. The same argument would be true if 99 percent of whites and 98 percent of minorities were successful, because whites would still be rejected half as often.

Like so much reporting on racial matters, cautious accuracy gave way to dramatic and inflammatory coverage. The eight-point gap between minorities and whites certainly invited suspicion, but the "half as likely" reference invited instant outrage. The actual rates of acceptance, by the way, were not included in the article, and since journalism is an industry proudly committed to recycling, the "half as likely" turned up in other newspapers as well. A third strange statistic in the news comes from Rep. Patricia Schroeder of Colorado, who says that about twenty-three women are dying in America from pregnancy-related problems for every 100,000 live births. This is a very high number, 2.3 times the actual rate based on six careful counting measures and reported by the Centers for Disease Control and Prevention. Schroeder intends to introduce a piece of legislation called the "Safe Motherhood Initiative," which turns out to be a bill that would prevent Congress from interfering with doctors' freedom to provide abortion services, including performing partial-birth abortions. To support her position, Schroeder cites a French study that claims an unusually high rate of maternal deaths, and she says the U.S. rate would be just as high if we gathered statistics better. But who would bother to gather any statistics when you can just make them up?

MEDIA BITES SELF

So many people are so mad at journalists these days that they don't notice how many journalists share their opinions. The self-flagellating panel discussion is almost a must at media conventions. Last Tuesday there were three such panels at the American Society of Magazine Editors meeting in New York, under the title "Why America Hates the Press."

Jerry Nachman, head of news for WCBS-TV in New York, pointed out that police conventions don't sponsor panels on the subject, "Civilians: Do We Beat Up Too Many?" and medical conventions don't spend long hours discussing the topic of "Patients: Do We Kill Too Many?" But editors and reporters are forever attacking their profession in panel discussions—a sure sign of health.

So much stomping of the press took place in the morning that the luncheon speaker, Ariana Huffington, author and wife of the defeated Republican senate candidate in California, Michael Huffington, had to discard some of her speech attacking the media. Most of it had already been said.

Much of the public is concerned about left-wing bias in the press. It's there all right, mostly in the treatment of social issues. On the day of the three panels, for instance, the *New York Times* ran a front-page article on New Jersey's new welfare cap—no extra funds for women on welfare who bear a second child. Right near the top the writer let us know that a few researchers "raised questions about whether the state can—or indeed should—regulate complicated sexual and reproductive decisions."

This clearly tipped off any moderately awake readers that they were about to read a political attack on the reform plan disguised as a news article. The whole piece was indeed shaped that way. Ten years ago, an article like this would not have gotten past the *Times* copy desk. Now it does.

But I disagree with conservatives who see consistent bias in national political coverage. No president has ever been savaged as relentlessly by the news media as Bill Clinton, and the savaging has been done by a press corps that basically voted for him en masse. This is why media discussions of media sins tend to swing away from the bias issue and focus instead on aggression, cynicism, and pack journalism.

Recent discussion revolves around two heavy-impact articles on the media, one in December in the *New Yorker*, one in the current issue of the *Columbia Journalism Review*. The *Review* article, by Paul Starobin of the *National Journal*, was a denunciation of the current crop of Washington reporters for cynicism and hip jadedness. It ran under the title "A Generation of Vipers."

After acknowledging that there is much in Washington to be cynical about, Starobin argued that the deep cynicism of reporters is tilting stories away from positive news and toward witty putdowns of the political class. He says reporters ignored or underplayed President Clinton's bill to establish a national service program because coverage might have made them look too positive or too pro-Clinton.

On the Republican side, he says, reporters barely told readers and viewers what was in Newt Gingrich's Contract with America because they considered it just a manipulative gimmick. He quotes Steven Waldman of *Newsweek* as saying that cynicism "not liberalism is the dominant ideology of the Washington press corps."

Adam Gopnik in the *New Yorker* focuses on a now famous *New York Times* lead sentence about President Clinton's visit to Oxford: "President Clinton returned today for a sentimental journey to the university where he didn't inhale, didn't get drafted and didn't get a degree."

That clever line, written by a great reporter, would have been fine in a column or an editorial. But it was all wrong in a news story, and it has launched a thousand discussions on journalistic ethics. For Gopnik, it was a bit of clever malice that reflected the "casual cruelty" and pointless aggression of the press. He writes: "The most distinctive thing to emerge in the American media recently has not been cynicism at all but a kind of weird, free-form nastiness—spleen without purpose, grayness with an attitude."

Pressure from tabloid papers and tabloid television is a factor. Reporters are supposed to present stories with an "edge," partly because everybody is presumed to have seen the story already on TV. All that reporters think they can do, Gopnik wrote, "is re-state the familiar story with a wink or a sneer."

There are other factors, of course. Competitive pressures are so high that reporters often feel they have to pump up a story to attract readers and please their bosses, something like carnival barkers shouting to get passersby into their tent.

Editors get involved in this screaming for attention too. Last week it was Tina Brown, editor of the *New Yorker*, who put an unusually trashy cover picture on her issue to mark Easter weekend and the April 15th income tax deadline. Believe it or not, it was a picture of a bunny crucified on top of a 1040 form. It was everything most people hate about "edge" journalism—aggressive, insulting, humorless, pointless, over the top, and therefore bound to be discussed. Can't we just cut this stuff out and get back to grown-up journalism?

A QUIZ FOR MEDIA MAVENS

Get your pencils. This is an important multiple choice test on current affairs.

1. Catatonia is better than watching the winter Olympics because:
   a. There's always a chance catatonia will end
   b. Catatonia doesn't require rotten weather
   c. Though quite serious, catatonia is rarely associated with the luge

2. The biathlon is a winter Olympic event combining cross-country skiing and rifle shooting. Because of its popularity, the next games will add this event:
   a. sitzbath-and-shoot competition (Jacuzzis and Uzis)
   b. bobsledding and grenade-throwing
   c. speed skating and bazookas
   d. ice dancing and fragmentation bombing

3. More than anything else, Gennifer Flowers needs:
   a. an ethics advisor
   b. a skilled hair colorist
   c. a spelling coach

4. To the best of our knowledge, America has been taken over and totally ruined by:
   a. The Japanese (Michael Crichton)
   b. A CIA military-industrial coup (Oliver Stone)
   c. Males (Susan Faludi)
   d. Columbus and all those old immigrants (Kirk Patrick Sale)
   e. All those new immigrants (Pat Buchanan)
   f. A crippling lack of self-esteem (Gloria Steinem)

5. Stanford University's first Ph.D. thesis in political correctness will deal with:
   a. Diversifying the so-called Founding Fathers: the Lesbian Feminist presence at the Constitutional Convention

b. Julius Caesar: the making of an Afrocentrist
c. Disease, death, and dinosaur extinctions: contributions of the white male

6. Oliver Stone's next movie will be:
   a. John Wilkes Booth—Mafia Patsy
   b. Harry Truman: Accessory After the Fact
   c. Cain, Abel, and the Grassy Knoll
   d. Innocent Bystander: the O.J. Simpson Story

7. In the Swarthmore College cafeteria, a student is overheard saying "Mexican food doesn't agree with me." How would the college react to this unexpected crisis:
   a. Following arrest by campus sensitivity cops, the offender would be required to attend grueling rap sessions on enchilada preparation and a revisionist history of the Alamo
   b. To demonstrate contrition, he would have to stand in the rain for an hour, holding aloft a delicious taco.
   c. He would write "Mexican cuisine is extremely agreeable to all persons" 8,000 times and then be suspended as a gustatory hate criminal.
   d. All of the above

8. Animal Rights activists believe that pets should be called "companion animals" or "other-than-human companions." Dr. Michael Fox of the Humane Society says that "pet owner" is offensive too, and should be changed to "human companion of the non-human companion." Therefore:
   a. The term "my pet peeve" becomes "my non-human peeve."
   b. The sentence "The other guy's dog bit one of my dogs" becomes "The other human companion's other-than-human companion bit my other-than-human companion but not my other other-than-human companion."
   c. Never mind

A LOVELY DAY FOR A HARANGUING

John E. Pepper, CEO and chairman of Procter & Gamble, didn't return any of my phone calls last week. Too bad. I hoped he could explain why P&G, a huge company with a conservative, almost stuffy image, is the major sponsor of two of the more atrocious TV talk shows, the *Jenny Jones Show* and *The Ricki Lake Show*.

In the first six months of 1995, P&G poured more than $11 million into advertising on these two programs, and millions more into their various clones and competitors.

Cultural degradation brought to you by major corporations headed by high-minded, socially aware executives is an old story. Ken Auletta of the *New Yorker* calls this a familiar "disconnect" in the minds of many titans of the business world—they often work hard for a better culture in their off hours, then undermine it by blindly promoting all the wrong cultural forces in their business decisions. From 9 to 5, the social conscience is apparently off duty.

John E. Pepper is active in charitable affairs and youth work, and so straight-laced that one colleague said he could have been a priest. He has been called "the soul and conscience of P&G" for so often that some at the company call him "Jiminy Pepper," a reference to the famed moral scourge, Jiminy Cricket.

On the other hand, he presides over a company whose ad dollars are certainly doing a great deal to prop up the stupid TV freak shows built around "I impregnated 30 girls, and I'm proud of it," and "I slept with my mother's boyfriend and his transvestite bookie and came down with herpes, so I gave it to my cousin." A September *Oprah* show featured a prostitute who had been raped 80 to 90 times, and a *Jerry Springer* show introduced a woman who had 251 men in one day.

This over-the-top programming has been begging for a public reaction. The ambushing and humiliation of guests and the mainstreaming of deviance and assaultive behavior are so gross that even Geraldo Rivera, an elder statesman of TV sleaze, says the programming makes him want to take a shower afterwards. (Perhaps using a Procter & Gamble soap advertised on *Ricki*?)

I should say that my efforts to reach Mr. Pepper resulted in a blizzard of phone calls from P&G public relations people. They wanted me to know that the company has standards and guidelines and that the company "closely monitors" the content of each TV show. "Close monitoring" turns out to mean they are told a bit about each show before any ads are locked in. P&G says it occasionally withholds ads and resumes advertising the next day, though no details about this were offered. But even if P&G keeps ads off a trashy show every now and then, its massive flow of ad dollars helps to keep these programs afloat, even the ones they say are too offensive to deserve their ads.

One spokesman told me P&G is cutting back on trash TV ads because the content of the shows seems to be getting worse. Maybe so, but the cutting back hasn't shown up yet in any available figures. For the first seven months of 1995, P&G advertising on seven of these shows more than doubled over the same period in 1994. For the *Jenny Jones Show*, P&G spending tripled, and for *Ricki Lake* (or "Ricki the Sicki" as Newsday critic Marvin Kitman calls her) it more than quadrupled.

I got the impression that P&G would probably be honestly reluctant to sponsor a televised beheading, or even a Christians v. Lions rematch, but anything short of that was probably okay.

Last week brought the first signs that advertisers are getting the message. Sears Roebuck said it has begun cutting back on daytime talk show ads to avoid alienating customers, but declined to identify the shows or say what the cutting back amounts to.

The *Wall Street Journal* quoted a spokesman for an unidentified pharmaceutical company saying that some makers of over-the-counter drugs "are concerned about the shows' preoccupation with sex and violence." The *Journal* reported that Unilever NV pulled ads from two talk shows and tightened its ad guidelines. And in the wake of the campaign against trash television by Senator Joseph Lieberman (D., CT.) and William Bennett, one station manager in California stepped forward and announced he was canceling the *Jenny Jones Show* on grounds of all-round loathsomeness.

It makes sense to shine the spotlight on the major advertisers (including such big names as Campbell Soup, Ralston Purina, Bayer, and General Mills) and the heads of the media conglomerates which are pushing all the trash: Mickey Schulhof at Sony Corporation of America (Ricki Lake), John Madigan of the Tribune Company (Geraldo), Sumner Redstone and Frank Biondi of Viacom (Montel Williams and Maury Povich) and Time Warner's Gerald Levin (Jenny Jones), who can't seem to keep his company out of these cultural pollution issues.

Eric Mink, the *New York Daily News* TV critic says: "When these guys—and/or their spouses—start to get hassled and harangued about the talk shows by their buddies on the golf course, at the health club, the boat yard, the hair stylist's, and the charity ball...THEN you might get some action." Good idea. Let the hassling and haranguing begin.

PART TWO

EDUCATION

TRUE LIES VS. TOTAL RECALL

The current issue of *Commentary* has a very funny article by Wendy Shalit, an undergraduate at Williams College, on how life among the politically correct goes these days on an elite campus. Much of the article deals with her fruitless search for a women's bathroom that doesn't have men in it (banning men from the premises would be "exclusionary of one gender," and might imply that males and females are somehow quite different—a no-no in the PC worldview).

Along the way she discusses the off-the-wall intellectual habits now being incubated on campus. She frequently hears her befuddled classmates say that the Holocaust didn't actually occur—rather, it "has purchase, compared with the currency derived from other events," or as one male student summed up, though it may not have happened, it's "a perfectly reasonable conceptual hallucination."

For only $24,000 a year, you too can ship your children to Williams and have them learn to think this way. The *New Yorker* book critic, James Woolcott, calls it "the blithe disregard for truth" in post-modern thinking. In the post-modern, post-everything worldview, there is no objectivity or truth. Everything is relative. Nothing is better or truer than anything else. Knowledge is politically constructed, an extension of power. As written by Western scholars, history is not a record of what happened. It is a political white-male story that must be replaced by other stories.

In their purest and therefore most lunatic form these ideas have not flourished in the real world, only on campus, our national holding pen for zany thinking. But they are always leaking out here and there, mixing with the new tribalism and the self-esteem movement to create real-world problems.

The textbook wars, for instance, show that each racial, ethic, and religious tribe now expects the power to judge and veto what is written about it. Some of this demand is normal democratic politics. But post-everything arguments provide the intellectual cover: if all stories are valid and all cultures are equal, then nobody but a member of the tribe can write its history. This is why you hear total silence from campus historians when, for example, Afrocentrists teach schoolchildren that Egyptian pilots were flying gliders around Africa in ancient times, and black astrologers were able to pick out a faint star (Sirius B) long before the telescopes needed to see it were actually invented. As some of Wendy Shalit's classmates might say, these ideas "have purchase" because they are strongly felt. Who cares if they are true? What's truth anyway?

This embarrassing development has led to two contradictory ideas: (1) nothing is true, but (2) what I say, or my group says, is true because it is so strongly held. The mantra of the sexual-abuse recovery movement is, "If you think you were abused, you were," because thinking makes it so. Here you needn't even believe very strongly to be guaranteed of truth. One of the movement's gurus, E. Sue Blume, says that doubts about whether abuse occurred, or the thought, "Maybe it's my imagination," are both symptoms of "post-incest syndrome." In any case, the truth doesn't really matter. As one repressed-memory therapist told *Frontline*: "I don't care if it's true. What actually happened is irrelevant to me."

A version of this pops up repeatedly in the anti-rape movement. Check back on all the recent notorious cases of fake rape allegations, and you will usually find somebody arguing that the truth doesn't matter. After the Tawana Brawley case, an article in the way-left *Nation* magazine said: "In cultural perspective, if not in fact, it doesn't matter whether the crime occurred or not."

At Vassar, false rape accusations against several males were no big deal to the assistant dean of students. She said coolly: "They have a lot of pain. but it is not a pain that I would necessarily have spared them." Her argument was that even if they weren't actual rapists, they should explore their potential for becoming rapists. And after a rape charge that tore the Princeton campus apart was shown to be false, anti-rape activists still rallied around the accuser, saying, according to one account, "Listen we can't hope to find truth in all these stories. The goal is to reveal these women as 'lenses of oppression' through which the crimes of the patriarchy can be exposed."

The key to this hard-line thinking is this: ever since the radical wing of feminism more or less ate mainstream feminism alive, the premise of the movement has been that women are everywhere under siege and oppressed by a common enemy: men. With this large truth in hand, it doesn't matter much whether this oppressor or that one is literally guilty of rape. This is penny-ante stuff. They are ALL guilty because rape is a paradigm of male-female relations under the evil patriarchy.

Nowadays it is best to be wary of movements with large blazing truths in hand and the firm conviction that petty, pesky, literal truth therefore almost doesn't matter. Our century has seen a lot of this argument—that dishonesty or indifference to truth is justified by one's commitment to a cause. Now we just have to deal with the current college edition of this, what Wendy Shalit calls the "corrupt moral and intellectual habits" being spawned on campus.

DON'T GET HYSTERICAL

Listen to the media and you will think that the sky is falling at the University of California, now that racial and ethnic preferences have ended. The *New York Times* detected a looming "white out" at the university, declaring that doors are closing to black and Hispanic students at an alarming rate.

An NAACP official said, "We are seeing these campuses revert to race-exclusive status." Columnist Carl Rowan saw a possible return of Jim Crow. An MSNBC headline announced a "Plunge in Minority University Enrollment" in the University system. Paul Conrad, the *Los Angeles Times* cartoonist drew a new seal for the university labeled "The University of Caucasians" with the motto "Let Truth Be White."

Reality check: there is no white-out, closing of doors, or a Caucasian University. In the eight-college University of California system, only two of five students are white. At Berkeley, the figure is one in three. (The "all-white" theorists manage to overlook Asian-American students, or simply dismiss them as whites). The dramatic "plunge" (for example, 64.3 percent fewer black freshmen admitted this fall at Berkeley) was only at the two leading campuses, Berkeley and UCLA. For maximum impact, pro-preference activists put out those numbers first. The system-wide data, released two days later by the University, show a more modest drop—18 percent for blacks, 7 percent for Hispanics. But this news never quite caught up with the selected numbers pushed by advocates and endlessly repeated in the media.

The University's official admission numbers on this fall's freshman class shows 675 fewer non-Asian minority students spread over the eight campuses, so the new freshmen admissions are 15.4 percent non-

Asian minority, compared with 17.6 percent for the 1997 freshman class, a decline of 2.2 percent. The drop may be even smaller, since the University doesn't know the ethnicity of the huge number of admitted freshmen (6,346) who declined to list their ethnicity on application forms this year. Non-checkers tripled this year to 14.3 percent of freshman admissions, partly, at least, because the new application form put the ethnicity box in an obscure place and made filling it out more difficult.

All these numbers must be treated with caution. But a decline of black and Hispanic freshman enrollment in the range of 2 percentage points is smaller than many expected. What the early reports treated as a mass exclusion of "underrepresented" students is actually a shift within the system—many students who had been pushed onto a faster track than they were ready for (Berkeley and UCLA) will now attend less prestigious but good colleges within the university system. In fact, the drive to raise minority numbers at the top two colleges had the effect of creating racial imbalances at the other six. Judson King, provost of the University of California, acknowledged this by saying that the end of preferences was "evening out" diversity across the U Cal system.

The fast-track problem becomes clear in the dropout rates. At Berkeley, the most selective public university in the country, the dropout rate for black students is 42 percent, more than double the 16 percent dropout rate for whites. This is an appalling statistic, and the most obvious way to interpret it is to conclude that diversity lobbyists cared far more about numbers than about graduation rates or actual learning. Stephan and Abigail Thernstrom, authors of *American in Black and White*, argue that the percentage of black and Hispanic students at the two elite colleges will fall in the short run, but the percentage who earn colleges degrees somewhere in the system will rise quickly. Remember too that California has a three-tiered system with the U Cal campuses on top, then the Cal State colleges and the community colleges, all allowing upward mobility through transfers. You don't have to start out at UCLA to end up with a UCLA degree.

Though there is no real shortage of hysterical commentary about the end of preferences, few people have bothered to talk about the strong positive aspects. For one thing, a great burden has been lifted from the shoulders of U Cal's black and Hispanic students: nobody can patronize or stigmatize them as unfit for their campuses. From now on, students in the system will make it on brains and effort and everybody knows it.

The end of preferences will help make the campuses far more open and honest places. The deep secrecy that surrounds the campus culture of racial preferences has compromised many officials and led to much deceit and outright law-breaking. Martin Trow, a Berkeley professor, spoke at a recent academic convention about all the cover-ups and lying that preferences have spawned, citing as one minor example an Iranian student at Berkeley who said he had been encouraged to list himself as Hispanic to qualify for a preference. No wonder that columnist William Raspberry says that the defenders of affirmative action preferences have lost the moral high ground.

Those defenders are determined not to notice the effects of racially polarizing policies installed without democratic input or honest debate. Whatever legitimacy the policies once had is gone. Soon the racial preferences will be gone too.

DUMBING DOWN TEACHERS

A reader sent in a list of teacher education courses at the University of Massachusetts, Amherst, along with a note: "This explains why 59 percent of prospective teachers in Massachusetts flunked a basic literacy test." The courses listed were: "Leadership in Changing Times," "Social diversity" (four different courses), "Embracing Diversity," "Diversity and Change," "Educating the Asian," "Multicultural Education," "Native American Education," "Latino Education," "Classicism," "Racism," "Sexism," "Jewish Oppression," "Lesbian/Gay/Bisexual Oppression," "Oppression of the Disabled," and (get this one) "Erroneous Beliefs."

The reader was referring to a basic tenth-grade test in language, math, and other subjects, given to 1800 would-be teachers in Massachusetts. Among other things, the 59 percent who failed often couldn't spell simple English words like "burned" and "abolished." Apparently they went into ed school without knowing much about anything, then came out the same way. But at least they are prepared to drill children in separatism, oppression, and erroneous beliefs.

Our schools of education have been a national scandal for many years, but it's odd that they are rarely front-and-center in our endless debate about failing schools. The right talks about striving and standards, the left talks about equal funding and classroom size, but few talk much about the breeding grounds for school failure—the trendy, anti-achievement, oppression-obsessed, feel-good, esteem-ridden, content-free schools of education.

For an article in *City Journal*, the journalist Heather Mac Donald recently visited New York's City College, to see how a modern education school manages to fill its class time without making the dread, professional mistake of having any actual content or clear purpose. She found the teacher talking about "building a community, rich of talk" and how ed school students should "develop the subtext of what they are doing." Each student wrote for seven minutes on "What excites me about teaching," "What concerns me about teaching," and "What it was like to do this writing." After the writings were read aloud, the teacher said, "So writing gave you permission to think on paper about what's there."

Then the students split into small groups and talked about their feelings. "It shifted the comfort zone," said one student, already fluent in ed-speak. Another said: "I felt really comfortable. I had trust there. "Let's talk about that," said the teacher. "We are building trust in this class." But what they were not doing was talking about anything in the real world, or about how to teach real lessons to real children. The credo for ed schools, Mac Donald says, is "Anything But Knowledge." "Once you dismiss real knowledge as the goal of education," she writes about the make-work silliness in ed classes "you have to find something else to do."

The education schools take for granted that education must be "child-centered," which means that children decide for themselves what they want to learn. Heavy emphasis is put on feelings and the self. An actual curriculum, listing things students ought to know is viewed as cramping the human spirit. Ed school students are taught to be suspicious of authority and the notion that teachers might be expected to know more than the children they teach, so the word "teacher" is in decline. The fad word is now "facilitator," part guide and part bystander watching the self-educating child.

The traditional ed school hostility to achievement currently hides behind the word "equity"—bright students must be tamped down so slower learners will not feel bad about themselves. Smuggled in along with equality is the notion that performance and learning shouldn't really count—they elevate some children at the expense of others. Grades and marks are bad too because they characterize and divide children. The result is that the brighter students get little help and are often the target of teacher resentment. Rita Kramer in her 1991 study of education schools, *Ed School Follies*, wrote: "What happens to those more capable or motivated students is hardly anyone's concern."

This lack of concern for achievement now has a racial cast. Asian and white children are often depicted as somehow out of step if they work harder and achieve more than blacks, Hispanics, and other minorities. Instead of working hard with children to reduce the racial gap, ed school theory calls for strategies to conceal it under group projects or simply to demonstrate that achievement doesn't matter.

Various experiments are under way to let bright college graduates bypass education schools. Connecticut has a program allowing graduates to switch into teaching from other careers simply by taking an eight-week summer course and a test. In New York, the Teach for America program produced a sudden infusion of very good teachers into public schools, also by bypassing the ed-school swamp. But the hidebound education industry is digging in to close these loopholes and protect its closed-shop monopoly. It makes no sense to force teachers through schools as bad as these. People should be able to qualify as teachers simply by passing rigorous tests in their area of competence. Scrapping the ed school requirement is clearly the way to go.

LET'S LOWER OUR SELF-ESTEEM

At the Kelly elementary school in Portland, Oregon, fifth grade girls are asked to make a list of eight qualities they like about themselves. Each good quality is written on a paper petal to form a flower, then a photo of each girl is placed in the center of her own flower.

Followers of educational fads will recognize this as a fairly conventional exercise in self-esteem training. Thinking up nice things to say about yourself is said to enhance confidence and therefore to improve scholastic achievement and citizenship in general.

Despite the back-to-basics trend and a strong backlash against self-esteem training in the early Nineties, the movement is still astonishingly strong and seems to hover over the schools like an established civic religion. The Los Angeles Times reports: "Indeed, few educators dispute the link between academic success and a student's self-confidence and self-regard."

Maybe so, but after more than 25 years of research there is virtually no evidence that such a link exists. Nobody doubts that adults can damage the confidence of young children, or that schools should respect and encourage their students. But there is almost zero evidence that failure to learn is tied to low self-esteem, or that massaging the psyche can improve learning.

Even the most ballyhooed effort to promote self-esteem, the $735,000 California Task Force on Self-Esteem, was accompanied by a book surveying all the research, which said frankly: "One of the disappointing aspects of every chapter in this volume...is how low the association between self-esteem and its consequences are in research to date." In fact, one common finding in the literature is that high self-esteem is often linked to low performance.

The data on race and self-esteem has also upset most expectations. The belief that the long history of racial oppression has left American blacks with a collective problem of low self-esteem turns out to be false. Study after study has shown that black self-esteem is about as high as that of whites, if not higher, and was only slightly lower before the civil rights movement, at the height of racism and segregation.

These studies tend to undercut public policies, including educational ones, based on the well-meaning desire to raise the self-esteem of blacks. That self-esteem is already high, apparently because blacks have historically been able to resist internalizing racist views of their abilities. "It may be that the low self-esteem argument has been poorly construed and overstated all along," said a 1989 academic study, directed by Stanley Rothman, head of Smith College's Center for the Study of Social and Political Change. That study was later published as *The Myth of Black Low Self-Esteem*.

Low self-esteem pops up regularly in other academic reports as an explanation for all sorts of violence, from hate crimes and street crimes to terrorism. But despite the popularity of the explanation, not much evidence backs it up. In a recent issue of *Psychological Review*, three researchers examine this literature at great length and conclude that a much stronger link connects high self-esteem to violence. "It is difficult to maintain belief in the low self-esteem view after seeing that the more violent groups are generally the ones with higher self-esteem," write Roy Baumeister of Case Western Reserve University and Laura Smart and Joseph Boden of the University of Virginia.

The conventional view is that people without self-esteem try to gain it by hurting others. The researchers find that violence is much more often the work of people with unrealistically high self-esteem attacking others who challenge their self-image. Under this umbrella come bullies, rapists, racists, psychopaths, and members of street gangs and organized crime.

The study concludes: "Certain forms of high self-esteem seem to increase one's proneness to violence. An uncritical endorsement of the cultural value of self-esteem may therefore be counterproductive and even dangerous....The societal pursuit of high self-esteem for everyone may literally end up doing considerable harm."

As for a prison program intended to make violent convicts feel better about themselves, "perhaps it would be better to try instilling modesty and humility," the researchers write.

In an interview with the *Boston Globe*, Baumeister said he believes the "self"-promoting establishment is starting to crumble. "What would work better for the country is to forget about self-esteem and concentrate on self-control."

In the schools, this would mean turning away from all the psychic boosterism and emphasizing self-esteem as a by-product of real achievement, never an end in itself. The self-esteem movement, still entrenched in our schools of education, is deeply implicated in the dumbing down of our schools, and in the spurious equality behind the idea that it's a terrible psychic blow if one student does any better or any worse than another. Let's hope it is indeed crumbling.

SORRY ABOUT THAT 1992 REPORT. WE MISSPOKE

After eight years, the truth is finally beginning to catch up with "How Schools Shortchange Girls," the influential but largely false 1992 report by the American Association of University Women.

The report, which swept though the world of education and led to girls-only financial plums of the Gender Equity Act, described the American classroom as a hellhole for girls. Females were allegedly invisible, ignored, silenced, and broken by a loss of self-esteem.

Media elites welcomed the report, often writing their stories directly out of the AAUW "executive summary." Few reporters seemed to notice or care that the AAUW synthesis of a thousand studies in the field ignored studies that didn't fit the "victim" thesis.

Reporters also overlooked the heavy ideological content of the report. The text was basically an expression of hard-line campus feminism which views relations between the sexes solely in terms of power and oppression. "School curricula should deal directly with issues of power, gender politics and violence against women," said the report, which deplored "the evaded curriculum" (gender issues).

The AAUW report is "politicized research" and "false political propaganda," says Judith Kleinfeld, professor of psychology at the University of Alaska. Kleinfeld deserves much of the credit for the report's sinking reputation. She undertook a long analysis of the AAUW study at the suggestion of the Women's Freedom Network, one of the promising antidotes to the hard-line campus feminism that has overtaken the AAUW.

Kleinfeld makes many of the points against the report that were made in 1992, but which somehow failed to penetrate the skulls of education reporters. From grade school through college, females in all ethnic groups receive higher grades, even in math, obtain higher ranks, are picked more often for gifted and talented programs and receive more honors in every field except science and sports.

In 1992, as in 1999, females lagged behind males in math and science test scores, but males are much further behind females in reading achievement and writing skills. By 1992 women had long since surged past men in college attendance (55 percent female, 45 percent male) and were flooding into the professions. By 1994 women attained almost half of professional degrees, up from almost none in 1961.

The most devastating charge in the AAUW report was the claim that teachers call on boys more often and allow them to call out answers eight to ten times more often than girls. This finding turned up everywhere, from TV and lectures to the Doonesbury comic strip. But it wasn't true. It comes from a mistake involving David and Myra Sadker, education professors and gender-bias specialists. In a 1981 article, the Sadkers reported that boys in Washington, D.C., public schools "receive eight to ten times as many reprimands as their female counterparts." Somehow the AAUW report garbled this finding into one saying that boys who didn't raise their hands got away with barking out remarks eight to ten times more often than girls, getting full attention and constructive comments from their teachers. But the Sadkers' original ungarbled article shows that this "extra attention" to boys was almost entirely scolding.

Most studies show that boys are not called on more often than girls. Kleinfeld shows that one of the AAUW's own studies ("Expectations and Aspirations: Gender Roles and Self-Esteem," 1990) finds it too: more girls than boys (59 percent to 57 percent) said they are called on often, and more boys than girls (67 percent to 63 percent) report that teachers won't let them say things they want to say.

The children do report bias, but it's bias against boys. "By overwhelming margins," the 1990 AAUW report said, teachers give more attention to girls. Nearly three quarters of boys and girls said teachers compliment girls more often, think they are smarter and prefer to be around girls. Apparently embarrassed by the incorrectness of its own study, the AAUW released it with no publicity and ignored it in the big 1992 report.

Amazingly, the AAUW is at it again, issuing another overwrought victim report, "Gender Gaps: Where Schools Fail Our Children." The main point is that "a new boys club" and "an alarming new gender gap" threaten to "cheat girls" because more females who are interested in computers take lower-level clerical and data entry courses and more males take computer science. The latest statistics, which go back to 1994, are not included in the report, but they show that females dominate in clerical and data entry and are close in computer science, with 10.96 percent of girls and 13.85 percent of boys taking full-year courses. A 2.89 gap between the sexes in four-year-old stats indicates an ominous "new boys' club"? Only at the AAUW.

The truth is that our schools have many flaws, but the oppression of females isn't one of them. The educational status of boys, not girls, is the real problem. Boys as a group, particularly minority boys, are falling behind, getting lower grades, suffering more emotional difficulties; getting punished far more frequently, dropping out and getting left back more often, reading and writing at levels that are appalling by girls' standards. One recent study finds that males account for 70 percent of all alienated students

The AAUW report was created by the Wellesley College Center for Research on Women, with a large input from Peggy McIntosh, the Center's oddest denizen. McIntosh thinks excellence is a dangerous, male ideal. Instead of the old "vertical thinking" (mastery, decisiveness, clear thought) she wants schools to push "lateral thinking," the aim of which is not to excel but "to be in decent relationship with the invisible elements of the universe." Life may be one tough battle against men, but McIntosh offers a few words of comfort to white males: it's not your fault; you were born that way. Somehow the media managed to miss all this in 1992. It's all still there folks. Take a look.

THAT SO-CALLED PYTHAGORAS

"Deep Thoughts" has been Jack Handy's running joke on TV's *Saturday Night Live*—a series of mock-inspirational messages about life that make no sense at all. Now "Deep Thoughts" are available on greeting cards, including one that pokes fun at the fuzzy new math in the schools. The card says: "Instead of having "answers" on a math test, they should just call them "impressions," and if you got a different "impression," so what, can't we all be brothers?"

Pretty funny. But it's hard for satire to stay ahead of actual events these days, particularly in education. The "New-New Math," as it is sometimes called, has a high-minded goal: get beyond traditional math drills by helping students understand and enjoy mathematical concepts. But in practice, alas, the New-New Math is yet another educational "Deep Thought."

Basic skills are pushed to the margin by theory and the idea that students should not be passive receivers of rules but self-discoverers, gently guided by teachers, who are co-learners, not authority figures with lessons to impart. Correct answers aren't terribly important. Detractors call it "whole math," because students frequently end up guessing at answers, just as children exposed to the "whole language" fad in English classes end up guessing at words they can't pronounce. "Although the Wicked Whole-Language witch is dying, the Whole-Math Witch isn't even ill," said Wayne Bishop, professor of mathematics at the California State University, Los Angeles.

Mathematically Correct, a San Diego-based group which strongly opposes whole math, recently posted a list of commandments on its Internet site, including "Honor the correct answer more than the guess," "Give good grades only for good work," and "Avoid vague objectives."

Those vague objectives include meandering exercises that have little to do with math, such as illustrating data collection by having second-graders draw pictures of their lunch, then cut the pictures out and put them in paper bags. Worse, the New-New Math comes with the usual stew of ed-school obsessions about feelings, self-esteem, dumbing down to promote classroom equality, and an all-round politically correct agenda.

Marianne Jennings, a professor at Arizona State University, found that her teenage daughter was getting an A in algebra but had no idea how to solve an equation. So Jennings acquired a copy of her daughter's textbook. The real title is *Secondary Math an Integrated Approach: Focus on Algebra*," but Jennings calls it "Rain Forest Algebra."

It includes Maya Angelou's poetry, pictures of President Clinton and Mali wood carvings, lectures on what environmental sinners we all are and photos of students with names such as Tatuk and Esteban "who offer my daughter thoughts on life." It also contains praise for the wife of Pythagoras, father of the Pythagorean theorem, and asks students such mathematical brain teasers as "What role should zoos play in our society?" However, equations don't show up until page 165, and the first solution of a linear equation, which comes on page 218, is reached by guessing and checking.

Jennings points out that "Focus on Algebra" is 812 pages long, compared with 200 for the average math textbook in Japan. "This would explain why the average standardized score is 80 in Japan and 52 here," she says. Marks do seem to head south when New-New Math appears. In well-off Palo Alto, California, public school math students dropped from the 86th percentile nationally to the 58th in the first three years of New-New Teaching, then went back up the next year to the 77th percentile when the schools moderated their approach.

The New-New Math has become a carrier for the aggressive multiculturalism spreading inexorably through the schools. Literature of the National Council of Teachers of Math, which is promoting whole math, is filled with suggestions on how to push multiculturalism in arithmetic and math classes.

New-New Math is also vaguely allied with an alleged new field of study called ethnomathematics. Most of us may think that math is an abstract and universal discipline that has little to do with ethnicity. But a lot of ethnomathematicians, who are busy holding conferences and writing books, say that all peoples have a natural culture-bound mathematics. Western math, in this view, isn't universal, but an expression of white male culture imposed on non-whites. Much of this is the usual ranting about "Eurocentrism" applied to math. *Ethnomathematics*, a book of collected essays, starts by reminding us that "Geographically, Europe does not exist, since it is only a peninsula on the vast Eurasian continent..." Before long, there is a reference to "the so-called Pythagorean theorem." Much of the literature claims that non-literate peoples indicated their grasp of math in many ways, from quilt patterns to an ancient African bone cut with marks that may have been used for counting.

It's all rather stunning nonsense, but this is where multiculturalism is right now. Unless you are headed for an engineering school working with Yoruba calculators, or unless you wish to balance your checkbook the ancient Navaho way, it's probably safe to ignore the whole thing.

LET'S ATTACK MERIT!

A good grade point average won't get you into the nursing program at Cuesta College, a community college in California. No, good marks are "artificial barriers" to nursing progress, according to the state's community college chancellor, so admission to the program is now by lottery. A working woman named Judy Downing didn't make the program, though she studied hard at night school and got straight A's in the required courses. But some candidates with C averages won the lottery and got in.

This is just one sign of the gathering assault on good grades, test scores, and nearly all known indicators of merit and academic achievement. Some of this is coming from a philosophy of radical egalitarianism (people must be treated as equal in all matters, regardless of talent or competence). But most of it has been drummed up to protect the excesses of an affirmative action movement in deep trouble with the courts and the American people.

Some examples: Lani Guinier has called for a lottery to determine admission to colleges, after minimal qualifications have been met by applicants. The president of the American Bar Association started a pilot project to de-emphasize the law SATs (LSATs) in law school admissions. A few colleges are abandoning use of the SATs and the Clinton department of education is investigating whether the University of California is violating anti-discrimination law by using these test scores. At CUNY, New York's City University, a cry was raised for a fuzzy standard of "multiple measures" to replace a 300-word essay that large numbers of graduating seniors were unable to write on a final exam. Texas now bypasses testing by admitting into the state university system the top 10 percent of students from all high schools, including de facto segregated schools where a large percentage of students can barely read or write.

Education journals regularly carry attacks on merit and tests. (Sample: *Change* magazine's article "Standardized Testing: Meritocracy's Crooked Yardstick.") The *New York Times*, an unfailing barometer of politically correct thinking, ran a long page-one article finding (surprise!) "wider sympathy" and "gathering data" calling the SAT tests into question. The *Times* revived the old charge of "cultural bias" on the SATs, as demonstrated by the test's use of the word "regatta." (Unmentioned by the *Times*: the test is endlessly combed for possible bias, and "regatta" hasn't appeared on a test since 1974.)

Colleges can no longer get around the Supreme Court's Bakke decision by pretending that race is just one factor in diversity admissions.

We now know too much about how those admissions really work, and the courts have upheld Proposition 209 in California and the Hopwood decision in Texas, a reverse discrimination suit by white applicants. So an effort is under way to circumvent or discredit all objective criteria for admissions.

The SATs in particular are under heavy attack because they consistently show 200- to 230-point gaps between test scores of whites and blacks. The argument here is that the tests can't be any good because not enough blacks and Latinos do well on them. But attacking the tests is like attacking thermometers because of cold weather. A ton of data tells us that they are merely reporting the truth—that depressingly large numbers of non-Asian minority group members arrive at college too poorly prepared to do well. When used as they are now (on a weighted basis with grades and other criteria), "the scores are the most reliable known predictor of academic success," as legal writer Stuart Taylor, Jr. recently wrote in a long analysis of the SAT issue.

Defenders of preferences now attempt to discount tests and grades by arguing that affirmative actions students do just about as well as better qualified students. One such study of law schools rippled through the media all year, hailed by Tim Russert ("blacks who were admitted under affirmative action performed just as well as whites"), *Time* ("graduation rates and bar-exam pass-rates similar to whites") and *Newsweek* ("no real difference in either graduation or bar-passage rates").

Well, not exactly. The study by educational researcher Linda Wightman carried the telltale title, "The Threat to Diversity in Legal Education," and muffled the negative evidence it found: 21.9 percent of black law students entering schools in 1990-1991 failed to get a degree, compared with 9.7 percent of whites. Far from showing that blacks admitted under affirmative action did "just as well" as strongly credentialed blacks, Wightman found that the blacks admitted under racial preferences were about three times more likely to drop out. And the affirmative action group had a shockingly high attrition rate—43.2 percent either didn't finish law school or finished but didn't pass the bar.

The "just as well" school of reporting reflects desire more than fact. People who defend preferences want what nearly all Americans want, a country in which no group is left behind. But they have fallen into a no-win strategy by fudging evidence and attacking all academic qualifications to cloak what is really happening. That attack, Stuart Taylor says bluntly, will descend on "every objective measure of cognitive capacity or academic achievement that has ever been devised, until more black and Latino children get decent educations in their early years." Sad, but probably true.

Don't Listen to Miranda

Parents: be on the lookout for Miranda the toucan. She shows up in *Here's Looking at You, 2000*, a health curriculum used in several thousand public schools. Because she knows that parents can't be trusted, Miranda encourages children to check the family cupboards for "poisons," including alcohol and tobacco. The busybody curriculum also urges them to confess "problems at home" by writing secret messages to the teacher.

Using students to "re-educate" their parents is standard fare now in the schools. Adults commonly joke about being "turned in" by their children for such crimes as drinking a glass of wine with dinner or failing to recycle a soda can.

Working on those "problems at home," which many schools consider part of their role, is a never-ending task for zealous reformers. In Petaluma, California, ninth-graders in a "human interaction program" were sent home with worksheets that judged whether their families worked on an "open" or democratic model or on a "closed, authoritarian" model.

In Tucson, high school students were asked in a health class "How many of you hate your parents?" Oregon parents testified that in a "values clarification" program, their children were asked "How many of you ever wanted to beat up your parents?" Discussing or judging parents is routine in heavily therapeutic "life skills" and "human interaction" programs. In the sex-education handbook, *Changing Bodies, Changing Lives*, parents are one of the "voices" students must weigh and judge. As in other textbooks, parents are either problems to contend with or examples of what to avoid.

Told by the schools to construct their own value systems, students are often led to challenge parental values or to dismiss almost any adult objections as illegitimate. Last week a friend here in New York saw this ethic in action. When she asked what her young child's school was going to do about a wave of bullying, including pushing classmates down a flight of stairs, the head of the school said no action would be taken because "children at this stage in their development do not welcome adult intevention."

Dana Mack's strong new book, *The Assault on Parenthood: How Our Culture Undermines the Family*, makes the case that the crisis of the public school system is not simply the familiar one of academic failure. It's also that a new ethic, dismissive of parents and traditional values, has descended on the schools. "At the heart of parents' frustration with the schools," she writes, "is a deep and unbridgeable chasm between the vocabulary of moral dictates, rules and authority that parents think are best for children and the vocabulary of autonomy and 'choices' that emanates from the classroom."

For generations, child-rearing experts have been suspicious or negative about the instincts and authority of parents. Mack makes the case that what used to be called the adversary culture—based on relativism, egalitarianism, "sexual diversity," a therapeutic view of the world, and hostility to family, authority and religion—has extended its control over the public schools.

Like a submarine slowly surfacing, this set of attitudes is becoming more visible each day as an official school ideology that nobody has ever voted for. In their franker moments, many educators admit that their real business is social transformation. In her book, *Ed School Follies* about the dominant philosophy at schools of education, Rita Kramer quotes the acting dean of the University of Texas ed school: "You can't NOT use the schools as agencies of social change. It's too convenient." The dean admitted that this emphasis on change "sometimes impedes learning."

Most of us would settle for schools that skip all the social transformation and just concentrate on teaching children how to read and write. It turns out that the modern touchy-feely "affective" curriculum, aimed at improving self-esteem or "getting children to think about themselves," tends to crowd out actual learning. The new ideology is heavily anti-achievement as well, sometimes actively hostile to brighter students because excelling is regarded as elitist, illiberal, and anti-democratic. Better to stay dumb, fit in, and feel good about yourself.

In the media, parental objections to all this usually come under the heading of condoms, school prayer, and the religious right. But behind the media screen, parents of all political stripes are getting the message and pressure is building. Alan Wolfe, one of our best public intellectuals, reviewed the Dana Mack book in the *New Republic* and didn't much like it. But he agreed with the central message. In his well-off suburb, he said, friends and neighbors are shopping around for alternatives to the public schools because of the schools' anti-intellectualism and hostility to parents. "If social trends can be proclaimed based on my personal experience," he wrote, "suburban public schools are about to face the same precipitous declines in enrollment suffered by urban ones." This is just one indicator that the problem isn't a regional, conservative, or religious one. Unhappiness with the social transformers in our schools is national, and it's growing.

GOOD HAIR, BAD CAKE

Ruth Sherman, a third-grade teacher at P.S. 75 in Brooklyn, is not going back to her class. Black and Hispanic parents denounced her for insensitively deciding to teach a certain book. She was called a cracker and a bigot. One parent said she was surprised that Sherman did not have a white hood on her desk. Another screamed, "We're going to get you." Sherman reported death threats. She intends to teach elsewhere.

The book is *Nappy Hair*, a critically praised children's story by a black professor about black self-esteem. In the story, a young girl's hard-to-comb hair becomes a metaphor for racial pride and the girl's fiercely independent spirit. Blacks do not like whites to use the word "nappy," a traditional racial insult. But it is, after all, in the title of the book. The author, Carolivia Herron, went on TV to support Sherman and said she would work with her to produce a study guide for the book.

Though Sherman is obviously a well-meaning teacher who did nothing wrong, support for her has been surprisingly scarce. The school district's first reaction was to yank her out of class while conducting an investigation. The Hispanic superintendent of the district told parents the book could be interpreted as racially insensitive. The high-profile chancellor of the city school system, who is black, was slow to speak out, though he sent Sherman a note asking her not to leave. School officials have had little to say about the scurrilous attacks on an innocent teacher and nobody seems to want to reprimand or even criticize the attackers.

Racial touchiness does not appear to be the reason for this odd squeamishness. Black and Hispanic officials, in particular, wouldn't risk much by defending a harmless black-inspired class exercise about self-esteem. The reason, I think, is that our schools have been permeated by the therapeutic culture, and in that culture it is incorrect to criticize feelings as wrong or bad. In the therapeutic culture, if a person feels affronted, then a real affront has taken place, even if the affrontee, like the Brooklyn parents, misunderstood the situation or got the facts wrong.

A clearer example of how feelings trump facts is the recent uproar at Swarthmore College over a mess found in the campus Intercultural Center. On November 8, students said they found excrement and vomit on the floor of the center's large meeting room. Students concluded that the mess was an attempt to divide the campus and lash out at minorities and gays.

By the end of the week, the campus learned that the vomit was real, but the excrement was not—it was actually chocolate cake with sprinkles. In the real world, this might have slowed the momentum of those who were sure the act was intentional vandalism and hate speech. But at Swarthmore it didn't.

Was the mess the result of drunkeness, a political statement, or a stupid prank? Nobody really knew, but on the modern campus, offenses are defined by feelings, not by facts or intentions. Since many students felt unsafe and violated, the mess was defined as an attack on the historically oppressed. College officials termed it an expression of hate, though they didn't explain how this determination was made. A rally against hate drew some 500 people. Cries of "respect, safety, unity" echoed across the campus.

The cake and vomit were described as the work of "a handful of people who are hateful and scared," and an act that "had the symbolic effect of a hate crime." Speakers effortlessly fell into the language of feelings and the therapeutic culture, talking about how empowered they now felt after feeling so vulnerable and unsafe because of the assault by cake and vomit.

"When you violate that space, you violate me," said one speaker. Another said he had cried all night—"I was overcome by tears and mucus...It wasn't a good cry: it was a bad cry." But because of the rally, he said, he now felt "tears of hope." The director of the In-tercultural Center drew tears from the crowd as she spoke halt-ingly about the painful healing process that she and Swarthmore now face. A list of ten years' worth of harassing incidents was read. One example was criticism aimed at a student because her boyfriend wore a dress.

The room where the cake and vomit were found is used for meetings of various support groups. (More therapized language. Students used to meet to discuss common interests or activities. Now they meet to sup-port one another.) One student I spoke to is a former member of the conservative women support group, which has been disbanded, partly because there are only six conservative women on campus. Though conservative, she too thought that the feelings of being attacked es-tablished that an attack had actually taken place.

Why not? The campus culture takes for granted that a real offense is what anyone feels offended by. Many campus speech and conduct codes were written that way. Sexual harassment policies too. Clear definitions of violations have given way to self-defined offenses and an implied right not to be offended. This is a weird culture, and it's gaining on us in the real world.

SEPARATE AND UNEQUAL

It's a common observation in the inner city: the public school is a mess, but the Catholic school around the corner is a great success.

How can this be? The conventional explanation is that the Catholic schools skim off the children from more motivated and more financially stable homes. Besides, they can expel troublesome students and the public school can't.

The only flaw in this rationale is that it's completely wrong. Consider the excellent assessment of this issue by Sol Stern in *City Journal*, a publication of the Manhattan Institute, the New York think tank.

As Stern writes, a study by the New York State Education Department found that Catholic and public schools have similar percentages of students from troubled families with low incomes, and another report shows that Catholic schools expel far fewer students than public schools.

He cites the experience of a wealthy non-Catholic benefactor, Charles Benenson, who guided both public school students and Catholic school students as part of the "I Have a Dream" program offering college tuition to minority children who finish high school. In the public high school class he "adopted" in the South Bronx, only 2 of 38 children made it to college. In the Catholic school class 20 out of 22 went to college.

"They were the same kids from the same families and the same housing projects," said Benenson. "In fact, sometimes one child went to public school and a sibling went to Catholic school. We even gave money to the public school kids for tutoring and after school programs. It's just that the Catholic schools worked and the others didn't."

None of this comes as a thunderbolt from the blue. Thirty years of research has consistently shown that Catholic schools outperform public ones, usually at a fraction of the cost. In New York City, Catholic schools operate on a budget of $2,500 per student, about a third of what the public school spends.

The only news is that our urban public school systems continue to avert their gaze from the success of the religious schools. When New York Mayor Rudy Giuliani said that Catholic schools should be the model for reforming the public system, the silence was deafening.

One reason why the unsuccessful refuse to study the successful is that they are wedded too closely to the factors that make them fail. The Catholic schools, like religious schools in general, have no paralyzing bureaucracies, no tenure guarantees, no rigid credentialing systems that keep out able and energetic teachers. And they are not at the mercy of the powerful teachers' unions that have enough clout to frustrate almost any sensible reform.

Stern thinks "it's hard to escape the conclusion" that the power of these unions, and their hefty contributions to liberal candidates, have a lot to do with the dominant liberal opinion that Catholic schools should be ignored, and get no government aid. An issue that purports to be about the separation of church and state is actually about control of a monopoly school system.

The other major reason why public school officials can't bring themselves to examine religious schools seriously is a moral one: religious schools are based on a shared moral vision, which generates respect among teachers, parents, and students, and lends a sense of common purpose that has disappeared from the vast majority of public schools.

By contrast, many public schools seems to envision students as basically rights-bearing individualists facing an endless series of consumer choices of classes to take. Stern is very sharp on this point, arguing that one key to the success of Catholic schools in New York is that they missed the so-called rights revolution, which eroded the authority of schools and discouraged the disciplining of students.

One study of the success of the Catholic schools came up with this assessment: Catholic schools take the position that "no one who works hard will fail," while the prevailing approach of too many public schools is that "no one who shows up will fail."

A communal culture also makes religious schools relatively immune to most of the disastrous fads that plague the public system: multiculturalism, dumbing down, the narrow obsession with self-esteem, use of bilingual programs to delay or avoid the mainstreaming of immigrant children.

Stern thinks it's folly to keep pouring all public funds into the school system that is failing our inner city children, while trying to keep every nickel out of the hands of schools that are succeeding. He says it's time to "tear down the wall of separation" by encouraging the flow of private money to religious schools, and by granting vouchers and tuition tax credits to religious as well as secular schools. This is the commonsense solution to the crisis of city educations. So watch for the politicians and union leaders to fight it tooth and nail.

KILLING OFF THE LIBERALS

As student uprisings of the Sixties go, the one at Harvard in 1969 was a second-tier, copycat effort with much less violence than usual. Only one building was taken. Some professors were roughed up by students. Some students were beaten by police. But the injury toll was low and the takeover ended quickly. One bomb went off harmlessly and an ROTC building was severely damaged by fire. The media hardly noticed.

Out of such unpromising material, Roger Rosenblatt has produced the most vivid memoir yet on the decade of campus upheaval (*Coming Apart: A Memoir of the Harvard Wars of 1969*). Every schoolboy knows that the Sixties polarized our politics. Rosenblatt goes further: in the process of trashing civility, tradition, and authority, the Sixties students destroyed liberalism. "They didn't reshape the moral nature of the country," he says. "They killed off the liberals and liberalism and left the scene."

Rosenblatt, a 28-year-old Harvard instructor at the time, played a key role in the controversy. He describes his 1969 self as politically unformed and much too eager to be loved by all sides. His popularity with students was so high that cheers went up when he was named to the faculty committee formed to deal with the disturbances. When he heard this "terrifying ovation," he writes, he knew that he was "a goner," because he had come to a very negative view of the student takeover at University Hall and so voted for discipline.

Though close to many of the students and young enough to identify with the generational reaction, Rosenblatt thought they had no sense of the fragility of institutions and the damage they were wreaking by physically manhandling professors and trying to wrest power from administration and faculty. Martin Peretz, then an assistant professor of government, now editor in chief of the *New Republic*, told Rosenblatt that the takeover marked the end of automatic and reflexive respect for teachers, and the beginning of his own political shift from left to right.

By 1969, one student tactic was obvious—by provoking authorities into calling the police to clear buildings, arrival of police on campus itself became the key issue, forcing liberals and moderates either to side with student radicals or the status-quo administration. At Harvard, President Pusey, who derided the radicals as "Walter Mittys of the left," went for the "fast bust." As predicted, moderates who had opposed the takeover called a mass meeting to decry the bust and large numbers of previously unsympathetic students converted to what one professor called a "dewy-eyed...solidarity" with the radicals.

By calling in cops, Harvard inflamed old town-gown resentments—police were working-class men who never had a chance to attend Harvard. Their brothers and friends were fighting the war that Harvard men were sitting out in their campus cocoon. Yet Pusey was clearly right that Harvard couldn't appease or tolerate those who used violence to interfere with the workings of a university.

Rosenblatt is very sharp in describing the faculty evasions, fussiness, and settling of old scores that accompanied the upheaval. Meetings thrived, all of them "huge, rancorous, silly." At one point the government department set up a Liberal Caucus, which was called the Radical Caucus by the Conservative Caucus, which liked to refer to itself as the Moderate Caucus.

In Rosenblatt's opinion, the faculty was "morally careless" in not speaking out clearly on the limits of acceptable protest. A "strange conspiracy" arose between those who wanted power and those who foolishly ceded it. He says, "Liberalism rolled over on its back like a turtle awaiting the end."

By belief and temperament, Sixties campus liberals were committed to reason, moderation, compromise, and seeing the other fellow's point of view. They were predictably baffled by student protesters who weren't much interested in any of this. From the first big uprising—Berkeley in 1964—liberalism was the declared enemy of radical protesters. The goal was confrontation and radicalizing by provoking repression. At Berkeley, leaders told students not to discuss or analyze issues, and at any rate, according to the popular slogan, "the issue is not the issue." (Among the non-issue issues that triggered major protests were free speech at Berkeley and a new gym at Columbia.)

"The left has failed because it was rooted in ideas," Jerry Rubin once said. "Our generation is in rebellion against abstract intellectualism and critical thinking." The goal was to dissolve traditional culture and its rational values.

These attitudes now tend to dominate the campus. Unable to transform the real world, large numbers of the Sixties activists and radicals decided to become professors and change the campus. They succeeded. As a result, what passes for liberalism in America today is a campus-based political correctness, often quite authoritarian in tone and style. The real liberals are no longer with us. As Rosenblatt says, they have been killed off.

Hey, we're no. 19!

First the good news: the IQs of students in the U.S. and other nations have been rising steadily, about three points every decade on standard tests. This undercuts any remaining belief that IQs are fixed or entirely genetic. Now the bad news: yet another big study shows that American students are well behind students of other industrialized nations in math and science. Among the 21 nations in the study, American high school seniors came in 16th in general science knowledge and 19th in general math skills. In physics, they were dead last in a field of 16. The U.S. performance was actually worse than it looked because Asian nations, which do particularly well in these comparisons, were not involved in this study. Otherwise America might have been fighting for 39th or 40th place in a 41-nation field.

About the IQs: no one knows for certain why they are rising, but one factor is surely the growing visual sophistication of each new crop of students. The gains are greatest on non-verbal, spatial tests—a rise of up to seven points per decade. Television, video games, and personal computers help teach these skills early. But some other popular hypotheses ring a bit hollow after the American performance in the 21-nation study: that IQs are going up because children today are benefiting from better nutrition, better access to good schools, and far more involvement of parents in their early education. How could these factors push our children to do better on IQ tests but worse on high school math and science tests, at least in relation to other students around the world?

The new survey is the Third International Math and Science study. It found that U.S. fourth-graders did fairly well on math and science and U.S. eighth-graders were mediocre or poor—they ranked in the middle of the pack on science and below the international average in math. The positive spin on this is that reforms are taking hold among the fourth-graders who will later do better as eighth- and twelfth-graders. But a more obvious explanation is that for whatever students are not building on early simple skills to develop complex ones, so the curriculum is subtly being dumbed down. The most popular rationalization of low scores, that they are solely a reflection of the democratization of our educational system, doesn't work here because even our best students did poorly by world standards. American advanced students in math came in 15th among 16 nations and American advanced science students came in 16th. Yes, poverty, weak family structure and the language problems of some new immigrants can retard school performance. But when the favored, self-selected few come in last or next to last in subjects critical to the nation's future, it is time to point the finger directly at America's schools and its methods.

What does the U.S. system have that other national systems don't? Well, for one thing it tolerates a high number of unqualified or barely qualified teachers—almost a third of math teachers and half of physics teachers did not major or minor in these subjects at college. Largely because of the culture of the teachers' colleges, our public education is pervaded by social attitudes that work against achievement. One is the heavy emphasis on feelings, subjectivity, and self-esteem at the expense of actual learning and thinking. College teachers complain that large numbers of freshmen now arrive on campus ready to explain their feelings and attitudes but unable to construct a rational argument. A number of surveys show that students feel a sense of self-esteem about their schoolwork, even when that work is poor.

Schools are flooded with progressive experiments and social agendas that either go down in flames or crowd out actual learning—whole language, cooperative learning, the politics of identity, outcome-based education, history as group therapy. An emphasis on egalitarianism in the classroom often has strange effects, making some teachers suspicious of achievement and any knowledge that "contributes to inequality." Some teachers now refer to themselves as "facilitators" because they believe "teaching" is an expression of dominance. Rita Kramer showed in her book, *Ed School Follies*, how pervasive these attitudes and fads are in the teachers' colleges. It's something like the many alternative and odd therapies on the fringe of the medical world. The difference is that faddists don't run the medical schools—they do run the teachers' colleges.

One sign of the times is the popular textbook *Secondary Math: an Integrated Analysis: Focus on Algebra*. It talks about the rain forest, Maya Angelou's poetry and student feelings about zoos, but doesn't get around to solving its first linear equation until page 165. Another is the long-awaited 1996 national English standards which turned out to set no standards at all. Instead we got a trendy tolerance for bad grammar and spelling and a lot of incomprehensible gibberish about "word identification strategies" and "writing process elements." Language skills of U.S. students are said to be even lower by world standards than their math and science skills. Should we find this surprising?

SHAKESPEARE VS. SPIDERMAN

I visited the Barclay School in Baltimore the same day that the new national "Standards for the English Language Arts" arrived on my desk in New York. This produced what the authors of the new Standards might call "dissonant cognitive process diversity," or what an English-speaking person would call a jumbled mind.

Barclay is a rigorous, structured, back-to-basics public school that combines confidence-building with high expectations. It gets results that elite private schools would be proud of, and it gets them from inner-city students, 85 percent of them black, 60 to 65 percent from single-parent homes.

While Barclay insists on plain English, the new standards are written in mind-bending jargon. They talk about "word identification strategies" (reading) and the use of "different writing process elements" (writing) but nothing directs teachers to teach specific rules of phonics, spelling, grammar, and punctuation (though the text says students "may wish" to explore ways of using punctuation more effectively).

At Barclay, these things are pushed hard and early. All consonant sounds are mastered before first grade. In the kindergarten I visited, a girl was sounding out words from a written list. In the first grade, I flipped through the assignment booklets hanging on the wall. All had well-written, grammatical one-page essays in clear, attractive handwriting.

Even in a special education class of older children, the written work was of good quality. I wouldn't have guessed that the writers had to be in a separate class.

The standards, on the other hand, feature a picture of a third-grader's rather crude one-paragraph essay. It has twenty mistakes of grammar, spelling, and punctuation. In current educational theory, these aren't errors, just alternate expressions and personal spellings. But Barclay aims at perfection, so they are errors. Any found in homework are corrected immediately the next day.

The standards are dismissive of "prescribed sequences" but Barclay is built around them: parents are told exactly what their children will learn each week and how they must help their children progress. At the end of the school year, parents and children visit the next grade, where they learn what will happen next term.

Barclay's approach is a rebuke to the reigning theories at our schools of education. It ignores whole-language theory. It believes in "direct instruction" (the dismissive educational term for actual teaching). It doesn't build self-esteem by excusing or praising failure. It ignores "learning strategies" and multicultural claptrap. All it does is churn out bright, achieving kids.

Unlike the notorious National History Standards, which were overly long and grandly contemptuous of the West, the English standards are short (one page with 69 pages of tortured explanation) and have been attacked on all sides as unreadable, even by the *New York Times*. They are the dubious work of the International Reading Association and the National Council of Teachers of English. These people are teaching our children how to write English?

It's a sign of the times at the NCTE that every key word in its title except "Council" is under attack from its membership: "National" (too nationalistic), "Teachers" (should be facilitators or guides) and "English" (non-inclusive of other languages). After reading the report, I'd take the word "English" out, too, as deceptive advertising.

But the problem goes well beyond prose style. As is so often the case, bad prose hides bad thinking. Buried in all the gobbledygook is a theory of education, derived from literary theory and the deconstruction movement on college campuses. It goes like this: schools treat literature and history as texts, but every form of expression is an equally important text worthy of study—CDs, TV, movies, comic books, ad slogans, graffiti, conversation. Children must explore all these texts in personal searches for meaning. This meaning is not inherent in any text—it is personally created in the mind of each child.

So books have no inherent meaning, and nobody can say that Shakespeare is more worthy of study than a baseball card or a cola jingle. There are no hierarchies of value and nobody is right or wrong about anything. In this meltdown of traditional learning, the teacher of course can't teach. He or she acts as a marginal but friendly guide to "critical thinking," which turns out to mean not the development of sharp and logical critical skills, but the easy accumulation of "divergent" views on all matters. In effect, learning becomes just another matter of "choice," a marketplace view of thought without thinkers.

With our SAT scores so low and our public schools in deep trouble, this is not a very good time to convince students that reading comic books is just as good as traditional schoolwork. The good news is that the publication of the English standards is exposing this awful stuff to a broad public for the first time. It has hummed along in the background without much opposition, mostly because few of us noticed it and fewer yet were inclined to demand an English-language version. Now it's out in the open and we all can throw mudpies.

EXPEL GEORGIE PORGIE NOW!

The kissing 6-year-old in Lexington, North Carolina, is not my favorite offender in the tot division of sexual harassment criminality. My favorite is still the third-grade boy accused of touching a girl on the breasts, though it is perhaps fairer to say that during a game of tag, he tagged her on the very spot where her breasts would presumably appear in three or four years. This is like being accused of robbing a bank that hasn't been built yet, a very serious offense despite the bad timing.

A close runner-up would have to be last week's story of the 7-year-old boy in New York City suspended for five days as a sexual harasser for kissing a classmate "because I like her" and then impulsively pulling a button off her skirt. When asked about the button, he brightly started talking about Corduroy, the bear with the missing button in the famous children's book. This was clearly a devious diversion, all too typical of today's hardened romper-room sex criminals. Or perhaps it was an effort to implicate Corduroy in his crime. Anyway, soft-headed school officials cut two days off his sentence, possibly time off for good behavior, possibly fallout from the discovery that the child is an innocent and has no idea what sex is.

We are deep into the McCarthyite phase of attending to the real problem of sexual harassment. The anti-harassment curricula and policies now being installed in our schools typically set no minimum age for offense and only the fuzziest standard for what should count as harassment and what shouldn't.

The faults of these policies usually copy the faults of the lobbying efforts that set them up. The lobbying efforts typically include alarming surveys on harassment. To drive the numbers up and show that harassment is an overwhelming and pervasive problem, nearly every known boy-girl behavior is counted as harassment. For instance, "Hostile Hallways," the 1993 report from the American Association of University Women, got the school harassment rate up to 81 percent by including glances and rumors as offenses. (With those standards, plus "body language," discussed as harassment in a new AAUW document, the rate should have hit 100 percent).

The high number is used to depict sexual harassment as uniquely awful, far more serious than other behavioral problems or girl-to-girl or boy-to-boy harassment, and in need of a strong curriculum reaching down to potential 5- and 6-year-old offenders.

In Minnesota, for example, "Hostile Hallways" triggered a similar state survey that found 2,220 elementary school offenses and resulted in a sex-harassment curriculum, "Girls and Boys Getting Along." Despite the happy title, the curriculum committed almost every known offense of the anti-harassment movement: it viewed almost all conflict through a gender lens, it centered on rights rather than mutual respect and civility, it treated small children as miniature adults, and it prepared tots for a future as aggrieved litigants by teaching 9-year-olds to draw up formal complaints.

The curriculum is still floating around in Minnesota and elsewhere, but it was derailed as a state program by a single complainant, Kathy Kersten of the Center of the American Experiment, a Minnesota think tank. Kersten argued that the whole project was profoundly undemocratic (installed without input from parents, community groups, or voters) and unpardonably crude. It warned first graders that teasing boys who want to jump rope is an expression of "homophobia." It called for asking 9-year-olds whether an abused girl can really be called "a whore" and featured "critical thinking" exercises in which a boy starts a rumor that two children in the class are having sex.

Most of all, an air of heavy-breathing indoctrination hung over the program, with children learning about sex for the first time as a source of offense and possible formal complaint. Another wrinkle came when Sue Sattel, one of the authors of the Minnesota curriculum, complained in 1993 about a California law allowing public schools to expel students in the fourth grade and up for sexual harassment because it left K to 3 children unexpellable. "California is sending a message that it's OK for very little kids to sexually harass each other," she said, sounding as though she would make short work of the infamous Carolina kisser and Corduroy's wayward friend in New York.

The harsh attitude toward tot-harassers is just one sign that sexual harassment policies are evolving oddly. It's true that crude sexual incidents occur in the schools, some reaching down to lower grades. But how should we respond? Many of the "gender-equity" and harassment specialists view all such incidents as expressions of society-wide female oppression. They are likely to stress punishment, training in gender oppressiveness, and litigation.

The rest of us, perhaps, are more interested in teaching mutual respect, emphasizing reconciliation rather than punishment, avoiding a girls-against-the-boys mentality, and trying not to sweep trivial offenses in with the real ones. Not all awkward expressions of pubescent sexuality are real offenses, and if we wish to avoid fanaticism, kissing first-graders don't really need to be expelled or have "sexual harasser" stamped on their school records.

EMPTY COLLEGE SYNDROME

My wife and I took our 16-year-old daughter and her girlfriend to see some colleges over spring break—ten campuses in five days, all in New England. If this is Tuesday, it must be Amherst, or is it Wesleyan?

Each college offers an "information session," usually followed by a tour. Out of deference to my daughter, I was on my best behavior at the information sessions, suppressing my instinct to ask embarrassing questions. Here's the question I managed not to ask at Brown University: Isn't it racialist, if not racist, to hold a separate freshman orientation for minority students? (Yale does the same thing. Call it basic training in identity politics.)

At Yale, I did not ask why the university refused to accept a $20 million donation from the Bass family of Texas for studies in Western civilization. Yale delayed and delayed until the Basses, sorely provoked, tried to force the issue. Yale took this opportunity to announce it could not be pushed around by contributors and turned down the money. But you can bet that if the $20 million had been earmarked for courses in queer cinema or a new department of gender studies, Yale would have snatched the check from the Bass lawyers before the ink was dry.

At Boston College, I awarded myself lots of moral credit for not bringing up Mary Daly, the high-status, man-hating, radical lesbian professor ("Males have nothing to offer but doo-doo," she was quoted as saying in the *Boston Globe*.) For over 20 years, she banned males from her class. The school finally told her to stop, but she took a leave of absence instead. Daly and her gender-war clones at other colleges help explain why the American campus has become a chilly place for males, as the academic magazine *Lingua Franca* pointed out casually a few years back.

The campus is very different from what it was fifteen or twenty years ago—heavily politicized, doctrinaire, obsessed with race and gender, contemptuous of all things white and Western. Do the fresh-faced students and their parents have any inkling of what they are getting into? Or are they chiefly interested in colleges as brand-name credentialing machines that happen to teach a few courses on the side?

As reading material on our trip, I brought along Alvin Kernan's new book, *In Plato's Cave*, a memoir and an assessment of what's happened to our campuses since World War II. Kernan, got to college on the G.I. Bill in 1946, talking his way into tweedy and elite Williams College. Later he taught at Yale and Princeton.

He delights in the increasing openness and democratization of the colleges, but as Kernan's tale nears the present, his light tone and winning anecdotes disappear. He notes "the growing irrationality" of the academy. Reason, in fact, is now a villain on campus. Feelings, identity, and personal opinion are kings.

Kernan explains how the campus social revolution of the sixties (challenging authority, books, professors, subject matter) turned into the philosophical revolution of the seventies and eighties: the breaking down the reality of language through the movement popularly known as deconstruction. Off-campus, linguistic philosophy is a dim and boring subject. But by undercutting the validity of language, deconstruction accomplished something truly radical: it announced that words were empty, grounded in no reality, thus discrediting all the word-built value systems that make the world real and stable. Because of deconstruction, and the broader post-modern movement, everything can be toppled. This is exactly what the West-bashing multiculturalists and male-bashing campus feminists wanted to hear.

The college guides don't mention it, and it never comes up at "information sessions," but the intellectual climate of meaninglessness and breakdown pervades our colleges. I recently heard from an old friend, a professor, who wrote that he is surrounded by a new crop of young professors who are total nihilists—"they don't believe in anything at all." This in the philosophy department of a fairly well-known Catholic college, no less.

Back to our campus visits. The college tour is obviously awkward for parents who realize that the modern American university is rooted in a disastrous new value system quite antagonistic to their own. "We are like a warrior caste that sends its children away to be raised by pacifist monks," says Norman Podhoretz, the critic and editor.

Why are the warriors paying the monks up to $36,000 a year to do this? Because they don't know what's going on, or because they don't know what else to do. A degree from a name college counts. It's still possible to eke out a decent education by navigating around the more disastrous departments and professors. And the hard sciences are still basically unsullied by monkish hands.

But pressures for more options are rising. "Why don't we organize some new universities?" writes Yale computer scientist David Gelernter. "When existing institutions are corrupt, it's natural to replace them— or at least to discuss replacing them." It's an idea that was bound to surface, drastic and in many ways unrealistic, but a perfectly rational response to the current crisis of the academy. We will hear more of this, I'm sure.

No TAKEOVERS, PLEASE

When people draw up their short lists of the nation's most politically correct campuses, the University of Massachusetts at Amherst is usually among the top five or six. Almost anything can happen there, from protests about the school's Minuteman mascot (he is military; he is white) to the regular takeover and trashing of offices, regularly followed by concessions to those who did the trashing.

Now U. Mass has hatched a plan that could send it to the top of PC lists everywhere. It's called "Vision 2000," a program drawn up by women's studies officials and other feminists at U. Mass and the five other land-grant universities of New England. The presidents of three of those universities, Vermont, New Hampshire. and Maine, have already endorsed the plan "in spirit." This is surprising, since the program seems to dissolve traditional academic freedom and call for a feminist overhaul of every campus department. Daphne Patai, a U. Mass professor of literature who co-authored *Professing Feminism*, a book on the odd development of women's studies, calls the plan "an attempted coup...a stunningly imperialistic move to put in place a questionable feminist agenda, thinly disguised as a plea for equal opportunity and fairness."

Ann Ferguson, director of women's studies at U. Mass, obviously disagrees, but acknowledges that traditional academic freedom would have to be modified. She told the U. Mass faculty senate that "we can't lose track of the wider goal in order to defend some narrow definition of academic freedom."

The plan, which the framers want to take nationwide, calls for "transforming the curriculum." This transformation would be "best conducted with guidance from an autonomous women's studies site." Every academic department would have to hold an annual seminar on gender issues and gender studies would be "introduced into all pertinent programs of institutional research." All students and professors would undergo gender sensitivity training. Faculty would be held accountable if men are "overrepresented" in the curriculum or if their "pedagogies" (teaching styles) are not "woman-friendly." And "woman-friendly pedagogies" must be used in all classes. Teachers who don't comply would be denied promotions and raises.

Other penalties are listed for any department with high female dropout rates, apparently a measure aimed at math and science teachers. The university would withdraw its support and recognition from any "group" with a higher rate of sexual harassment or sexual violence than the campus average. So presumably fraternities, sports teams or social clubs which exceed an average number of reported harassments would be eliminated.

The document's ban on the "overrepresentation" of males in the curriculum could mean, for instance, that a course of Renaissance art would somehow have to find that half of the great artists of the period were female, though 99 percent were male, since women were excluded or discouraged from artistic work at the time. Presumably a course on 19th-century American quilt-making would have the opposite problem of finding a correct retroactive quota.

The apparently innocent term "women-friendly pedagogies" might be enough to revamp the campuses all by itself. At colleges and law schools around the country some feminists have argued that abstract argument, debating, logic, grading, and calling on students in class who don't wish to be called upon are all male techniques that many women resent. In this view, "female" knowledge depends heavily on personal experience, feelings, and cooperation rather than competition or striving for excellence.

Campus feminists, like most multiculturalists, tend to believe that all knowledge is constructed, and that college women are being spoon-fed "male" or "white male" knowledge that must be deposed and replaced by "new knowledges" created by women and minorities. This worldview turns the debate away from learning and toward a politicized power struggle to control the curriculum. "Vision 2000" wants to "utilize institutional research capacity to produce the data necessary to raise consciousness, instigate action and monitor progress," a clear indicator that even the collection of data must now be politicized. Money, too, is supposed to follow the new politics. The plan calls for the universities to divert funds toward "marginalized and underrepresented groups."

A few of the women's studies programs seem to be serious academic programs, interested in ideas, evidence, debate, and an open search for truth. But most aren't. Most are part therapy group, part training grounds for feminist cadres to fight the patriarchy. It's a close question whether these politicized outposts should be academic departments at all. The "Vision 2000" proposal to make them campus-wide supervisors of courses and faculty is stupefying. The modern university is not known as a place of great courage or common sense. Let's hope enough of both are found on the six campuses to put this plan to sleep.

THE ANSWER IS 45 CENTS

The latest in a long line of depressing reports on the condition of our colleges is "Declining Standards at Michigan Public Universities," put out by the Mackinac Center for Public Policy.

The report finds that Michigan's state universities are "suffering from a general erosion of academic standards and a radical politicization of the undergraduate curriculum." Nothing new there. A 1996 report on New York state's universities said much the same thing and the National Association of Scholars put out a devastating national analysis of the dumbing down of the modern curriculum, which now bulges with things like "queer theory," the works of Pee Wee Herman, and watching *Oprah* or *Montel Williams* for credit.

No wonder that a Department of Education study three years ago showed that more than half of American college graduates can't read a bus schedule. Exactly 56.3 percent were unable to figure out how much change they should get back after putting down three dollars to pay for a 60-cent bowl of soup and a $1.95 sandwich. (Listen up, college people: the correct answer is 45 cents. Take my word.)

What caught my eye about the Michigan report is how the new stupidity shows up in college writing classes. The report finds that the "process" school of composition seems to dominate 133 of 140 freshman writing classes at state institutions. According to this school of thought, writing is a continuous process with much re-writing, growth, and self-discovery. So far so good. But embedded in the theory is the notion that standards, grammar, grades, and judgment are bad. Self-expression, self-esteem, and personal rules are good. Students sometimes talk about their "personal languages" and "personal spellings," all of which are presumably just as good as anyone else's language or spelling.

Writing in the *Public Interest*, Heather Mac Donald reports that "Students who have been told in writing class to let their deepest selves loose on the page and not worry about syntax, logic, or form have trouble adjusting to other classes"—the ones in which evidence and analysis are more important than personal revelation or feelings.

In "process" teaching, the gush of feelings about the self often gets tangled up with radical politics and multicultural makeover of the colleges. Rules, good writing, and simple coherence are sometimes depicted as habits of the powerful and privileged, sometimes as coercion of the poor and powerless. A collection of papers prepared for a course at Central Michigan University takes this politicized stance: "Traditional grammar books were unapologetically designed to instill linguistic habits which were intended to separate those who had made it from those who had not."

So the Michigan report complains about "the politically motivated dismissal of correct, formal prose as oppressive or intimidating to students." Those winds are certainly blowing through the colleges. James Sledd, professor emeritus of English at the University of Texas, writes in *College English* that standard English is "essentially an instrument of domination." Arguing against knowledge of grammar and logic, Jay Robinson of the University of Michigan says that "the myth of basic skills" helps sustain a rigid and evil class structure. What college students really need, he says, is reaffirmation as "members of racial, social, and linguistic minorities."

A better example of this school of thought is an article in the *English Leadership Quarterly* urging teachers to make intentional errors in English as "the only way to end its oppression of linguistic minorities and learning writers." The pro-error article, written in disappointingly good English by two professors at Indiana University of Pennsylvania, actually won an award from the quarterly, a publication of the National Council of Teachers of English. The NCTE, a group that sometimes seems to be moving rapidly away from any contaminating association with actual English, was co-author of last year's goofy national English standards, attacked on all sides as empty and unreadable, even by the *New York Times*.

In some ways, this anything-goes movement is an attempt to patronize a new wave of unprepared college students, largely members of minority groups, by saying that standards aren't really very important after all. Mac Donald writes: "Confronted with a barrage of students who had no experience in formal grammar or written language, it was highly convenient for professors to learn that students' natural way of speaking and writing should be preserved, not corrected."

But the good-hearted professors who disparage "the myth of basic skills" are doing the students no favors. At some point students have to leave the university and find a job, usually one offered by a company that cares less about oppression and feelings than about those basic skills. "Recruiting Trends 1994-95," by Michigan State professor L. Patrick Scheetz, is one of umpteen studies showing how disappointed employers are by so many college grads. Scheetz finds that "not enough graduates have the ability to write, speak, reason, and relate to others in a satisfactory manner" to hold down a job. Should we correct this, or just order up more feel-good, anti-English theory in the colleges?

How the West Was Lost at Yale

Campus culture being what it is these days, Donald Kagan's 1990 speech to incoming freshmen at Yale College was amazingly controversial: he said the study of Western civilization ought to be common and central. Kagan, then dean of the college, said that the West's flaws—including war, slavery, exclusion of women—were common to other civilizations, but its achievements have been unique, including great emphasis on law, equality, liberty, and conscience.

Naturally enough, he was widely denounced on campus as a backward-looking white male and a racist. But in the wake of his speech, the then president of Yale, Benno Schmidt, approached one of the university's wealthy contributors, Lee Bass, and asked for money to establish a Western civilization program.

Yale had many courses in Western thought and culture, of course, but the idea was to offer an integrated program as an option to just picking cafeteria-style among individual courses. Schmidt thought it could be a model for programs at other universities around the country. Bass gave $20 million, touching off almost four years of academic wrangling that ended this month with Yale promising to give the money back, with interest.

Almost from the beginning, a lot of faculty opposition arose. Most of it claimed to be non-ideological—the faculty hadn't been consulted, funds were needed for other departments, the university was already strong in Western studies. Interestingly, Professor Harold Bloom, author of *The Western Canon*, agrees with this line of reasoning. "The dragon is out there all right," he said. "They've destroyed literary studies at all but four or five universities, reading Alice Walker instead of Spenser, Milton and Shakespeare. But it's not happening here. We have always been strong in the study of the Western humanities and we still are."

Still, the conventional ideological opposition to the West is there. Professor Sara Suleri, a veteran West-baiter, said: "Western civilization? Why not a chair for colonialism, slavery, empire and poverty?" Peter Brooks, head of the Yale Humanities Center, fretted about other programs being pre-empted by "something called Western civilization." Historian Geoffrey Parker, who teaches some of the Western courses that Yale is so deep in, was quoted as observing that "The major export of Western civilization is violence." And though the multicultural smog at Yale may indeed be thin by the standards of other campuses, in 1991 the *Boston Globe* quoted one of Donald Kagan's "implacable enemies" as saying that Kagan is 90 percent right about the damage done to Yale in the 1970s by fads like structuralism and deconstruction.

Whether because of ideological opposition or normal academic squabbling, Yale went years without implementing the program. The original committee, dominated by Kagan's allies, disbanded when the university refused to authorize money to hire four new faculty members for the program. With Schmidt gone and Kagan no longer the dean, Yale president, Richard Levin, named a new committee made up of professors much less friendly to Kagan's original plans.

An undergraduate, Pat Collins, then published an article in a conservative campus magazine, *Light and Truth*, charging that "all serious efforts" to implement the program had been effectively ended by Levin, and that "a number of faculty have even tried to have the funds redirected to their own projects or departments after succeeding in killing the original proposal." A *Wall Street Journal* editorial picked up the issue and blasted Yale. It reported that Michael Holquist, acting head of comparative literature, believed there could be "fusion" between Bass courses and classes on such issues as gender studies. In other words, the new Western civ program might end up being part of the same multicultural mush it was supposed to counter.

The exasperated Bass apparently had lost so much faith in Yale (Bass, Levin, and other principals in the case declined to be interviewed) that he asked for new assurances and made the tactical mistake of asking to approve the professors named to the program. But no university can allow outsiders to pick faculty. This offered Yale a way out of its self-created mess—it could reject the Bass grant on principle and spin the story to the press as if it centered on a rich alumnus trying to tell Yale what to do. (The *New York Times* and the *New Yorker* dutifully played the story this way.)

The heart of the story is this: how is it that Yale, which receives hundreds of millions of dollars a year and funds hundreds of programs, singled just this one program out for a four-year brouhaha? This was never conceived as a closed or celebratory project—it was expressly described as ranging from the rise of Mesopotamia to the rise of the Nazis and the Holocaust. And unlike the mandatory multicultural courses on many campuses, the courses here were optional—any student could avoid them.

Yale gave up $20 million in funding, and perhaps another $20 million in lost donations from disillusioned alumni, according to one source. Losing that much money in one failed adventure may well cost President Levin his job. It's a reminder of how far the modern university president will go these days to avoid hurting the feelings of the campus left.

Miss Piggy Was a Smarter Choice

Kermit the Frog won an honorary degree from Southampton College the other day, a "doctorate of amphibious letters." Apparently the first non-mammal to earn a degree on Long Island, Kermit was nice enough to deliver the keynote address, most of it in his familiar rat-a-tat comedic style. ("Don't let my spindly arms fool you. I can slam dunk one mean basketball.") Not to give away any trade secrets, but a muppeteer was scrunched down inside a specially constructed podium, while a mini-version of the college's academic robes were draped over his green and froggy hand.

A hundred or more students threatened to turn their backs on the Sesame Street star to show their displeasure with the college's publicity stunt. It isn't easy being green. At the last minute the rebellion faded, though a fair amount of muttering occurred. After five years of hard work, said Samantha Chie, a marine biology major, "now we have a sock talking at our commencement. It's kind of upsetting."

Over at Montclair State, honorary degrees went to Bruce Willis and Yogi Berra. Showing a grasp of popular culture, Montclair State president Irvin Reed said school loyalties "die hard" for Willis, whose life reads like "pulp fiction." (We get it.) Berra, who never went to college or high school, once again cast himself in his familiar role of Mr. Dim. Festooned in cap and gown, he read a series of Yogiisms, all originally concocted and polished to make him seem as stupid as possible. Among those he read were "When you come to a fork in the road, take it," and a mangled version of his well-known one-liner, "Nobody goes to that restaurant any more; it's too crowded."

Welcome to the modern commencement ceremony, where colleges strive to close any remaining gap between education and entertainment by spraying out honorary degrees to any available performer with recognizable name.

Among those who won degrees this year are Arnold Schwarzenegger (University of Wisconsin at Superior), Donald O'Connor (Chapman University), and Neil Diamond (NYU). Dodger Manager Tommy LaSorda gave the commencement address at Cal State, Long Beach.

Comedians usually do very well. Bill Cosby has a number of degrees, and added at least three this spring. Other honorees include Jerry Seinfeld (Queens College), Chevy Chase (Bard), Dan Ackroyd (Carleton University), Da Fonz (Henry Winkler, Emerson College), and Jackie Mason. For some reason, Oxford, possibly the world's most prestigious and least frivolous university, just gave Mason a degree. Go figure.

Anyone attending a graduation these days must prepare for the perplexing sight of academic robes being placed on the shoulders of who-is-he-again? minor characters from sitcoms and other TV shows. This is indeed a strange phenomenon, but there is a reason. Many students are delighted to see their TV friends right there on campus. Many administrations are delighted because any kind of celebrity will create buzz. If the big stars can't be bothered, or if they demand huge appearance fees to come get a degree, it's smart to go with lesser lights.

The granting of honorary degrees is an odd business at best. It's supposed to be done to recognize intellectual excellence, but variety is important on an honors list. Does it matter much that Barbra Streisand is now Dr. Streisand thanks to Brandeis University, or that Captain Kangaroo (riding the nostalgia boom) is one of our leading collectors of such degrees, with 18?

Probably not much. Finding 2,500 commencement speakers every year is a daunting job. Often a degree has to be dangled to attract a well-known speaker, and graduates pay so little attention to commencement talks that few will care (or remember) whether the speaker was Mother Theresa or Rocky and Bullwinkle. Bill Buckley calls the commencement speech "the last great obstacle to liberation." The form is so tired, the rhetoric of youth facing the future so cliche-ridden, that colleges might be forgiven if they import a Trekkie or a talking frog once in a while.

Still, it seems clear that colleges no longer show much ability to resist entertainment values and the marketing power of the celebrity culture. In this culture, any muppet or famous cartoon character can put a college on the map in a way that most doctors, scientists, lawyers, or public officials can't. This same procedure has invaded the curriculum too. Since colleges tend to be financially desperate consumer-driven places now, the curriculum is now more entertaining, more open to popular tastes and what students already know and want to hear more about. Courses on Batman, comic strips and TV shows are routine. Yale offers one on "Troubadours and Rock Stars," possibly covering the career of Dr. Sting, a recent honorary degree winner.

Look for more honors to go singers and sitcom characters. In the past few years, academic degrees have gone to Cliff the mailman from *Cheers* (Sacred Heart University), George the fall guy from *Seinfeld*, and this year, Vivian and Uncle Phil from *Fresh Prince of Bel Air* (Norfolk State, Virginia State) and Billy the hunk from *Melrose Place*. Coming next May to a university near you: the former key grip man from *Gilligan's Island*.

COP-KILLER AND COMMENCEMENT SPEAKER

Until last week, the worst choice of a college graduation speaker was probably Kermit the Frog, the well-known fictional amphibian and green sock who clowned around with departing seniors at Southhampton College in 1996. On Friday, Evergreen State College in Washington State set the modern record for commencement foolishness. It heard from Mumia Abu-Jamal, the convicted cop-killer, who spoke via audiotape from death row in Pennsylvania.

Abu-Jamal is the only classic radical chic cause to survive into the 1990s. He is the focus of arguments about race, the death penalty, and radical attempts, here and abroad, to depict America as a vindictive, racist nation. One overwrought supporter wrote that his death would be "the first explicitly political execution since the Rosenbergs were put to death in 1953."

His case has been taken up by the usual Hollywood suspects (Ed Asner, Whoopi Goldberg, Susan Sarandon, Oliver Stone, among others). Because Abu-Jamal has a powerful intellect and writes well, the more sophisticated segment of the cultural left quickly took to him too. Professor Cornel West compared him to Dr. Martin Luther King, Jr. Norman Mailer, who has celebrated two other convicted killers in his writings, added Abu-Jamal to his list. The *Yale Law Journal* published one of Abu-Jamal's articles. National Public Radio hired him to do commentaries on prison life, then dropped the idea when protesters questioned the wisdom of featuring an unrepentant cop-killer as an NPR analyst. (Would NPR hire Hannibal Lecter to cover eating disorders? Why not? He has a powerful intellect too, and he knows the subject.)

The Abu-Jamal case has unfolded on two levels. One level features the media circus to convert him into a celebrity, a political martyr and living indictment of modern America. The other level, much less interesting to both sides, deals with actual facts of the case, and here some sound arguments can be made on Abu-Jamal's behalf. He is, in my opinion, surely guilty. But some procedures were unfair and the way the death penalty was imposed was indefensible.

The unchallenged facts in the case are these: at 3:51 A.M. on December 9, 1981, in a seedy area of Philadelphia, Officer Daniel Faulkner stopped a Volkswagen driven by Abu-Jamal's brother, William Cook, apparently for driving the wrong way down a one-way street. He radioed for backup, then added, "On second thought, send me a wagon," intending to arrest Cook. When Cook turned and struck Faulkner, the officer began beating Cook with a seventeen-inch flashlight. Abu-Jamal, who was moonlighting as a taxi driver, came running over, armed with a .38 (his presence at the scene was never explained). Five shots were heard and Faulkner was hit twice. The fatal shot was fired directly into his face at close range. Less than one minute later, police arrived and found Abu-Jamal, shot once by officer Faulkner, four feet from the police officer's body. Abu-Jamal was wearing an empty shoulder-holster and an empty .38 was nearby, containing five spent shell casings.

There was no definite match between Abu-Jamal's gun and the bullets that hit Faulkner—the bullets were hollow-points that fragment in the body. Police neglected to test Abu-Jamal's hands, to determine whether he had fired his gun, and they didn't smell the gun barrel to see if it had just been fired. An eyewitness, cabbie Robert Chobert, said he saw Faulkner fall, with Abu-Jamal "standing over him firing more shots into him." But there were contradictions in his account—he first said that the shooter had run away from the scene before being caught and arrested, though police said Abu-Jamal hadn't run at all. And Chobert needed to stay on the good side of police. He was facing charges of arson and was driving that night with a suspended license. Two other eyewitnesses testified, also with contradictions and problems in their testimony.

One of the oddities of the case is that Abu-Jamal has never explicitly denied that he shot Faulkner. The closest he came was at the sentencing hearing, when he said, "I am innocent of these charges." Nor has he or his brother given any explanation of what did happen that night. Stuart Taylor, Jr., of *National Journal* thinks Abu-Jamal may have remained silent for seventeen years because he is an honest man who did shoot Faulkner and refuses to lie about it.

Taylor, in a long and brilliant analysis of the case in the American Lawyer in 1995, concluded that Abu-Jamal's trial was "grotesquely unfair." Only two blacks made it onto the jury in a city that's 40 percent black. Taylor thinks an unfair trial was guaranteed when it was assigned to Judge Albert Sabo, who is believed to have sent more defendants to death row—thirty-one—than any other judge in America. As Taylor tells it, the sentence was "pushed though by Judge Sabo in less than three hours on the Saturday of the July 4 weekend," in a proceeding "riddled with constitutional flaws," including introduction of an inflammatory statement Abu-Jamal had made as a Black Panther twelve years earlier at age fifteen.

Abu-Jamal is not Martin Luther King, Jr., not a folk hero and not anyone who should be honored at a college commencement. But he ought to get a new trial.

BOLD WORDS FOR A NEW GENERATION

Nobody asked me to give a commencement speech this year, but I had this one ready, just in case.

* * *

Let me say that I am pleased and privileged to be here, honoring you, the graduating class, on this, your day of days.

As I gaze out at your sea of bright and shining faces, it goes without saying that you will not just live *in* the future; you are that future.

I feel certain of this, just as I feel certain that you will fill that future to the brim with the distinguished gifts and talents that are so very much uniquely yours.

I believe it was Robert Frost, or perhaps Plato, who said, "Old men dream dreams; young men see visions." What lesson can we take here from Frost, or Plato, apart from the obvious sexism of the reference to "men" instead of "persons"?

I believe it is this. I believe this quotation enjoins you all, as it must, to dream the impossible dream, to be all that you can be, to empower yourselves, to get in touch with your inner child and make it your own best friend, to feel each other's pain while looking out for number one, to know no boundaries, to not stop thinking about to-morrow, to explore strange new worlds, to boldly go where no one has ever gone before. Imagine all the people, living for today!

This much is obvious, as you know. If you are at all like I was at your age, I imagine that you feel a mixture of hope and apprehension, partly because you aren't sure how long this speech is going to go on.

Now you are on your own. Years from now, when you leave your parents' homes and get your first jobs, I hope you will reflect back on what happened here, not on this ceremony itself, or on my poor words, or on the lousy economy and the crushing debt we have inadvertently dumped on you, but on what you yourselves have accomplished.

The president of your university assures me that he graduates no mind before its time, so the fact that you are here today surely indicates that he feels it is time for you to leave. Of course, there is always graduate school...

Now you embark on one of the more significant legs of that endless series of connecting flights we call life. Just as all Delta flights go through Atlanta, for some reason, even the ones from San Francisco to Los Angeles, so too may all of your life's short hops fly you spiritu-ally through the values of your alma mater. And remember, since bag-gage has a way of getting lost now on almost all flights, may these values always be with you as carry-ons.

You should know that, in a sense, you are not really leaving this university today, for a university is more than buildings and bricks and mortar and sexual harassment hearings and pointless tribal conflict observed from afar by college administrators.

It is also a long line of the many generations who have walked these campus paths, stretching from the distant past to the equally distant future and beyond.

What will the future be like? No one knows of course, but I believe there will be a great deal of change. Paradoxical as it may sound, I believe that change is the one constant in life. Make it your friend and not your enemy. As Heraclitus, the great Greek philosopher once observed, "You can't step twice into the same river." This may have been a reference to water pollution. Nobody knows for sure.

You are entering a world far different from the one my generation entered. My generation grew up with no MTV, no computer nerds, no millionaire utility infielders, no Maury Povich, no college loan deadbeats, no AK-47s, no $175 sneakers, no underwear worn in public, and very little jewelry worn on the tongue. Yet somehow we broke through and achieved all these things and more.

I believe that your generation is far more humane and caring than my own. You ask questions: "What is the meaning of life?" "How can I make a fortune in cattle futures with almost no money down?" "Why do we have to sit around in the hot sun listening to a commencement speech?"

I do not recall who it was who spoke at my own graduation. Whoever it was, I know I looked to him for wisdom and guidance, just as you now look to me. I suppose if there is one single message I'd like to leave with you, it is this: Concentrate on what you are doing.

If you do it well, you will ultimately be successful, unless you are trying to manage the Mets, eliminate the federal deficit, or establish an indoor smoking zone.

Act boldly. Do not fear making mistakes, though if you make one, look out. Frankly, the fast-food industry is filled with people hoping you will fail at your McJob.

Make a difference. Even though 70 percent of you will be lawyers, engaged in suing or defending the other 30 percent from one another, still I say to you: try to do something useful with your life, if only in your spare time.

In a very real sense, your graduation here today is not an ending, but a beginning, literally a commence-ment. If I may say so, this is, in fact, the first day of the rest of your lives. I realize it is startling to look at graduation this way, but I believe we must. Thank you and lots of luck. You'll need it.

MAINSTREAMING DEVIANCE

Jimmy Peters, age 6, is described vaguely as "communicatively handicapped." He speaks only in disconnected words. According to teachers, when he's frustrated, he lashes out. In his kindergarten class in Huntington Beach, California, teachers say he threw chairs, toppled desks, repeatedly bit and kicked other children and teachers, and disrupted class by throwing temper tantrums.

The Ocean View School District wanted to transfer Jimmy to a special education class. His father said no and denies his son is violent. The District sued to remove the boy. A county judge temporarily barred Jimmy from class, but a federal judge ruled that Jimmy is not an immediate danger to himself or others and ordered him readmitted.

Jimmy's teacher went on medical leave, saying she couldn't take the stress any longer, and 12 of the 31 children in Jimmy's class were removed by their parents because of the boy's return. "We're not against inclusion," said Karen Croft, one of the parents. "But if a child is going to be included in a class, he has to behave."

The Jimmy problem is a byproduct of humane reform: the mainstreaming of hundreds of thousands of disabled youngsters into ordinary public school classrooms. The downside of the movement is that schools have lost much of their ability to maintain order. The State of Virginia is currently battling the U.S. Department of Education to preserve school boards' authority to expel disabled students for behavior unrelated to their disability, such as bringing guns, knives, or drugs into school.

In 1988, the U.S. Supreme Court ruled that public schools may not expel or remove disruptive, emotionally disturbed children from their classes for more than 10 days, even to protect others from physical assault, unless they get permission of the parents or a judge. Writing for the majority, Justice Brennan said that when school officials sue to remove a disturbed child, they have the burden of proving the child is dangerous.

This has had the effect of turning placement decisions—whether a child goes to a regular class or a special ed class—over to lawyers and judges. And the high hurdle of having to prove dangerousness to self or others, the same hurdle that keeps some of the wilder deinstitutionalized mental patients on our streets, means that the schools will usually lose such suits in court.

More astonishingly, the right of all schoolchildren to a chaos-free classroom is not taken into account. If proving dangerousness to a judge is the only way to remove a disturbed child, then presumably the child could run around class shrieking every day, toppling desks, and shredding schoolbooks in a non-dangerous manner without running afoul of the Brennan rule.

"At what point do we raise the question, 'Can the rest of the class function?'," asks Robert Berne, dean of the Wagner School of Public Service at New York University. "If mainstreaming is slightly better for the disturbed child, but much worse for everyone else, we have to deal with that."

The problem is becoming worse as the call for "full inclusion" grows. In the 1980s, many school districts started mainstreaming children with mild disabilities, often without special help. Since then children with severe mental, physical, and behavioral problems have been placed into regular classes. The argument is now made that the "exclusion" of any youngster, no matter how seriously impaired, is simply unjust.

There's a more cynical explanation for the sudden mainstreaming of very serious cases: since special-education students are heavily funded, school districts can save millions by "dumping" these students into regular classes without providing the support of expensive aides and special teachers.

Albert Shanker, president of the American Federation of Teachers, says a lot of dumping is going on. The AFT believes that many teachers are either afraid or skeptical of the inclusion policies. An AFT poll of West Virginia teachers shows that 78 percent of respondents think disabled students won't benefit from the inclusion policy; 87 percent said other students won't benefit either.

The Toledo AFT points out that some severely disturbed children are already in regular public schools, though still segregated in special classes. Among them are students in diapers, others fed through tubes, suffering from obsessive-compulsive disorders, or extremely violent and destructive. One 9-year-old, whose mother had sued for him to be mainstreamed, had broken the jaw of one staff member and three ribs of another. A high school student urinated on the floor, banged her head against the wall and tore off her clothes and shredded them when she did not get her own way.

The call for "full inclusion" should surely lead to some discussion about when exclusion is justified, what the financial and social costs of the program will be, and what kind of learning will go on in classes where severe disturbance is allowed to set the tone. This movement has rolled along without enough input from the public. If it goes much further, it may turn out to be yet another advertisement for school choice programs.

AFFIRMATIVE ACTION HISTORY

Gilbert Sewall, head of the American Textbook Council, has touched off a controversy over a newly multiculturalized version of a famous old high school history book.

Writing in the *Wall Street Journal*, Sewall argues that Todd and Curti's *The American Nation* (Holt, Rinehart and Winston) is unfair to the Reagan years and too devoted to "radical gestures and trendy global 'concerns,'" with a text that has been dumbed down and jazzed up with lots of pictures.

Maybe so, but that doesn't go to the heart of the current textbook problem. I think the problem is this: how can the story of minorities and women be told more fully and honestly without pulling the main story of America's development out of whack?

Paul Boyer, the University of Wisconsin historian who wrote the text, said he wanted to make up for "the unconscionable neglect" of outgroups. The editorial director of the project, John Lawyer, said he wanted to treat each of these groups in every era of American history and not relegate them to corners of the book. Fine. But there's a price to be paid. Stressing these groups over and over has some strange effects. So does the barrage of pulse-taking study-guide questions on how they are doing.

What happened in the Fifties? "Rural residents, African Americans, Hispanic Americans, and Native Americans continued to endure poverty and prejudice."

How about American Independence? Well, it "failed to benefit" women, blacks, and Native Americans. The study questions include these: How were African Americans and Mexican Americans affected differently by the Depression? How did the New Deal affect African Americans and Native Americans? What gains did African Americans and Mexican Americans make during the war?

This is carried on so relentlessly that it eventually takes on a comic effect. What's next? Maybe, "Describe the impact of the Los Angeles Earthquake on Polish-Americans" or "Explain how Swedish people living in Minneapolis feel about Rodney King."

It drives home a balkanized view of America as seen through the race-and-gender lenses that are standard issue on campuses these days. And the book never explains why certain groups—basically those covered by affirmative action programs—are worth so much more attention than, say, religious minorities or other ethnic minorities.

As an Irish-Italian-American, I managed to spot pictures of two Irish-American men (one ward boss and Jack Kennedy) and two of Italian descent (Sacco and Vanzetti). But there are 75 to 80 illustrations of Indians and Indian culture running through the book, about three times the pictorial treatment given to the Irish, Jews, Swedes, Italians, Poles, Germans, and Arabs combined.

The race-and-gender allocation of biographies in the back of the book is worth noting, too. By my count, of the nearly 200 Americans considered worthy of short biographies, 56 are white females, 71 are white males, and 68 are nonwhites. Of the white males, 41 served as president, so white American males who failed to become president account for about 15 percent of all the profiles. Two of these lucky 30 who made the list were Julius Rosenberg, executed as a spy in 1953, and General George Custer. Of the 13 religious leaders on the list, two are non-Hispanic white males—Brigham Young and Ralph Waldo Emerson.

As in all these books, the desire for accuracy mingles with market pressures and an urge to compensate certain groups for their virtual exclusion from earlier texts. So the allocation of space and emphasis pushes the book toward a kind of affirmative action history. Senator Margaret Chase Smith is cited for challenging Senator Joseph McCarthy. While one of the early critics, she didn't have much to do with bringing McCarthy down. She is presumably included here—given prominent play and a photo—to get a woman into the narrative.

The race-and-gender approach is bound to wear down all but the most devoted admirers. Television, the book says, "often reinforced stereotypes of ethnic groups, women and American life." The Clinton administration is hailed for "the most racially diverse and gender-balanced cabinet in U.S. history." Before the upheaval of the 1960s, the book says, America's popular culture "emphasized that to be American meant to be white and middle class."

Like many such texts, the book is flooded with an extraordinary amount of harmless, esteem-boosting multicultural filler (1853: Native American chef George Crum makes first potato chips.) More seriously, America's long racial crime against blacks often becomes the only prism through which the nation is viewed.

The game of baseball comes up three times in the text, twice to remind us that blacks were excluded for 60 years. Similarly, an essay in the book says that Thomas Jefferson has been brought down a peg by revelations of his possible affair with a slave. The essay suggests that his "enshrining" was tied to an older school of history, leaving his reputation as mixed today as when he was alive and critics were calling him "Mad Tom."

The book won't do. Our students deserve better than this.

No Books, Please; We're Students

Incoming college students "are increasingly disengaged from the academic experience," according to the latest (1995) national survey of college freshmen put out each year by UCLA's Higher Education Research Institute. This is a rather dainty way of saying that compared with freshmen a decade or so ago, current students are more easily bored and considerably less willing to work hard.

Only 35 percent of students said they spent six or more hours a week studying or doing homework during their senior year in high school, down from 43.7 percent in 1987. And the 1995 survey shows the highest percentage ever of students reporting being frequently bored in class, 33.9 percent.

As always, this information should come with many asterisks attached: the college population is broader and less elite now, and many students have to juggle jobs and heavy family responsibilities. At the more selective colleges, short attention spans and a reluctance to read and study are less of a problem. But a lot of professors are echoing the negative general findings of the freshmen survey.

"During the last decade, college students have changed for the worse," chemistry professor Henry Bauer of Virginia Polytechnic Institute said in a paper prepared for an academic meeting this week in Orlando. "An increasing proportion carry a chip on their shoulder and expect good grades without attending class or studying."

Bauer has kept charts since 1986, showing that his students have done progressively worse on final exams compared with mid-semester quizzes, even though they know that the same questions used on the quizzes will show up on the finals. He thinks this is "indisputable" evidence of student decline, including a simple unwillingness to bone up on the answers known to be coming on final exams.

His paper is filled with similar comments from professors around the country. A retired Marquette professor complained that "sleeping in my classes was common and attendance was under 50 percent except before tests." "The real problem is students who won't study," wrote a Penn State professor. A retired professor from Southern Connecticut State said: "I found my students progressively more ignorant, inattentive, inarticulate." "Unprecedented numbers of students rarely come to class," said a VPI teacher. "They have not read the material and have scant interest in learning it." Another VPI professor said that many students only come to class when they have nothing better to do. At one of his classes, no students at all showed up.

So far the best depiction of these attitudes is in the new book, *Generation X Goes to College*, by "Peter Sacks," the pseudonym for a California journalist who taught writing courses to mostly white, mostly middle-class students at an unnamed suburban community college.

Sacks produces a devastating portrait of bored and unmotivated students unwilling to read or study but feeling entitled to high grades, partly because they saw themselves as consumers "buying" an education from teachers, whose job it was to deliver the product whether the students worked for it or not.

"Disengaged rudeness" was the common attitude. Students would sometimes chat loudly, sleep, talk on cell phones, and even watch TV during class, paying attention only when something amusing or entertaining occurred. The decline of the work ethic was institutionalized in grade inflation, "hand-holding" (the assumption that teachers would help solve students' personal problems) and "watering down standards to accommodate a generation of students who had become increasingly disengaged from anything resembling an intellectual life."

Engulfed by an amusement culture from their first days of watching *Sesame Street*, Sacks writes, the students wanted primarily to be entertained, and a majority said so in a poll he took. The word "fun" turned up often in student evaluations of teachers, which exerted powerful sway over a teacher's career. At one point, a powerful faculty member suggested that "Sacks" take an acting course so he could improve his student evaluations.

The entertainment factor is popping up at many colleges these days—courses on *Star Trek*, use of videos and movies, even a cartoon music video on the economic theories of John Maynard Keynes. Economics light for non-readers.

But the book goes well beyond conventional arguments about slackers, entitlement, and dumbing down. Students, he says, now have a postmodern sensibility—distrustful of reason, authority, facts, objectivity, all values not generated by the self. "As children of postmodernity, they seem implicitly to distrust anything that purports to be a source of knowledge and authority."

Sacks and some of his fellow teachers concluded they were "in the midst of a profound cultural upheaval that had completely changed students and the collegiate enterprise from just ten years earlier." Oddly, he presents his Boomer generation as the defender of the traditional order against Generation X, but the heavy campaign against authority, objectivity, and an adult-run university were Boomer themes of the Sixties now rattling through the whole culture. But he's right about the depth of the upheaval. We can expect greater campus conflict and upheaval in the years ahead.

LET'S LOWER THE BAR

When you think about the Americans with Disabilities Act, think about the case of Marilyn Bartlett. Bartlett wants to be a lawyer, but she has failed the New York bar exam five times. From the first, she applied for special accommodations under the American with Disabilities Act, claiming that she suffers from a learning disability that impairs her reading and her ability to be able to work as a lawyer.

Bartlett's claim of severe difficulty in reading would seem to disqualify her from becoming a lawyer. After all, lawyers need to assimilate lots of information, most of it by reading. Bartlett reads very slowly and tends to lose her place often. While reading aloud in court, she confused the words "indicted" and "indicated."

Should she get special advantages in trying to pass the bar exam? The New York State Board of Law Examiners said no, on the findings of a reading specialist who tested her and decided that her problem was a mild one, not qualifying as a disability. Bartlett sued in federal district court and won. A judge ruled that she had a right to help because she couldn't read nearly as well as other aspiring lawyers. The judge found that Bartlett has a "defect that significantly restricts her ability to...decode the written word." The judge also said that reading is not essential to being a lawyer, since some attorneys are blind. (But blind attorneys do read—in Braille.) One legal commentator called this decision "counterintuitive," which is a fancy way of saying "very strange."

Bartlett took the bar exam with accommodations, including 50 percent more time than other test-takers, questions printed in large type, use of a computer, a private room and an assistant to help her with the test. She failed anyway, complaining that the assistant distracted her with unnecessary noise, mostly by unwrapping food and munching loudly. A few weeks ago, on an appeal by the Board of Legal Examiners, Bartlett won again. Now she will take the test a sixth time, with no assistant but double time allowed. If she fails, her lawyer says, she might go back to court for more accommodations.

What's wrong with this? With the help of its own people (judges) the legal profession is losing control of its minimum standards for entering the field. Law firms do not believe that ability to read and analyze texts with reasonable speed is optional, but the courts thought so in this case, and so the standard is being lowered. Under pressure of ADA litigation, look for accommodations to be granted to apparently unqualified candidates for medical board examinations and other forms of licensing. The traits that used to disqualify candidates—inability to function on crucial tasks—are now legally positioned as advantages or as conditions that call for various forms of extra help. For example, a law firm may be required to hire a reader solely to help a lawyer with a reading problem.

The cost of litigation will play a role, too. Fighting cases like Bartlett's means high legal bills and the possibility of paying compensatory damages as well. Under this pressure, it may be easier for the professions to shrug and grant accommodations to most applicants.

Walter Olson, an expert in employment law, sees the prospect of two different tracks for doctors and lawyers—one for those who meet announced professional standards, another for those meeting more relaxed performance levels because of ADA litigation. And it might be hard for clients and patients to discover which track their own lawyers and doctors took to become professionals. "ADA has the potential to force the rethinking—and watering down—of every imaginable standard of competence, whether of mind, body or character," Olson writes in his book, *The Excuse Factory.*

Objecting to a character flaw is dicey because almost all bad behavior can be construed as the result or expression of a disability. Rude behavior, for instance, might be the result of missed social cues or boorishness, known as dyssemia. Just as the psychiatric profession now lists all sorts of behaviors and minor problems as official disorders, the American Council on Education lists things like "a short attention span" and "difficulty being on time" as symptoms of learning disability. So almost any punishment of objectionable behavior can be a violation of disability law.

The broader problem is that nobody is quite sure how to distinguish between people with genuine learning disabilities and those who are underachievers, lazy, not too bright or just faking it to take advantage of ADA. Some creative students claim dubious disabilities such as dysrationalia (illogical thinking) or dysgraphia (bad handwriting). In many high schools, claims of learning disability have become a competitive sport played by parents who want their children to have the extra edge of more time on tests and therefore a chance to get higher marks. Often it takes no more than a note from a psychologist or a doctor. A large wave of students who came to rely on these accommodations in high school is now hitting the colleges. Graduate schools and the professions are next.

READY FOR BETTY THE YETI?

First the Oscars, then the Tonys and Grammys, now the "Pollys"—the new Campus Outrage Awards for berserk political correctness. OK, so maybe these awards aren't worth four hours of national TV, complete with six or seven paralyzing dance sequences. But the Intercollegiate Studies Institute, a conservative think tank based in Delaware, went to the trouble of thinking them up to honor what the American campus does better than any other institution: screw up its people with soul-crunching correctness. So please try to pay attention. There are five awards and the grand prizewinner is...(drum roll...dramatic opening of the envelope)...the Arizona State University Department of Theater for firing one of its professors, Jared Sakren.

Sakren, a graduate of Juilliard who taught at Yale, was recruited from the Alabama Shakespeare Festival four years ago and put in charge of ASU's graduate acting program. He says he began to get the flavor of his new department when he overheard some female students coming out of a feminist drama class talking about the genetic inferiority of males. Still, he won glowing approval from the department at the end of his first year, which happened to include the staging of Shakespeare's Taming of the Shrew. Lin Wright, the department chair, wrote: "You should be very pleased with the excitement and effort you have generated in your faculty."

The praise turned to criticism a few months later, during the 1995-1996 academic year. Sakren got a memo from Wright saying that "the feminists are offended by the selection (of) works from a sexist European canon." These included plays by Shakespeare, Moliere, Ibsen, Chekhov, and Aeschylus. Earlier Wright had written a memo, cited in Sakren's complaint to the university, which boasted: "It is probably the feminist view point that will kill off the classics, not media or a global society."

Sakren says he kept hearing from his colleagues that he wasn't innovative enough, that he should "reinterpret" plays or see than "in a new light, so as not to offend feminists." His staging of Shakespeare's *The Comedy of Errors* was called disappointing and Wright complained that "casting was a fiasco." Besides, it was another of those white male plays that irritate campus feminists. Sakren wasn't sure what he was supposed to have done to improve *The Comedy of Errors*, except maybe transform it into a symposium on domestic violence. He says that was basically what had happened to the Greek myth of Jason and Medea in an ASU production called *The Medea Project*. As Sakren recalls it, the play featured six Medeas (but no Jasons), all of them screaming about domestic violence.

Another play staged by the department was *Betty the Yeti*, the story of a logger who meets an abominable snowwoman high in the western mountains, "a creature that represents all the mystery and beauty of the ancient forest." The logger has sex with her, and is transformed into an environmentalist. ("Garbage," Sakren says.)

Wright wrote that "In virtually every area of his work at ASU, Mr. Sakren has been oblivious of, or has contributed to, a climate of sexism." As columnist John Kolbe wrote last fall in the *Arizona Republic*, "A stack of performance evaluations, departmental memos, probationary reviews, and formal findings reveal that Sakren has run headlong into the rubble of feminist 'deconstruction' despite glowing endorsements from students and co-workers."

In a performance review, Wright said that Sakren had discriminated against a disabled student and had showed insensitivity toward a woman doing a partial nude scene in a play about breast cancer. But both students said in writing that the allegations were false and praised Sakren for his sensitivity. Wright said, "I have serious reservations about his view of women." In a complaint to the university, Sakren says the department tried to replace him as director of the play about breast cancer after it opened to favorable reviews and won an award.

A student dramatist weighed in with a letter describing the overbearing feminist tone of some professors. One such professor, she wrote, talked about "getting me to throw (my) script away because it did not forward her vision of the feminist movement. She told me that my play followed the male paradigm of conflict and action, and that I'm on the 'boys side.' She told me I should put this play away, read some feminist theory, and then use my good play writing skills to write feminist plays."

A source in the department says there are legitimate differences of opinion in the Sakren case: the department wanted an emphasis on new work and Sakren favored the classics. Still, he was recruited from a Shakespeare festival so his approach was well known. "Political correctness was part of his firing," the source said. And "the fact that he is a white male had something to do with it. If he were a minority or a woman, he would still be working." The university responds that the Sakren case is "not about academic freedom or disagreements about his philosophy..." Sakren has filed a formal complaint against the university. Whether he wins or not, Arizona State seems a deserving winner in the PC sweepstakes.

TONGUE-TIED BY AUTHORITY

Universities keep telling us how committed they are to freedom of speech. But once the politically correct people start howling about the wrong sort of speakers, administrators usually fall in line to find a way to cancel or discourage the talks.

This happened to me a week ago at Columbia, and it happened to conservative author Dinesh D'Souza and six other speakers. We were invited to talk at Columbia's Faculty House by Accuracy in Academia, an offshoot of the conservative media watchdog group Accuracy in Media. We ended up off-campus, speaking to a tiny crowd on a sidewalk, surrounded by cops and protestors.

As I walked up, one of the protestors recognized me and silently mouthed the words, "I'm sorry." So at least one person on the left figured out that there was something wrong with the way Columbia treats dissenters.

Our Saturday speeches were scheduled to follow a Friday night invitation-only dinner talk by Ward Connelly. He was the leader of the successful referendums against racial and gender preferences in California and Washington State, so the campus thought police were naturally angry that he was allowed to speak. Letters to the campus newspaper, *The Spectator*, warned darkly that the "racists" were coming where they didn't belong.

Connelly's speech, and the whole two-day event, had been scheduled since August, and Accuracy in Academia had paid a quite high fee for use of the hall. Seven hours before Connelly's speech, Columbia decided that the group had to pay an extra $3,100, immediately, for beefed-up security protection. Late charges like this are a conventional way of stopping incorrect speech, but someone produced a credit card and the surprise fee was paid.

A crowd of 250 protestors showed up at Faculty House denouncing Connelly as a bigot and an Uncle Tom. One demonstrator shouted, "Let's force our way in," or words to that effect. Nobody tried, but the protestor's shout became the source of a lot of official concerns about safety for the speakers and their audience the next day.

These safety concerns ended up pushing the Saturday speakers off campus. University officials said they had no idea that Accuracy in Media had invited college students from around the New York area. What would happen if 700 or 800 people, perhaps many of them disruptive, showed up to fill a 200-person hall? A hand-wringing session was held at the home of Columbia's president, George Rupp.

Did the University decide to move the event to a larger hall, or simply give the speakers a bullhorn and let them speak to a standing crowd in Columbia's enormous quadrangle? No. That would have made sense. Instead, Columbia decided it would cut the crowd at Faculty House down to size by banning everyone who didn't have Columbia I.D. Unsurprisingly, Accuracy in Academia said "No thanks." It would have meant stiffing all non-Columbia invitees, perhaps two-thirds of the crowd. Since they concluded that they were being manipulated by an unprincipled administration, they moved the talks to a sidewalk off-campus as a protest.

The demonstrators understood that a form of censorship had just been imposed. That's why they chanted lines that included, "Ha, Ha, you're outside," and carried signs that said, "Access denied—we win."

As it happens, my speech was going to be about the lack of free expression on the modern politically correct campus—how colleges learn to use speech codes, conduct codes, and sexual harassment rules to intimidate and silence dissenters. It didn't need many changes to fit Columbia's tawdry treatment of Accuracy in Academia. I said that the crowd was witnessing a sophisticated version of the heckler's veto—using safety concerns to squelch unwanted speech. If I'm wrong about this, and if Columbia and its president turn out to believe in free speech after all, they can show it by making sure that Accuracy in Academia is invited back on campus, minus the rule changes, the extra fee, and the heckler's veto.

PART THREE

FAMILY AND GENDER

MARS TO VENUS: BACK OFF

A famous television newswoman told this joke last month at a fund-raising dinner for a women's college: A woman needed a brain transplant. Her doctor said two brains were available, a woman's brain for $500 and a man's brain for $5,000. Why the big price difference? Answer: the woman's brain has been used.

Most in the audience laughed, but one man stood up and booed. "What's wrong?" asked a woman at his table. The man said, "Just substitute woman, black or Jew for 'man' in that joke and tell me how it sounds."

At about the same time, American Greeting Cards launched an ad campaign in *Newsweek*, *Life*, and other magazines. One ad featured a "Thelma and Louise" greeting card, pasted into the magazines, that said on the front, "Men are always whining about how we are suffocating them." The punch line inside the card was this: "Personally, I think if you can hear them whining, you're not pressing hard enough on the pillow."

The newswoman, who is a friend, seemed shocked when I phoned and raised questions about her joke. "The poor, sensitive white male," she said. A spokesman for the greeting card company saw nothing wrong with a humorous card about a woman killing a man. He faxed a statement saying the card had been pre-tested successfully and besides, "We've heard no protests from consumers who are buying and using this card." But would American Greetings print a card with the sexes reversed, so the humor came from men joking about suffocating a woman? No, said the spokesman, because 85 to 90 percent of cards are bought by women. There is no market for a reverse card.

In truth, no man could get up at a fancy banquet and tell a joke about how stupid women are. And a greeting card joking about a woman's murder would be very unlikely, even if surveys showed that millions of males were eager to exchange lighthearted gender-killing greetings. The obvious is true: a sturdy double standard has emerged in the gender wars. "There used to be a certain level of good-natured teasing between the sexes," says Christina Sommers, author of *Who Stole Feminism?*: "Now even the most innocent remark about women will get you in trouble, but there's no limit at all to what you can say about men."

Men's rights groups phone me a lot, and I tell them my general position on these matters: the last thing we need in America is yet another victim group, this one made up of seriously aggrieved males. But these groups do have an unmissable point about double standards. On the *Today Show* last November Katie Couric suddenly deviated from perkiness and asked a jilted bride, "Have you considered castration as an option?" Nobody seemed to object. Fred Hayward, a men's rights organizer, says: "Imagine the reaction if Matt Lauer had asked a jilted groom, 'Wouldn't you just like to rip her uterus out?'"

The double standard is rooted in identity politics and fashionable theories about victimization: men as a group are oppressors; jokes that oppressors use to degrade the oppressed must be taken seriously and suppressed. Jokes by the oppressed against oppressors, however, are liberating and progressive. So while sexual harassment doctrine cracks down on the most harmless jokes about women, very hostile humor about men keeps expanding with almost no objections. Until recently, for example, the 3M Company put out post-it notes with the printed message: "Men have only two faults: everything they say and everything they do." Anti-male greeting cards are increasingly graphic, with some of the most hostile coming from Hallmark Cards' Shoebox Division. (Sample: "Men are scum....Excuse me. For a second there I was feeling generous.") *Detroit News* columnist Cathy Young sees a rising tide of male-bashing, including "All Men Are Bastards" and "Men We Love to Hate" calendars and a resentful "It's-always-his-fault" attitude pervading women's magazines.

Commercial attempts to increase the amount of sexual antagonism in America are never a good idea. And if you keep attacking men as a group, they will eventually start acting as a group, something we should fervently avoid. But the worst impact of all the male-bashing is on the young. Barbara Wilder-Smith, a teacher and researcher in the Boston area, was recently quoted in several newspapers on how deeply anti-male attitudes have affected the schools. When she made "Boys Are Good" t-shirts for boys in her class, all ten of the female student-teachers under her supervision objected to the message. (One, she said, was wearing a button saying "So many men, So little intelligence.") "My son can't even wear the shirt out in his backyard," she said. "People see it and object strongly and shout things. On the other hand, she says, nobody objects when the girls wear shirts that say "Girls Rule" or when they taunt the boys with a chant that goes "Boys go to Jupiter to get more stupider; girls go to college to get more knowledge." Worse, she says, many adolescent boys object to the "Boys are good" shirts too, because they have come to accept the cultural message that something is seriously wrong with being a male. "The time is ripe for people to think about the unspoken anti-male 'ism' in our colleges and schools," she says. And in the rest of the popular culture as well.

Marriage bashing à la mode

One of the problems in shoring up the institution of marriage is that so many of the professionals who teach and write about it—the counselors, therapists, academics, and popular authors—really don't support marriage at all. Some depict it as archaic and oppressive. Others give it tepid support as just one of many acceptable adult arrangements.

Another study showing this trend will be released this week: "Closed Hearts, Closed Minds," a report from the Council on Families, a project of the "I find marriage physically threatening," will very likely find it psychologically stifling. Glenn finds the books riddled with glaring errors and distortions of research.

Last week I read eight of these books and concluded that Glenn is right. The books generally portray families as loose collections of rights-bearing individuals. One book complains that the traditional view of family "collapses the interests of all family members into one whole." Marriage is depicted more as a convenience than as a commitment. As a result, children appear in the books as almost incidental to marriage, and authors expend great energy to show that they don't need two parents and aren't really harmed by divorce.

Families and Intimate Relationships by Gloria Bird and Keith Melville strongly argues that most problems showing up in children of divorce actually precede the marital breakups. Only one of the eight books focuses on the enormous accumulation of evidence that children in single-parent homes are far more at-risk than children in two-parent homes. Most treat the single-parent home as an inescapable fact and glide swiftly past the findings of high risk.

The effects of children on parents is handled oddly too. In the opening pages of *Marriage and Family: The Quest for Intimacy*, Robert H. Lauer and Jeanette C. Lauer casually mention that children "clearly do not always increase satisfaction." They say "most studies show that marital satisfaction decreases" during child-rearing years, although (here comes their good news) "parents may find their marital satisfaction returning again" after the children grow up and leave home. Later, however, they say 130 studies show that "the tendency for married people to be happier and healthier is long-standing." They also cite a Gallup poll showing that 95 percent of Americans say family life is very important to them, compared with 61 percent saying that about work, and 41 percent about religion.

But in all twenty books surveyed, Glenn found that this positive news is muffled or omitted. He writes that "almost half of the meager space devoted to marriage effects is taken up with discussions of how marriage hurts women."

The worst of the books, Judy Roote Aulette's *Changing Families*, is a Marxist-feminist analysis mostly devoted to the question of whether Marxists or radical feminists are more nearly correct about marriage as an inherently oppressive institution. At one point, she suggests that a husband should have no input on a wife's decision whether or not to have a child. Any wife who listens to Aulette will probably want to stay childless anyway, since she too tells us that "research shows that children have a detrimental effect on parents' mental health." Aulette approvingly cites Marx's intellectual ally, Friedrich Engels, arguing that marriage was "created for a particular purpose: to control women and children."

In these books, what many of us see as the gradual collapse of the family is just an adjustment to social and technological change. In many passages, this collapse is portrayed as an achievement: the two-parent family isn't especially good for children, but luckily it is fast disappearing.

That view has been in retreat for a decade now, as evidence has piled up that family form matters. James Q. Wilson writes that when the American people "look at the dramatic increase in divorce, single-parent families, and illegitimate children that has taken place over the last thirty years, they see families in decline. They do not need studies to tell them that these outcomes are generally bad." But that message hasn't gotten through to the tiny and determined minority that Wilson calls "the high culture," Maryann Glendon calls "the knowledge class," and most of the rest of us call "the cultural elite." They are still tossing out the old "Ozzie and Harriet" taunts and grinding out the same ideological tracts. The battle for public opinion may be over, but the losers are still writing the textbooks.

BOY, GIRL, BOY

"John" was an 8-month-old infant when his penis was destroyed in botched surgery. On the advice of doctors at Johns Hopkins Medical School, his parents decided to change him into a girl so he might one day have a normal sex life. His testicles were removed, a rough version of a vagina was created, and "John" was raised as "Joan."

This is a famous case in sexual medicine, if medicine is the correct term for what was done. One reporter who covers such matters calls it "the Wolfman of Sexology," meaning that the case is as central to sex and gender research as Sigmund Freud's "Wolfman" case is to Freudian psychology. It has been cited over and over in psychological, medical, and women's studies textbooks as proof that, apart from obvious genital differences, babies are all born as sexual blank slates—male and female attributes are invented and applied by society.

Now all those texts will have to be rewritten. More than thirty years after "John" became "Joan," word finally comes that the change was a failure from the start. "No support exists" for the blank-slate theory "that individuals are psychosexually neutral at birth." This conclusion is reported in the Archives of Pediatric and Adolescent Medicine by Milton Diamond, a sexologist, and Keith Sigmundson, a psychiatrist.

The young "Joan" picked trucks and a machine gun as toys, frequently ripped off her dresses and imitated her father shaving. Despite the lack of a penis, she insisted on urinating standing up. Thrown out of the girl's bathroom at school, she moved to the boy's lavatory and used a urinal. At 12, she received hormones to make her breasts grow, but she hated her breasts and refused to wear a bra.

Therapists couldn't convince "Joan" to accept her role as a girl, as theory said she should. Instead, she "felt like a trapped animal" and threatened suicide. When she was 14, her father tearfully told her she was a boy. "All of a sudden everything clicked," "Joan" said. "For the first time things made sense and I understood who and what I was." "Joan" had a mastectomy, got male hormone shots and began living as a boy. At age 16, he bought a van with a bed and a bar and started to pursue girls. At 25, he married a woman with three children and now at age 34 he reportedly is self-assured and content, though bitter that his castration means he can never have a child of his own.

Why was this disastrous experiment undertaken? One reason is that it's easier to construct a vagina than to reconstruct a penis. But another reason is just as obvious: it was a chance to prove a rising academic and feminist theory about gender. The doctor in charge of the case at Johns Hopkins was John Money, a medical psychologist and a well-known figure in sexology who believed that all sex differences are culturally determined.

In December, 1972, when "Joan" was about to turn 10 (and as we now know, fiercely fighting her life as a female), Money reported at a scientific convention that "John's" change was an apparent success. *Time* magazine noted that "this dramatic case...provides strong support for a major contention of women's liberationists that the conventional patterns of masculine and feminine behavior can be altered. It also casts doubt on the theory that major sex differences, psychological as well as anatomical, are immutably set by the genes at conception."

The John-Joan case is a classic example of how an untested idea, backed up by no evidence at all, can be used by well-meaning people to ruin someone's life. "It might have been the zeitgest," Diamond said in an interview, referring to the "flower-power, you-can-be-anything-you-wish" ethic of the 1960s and 1970s. Though many attempts have been made to turn infants with damaged or ambiguous genitals into females, Diamond and Sigmundson say there is no known case where "a 46 chromosome, XY male, unequivocally so at birth, has ever easily and fully accepted an imposed life" as a heterosexual female. Money has given no interviews, on ground that "John" has not given written permission for him to speak.

On the broader issue of sexual differences, the pendulum that began to swing so strongly against disparities in the 60s and 70s is now swinging the other way. Since biology and male-female differences were used so long to disparage women, feminists argued strongly that true distinctions didn't exist. On campus, the old debate over male and female characteristics mutated into "gender studies," it was simply assumed that differences were either trivial or socially constructed by males to oppress women.

Daphne Patai, co-author of *Professing Feminism*, writes that some hardline campus feminists believe that even morning sickness and the pain of childbirth are socially created by the patriarchy. She predicts that they will just shrug off the "John-Joan" case. "The whole point of being an ideologue is that new information doesn't disturb your worldview," she says. Now, brain studies are showing many innate differences. As Diamond and Sigmundson write, "The last decade has offered much support for a biological substrate for sexual behavior." The "John-Joan" case may not be the last of its kind. But it looks like something left over from a different era.

PARENTING WITHOUT A CARE

Judith Rich Harris's book, *The Nurture Assumption*, is apparently a commercial and talk-show success. That leaves publishers, critics, and psychologists scratching their heads and struggling mightily to figure out why. Harris argues that parenting doesn't matter—nothing much that mothers and fathers do will have any long-term effect on their children. She thinks parents are essentially non-players in their children's lives. Genes and peer group pressures are the real formative factors.

This is a very abstract argument, and readers may find it hard to believe that Harris has managed to hold on to her theory while raising two children of her own, or rather, standing by while genes and peers raised them. As she is quick to say in her book, Harris is not a psychologist or a social scientist of any sort. She is what journalists call a "rewrite man," someone who takes the work of others and puts it into plain English for popular consumption. Until recently, she did this as a textbook writer. Now she has rewritten the literature on a continuing debate in the social sciences—how much of personality and character is due to nurture (parents and environmental factors) and how much is nature (genetic and evolutionary in origin).

This debate has been going on for decades. Researchers point to a genetic base for traits such as shyness, nurturance, and aggression, and even for behaviors such as suicide and divorce. Harris's contribution, if you want to call it that, has been to take this debate and inject it into the national conversation in the most extreme and simpleminded form possible.

Along the way, she makes many of the conventional mistakes of the rewrite man, who is often distant from the actual work being rewritten. She accepts fuzzy concepts such as "intelligence" and "personality" as if their meaning were absolutely clear, takes what people say on questionnaires at face value, and ignores findings that don't fit her thesis. One of these is the consistent finding that when parents make a strong effort to talk to and read to their young children, the children turn out to be more verbal and get better grades (and eventually, better jobs) than other children. "That fact alone is enough to discredit her thesis," said Harvard's Jerome Kagan, a leading expert in child development. T. Berry Brazleton, another well-known child expert, says Harris's book is "absurd."

So how did a shaky, naïve, and extreme book by an unknown with no credentials in the field come to be such a success? The poor performance of the elite media obviously played a role—the *New Yorker* and *Newsweek* both put the story on their covers. So did the fact that the book came along in August, a dull news month when otherwise rational editors scramble after marginal and stupid stories.

Some editors waved off objections by pointing out that the American Psychological Association gave Harris an award for an article that became the basis for her book. But the APA gives out prizes like soup lines give out soup. The organization has 52 divisions, each of which give two, three, or four awards a year, for a probable total (the APA keeps no figures) of 200 or more a year. And this doesn't count the more prestigious association-wide awards given above the division level. Harris was rejected for one of these 200 awards in 1996, but someone pushed her case and she got one of the 1997 prizes, bestowed at the 1998 APA convention in August, just in time to help market the book.

Then, too, the book was perfectly geared to our talk-show culture, which loves passionate controversy over "high concept" topics that can be explained in ten words or less. Samples: "The Holocaust never happened," "Scientists are lying to us—the earth is flat," and "Parents don't count—genes and peers do." Clearly a more nuanced book on the complexities of the nature-nurture controversy would have failed to entrance Geraldo.

There's another obvious factor. Many anxious parents want reassurance that their child-rearing habits haven't hurt their children. And self-absorbed parents with a track record of putting their own desires ahead of their children's needs want absolution, now available in book form for only $26.

Publishers have been feeding the market for parental absolution for some time. Books and articles explained to us that divorce doesn't matter to children (it's better to separate than to argue in front of the kids), and that the amount of time spent with the children doesn't matter ("quality time" will make up for the loss of old-fashioned quantity time). Now comes the ultimate gift in the marketing of parental absolution: nothing you do or don't do matters at all.

The ultimate message here is that sacrifice, concern, and loving treatment of one's children no longer makes sense. Why bother, if genes and peer groups are doing the real parenting? Our society is hip-deep in evidence of the pain and loss of underparented and unparented children. It's no time to celebrate a foolish book that justifies self-absorption and makes non-parenting a respectable, mainstream activity.

THE JOY OF SEXUAL VALUES

Faye Wattleton, former head of Planned Parenthood, was crushed to learn that women's attitudes on abortion are not what she supposed they were. A poll conducted by Wattleton's new group, the Center for Gender Equality, found that 53 percent of American women think abortion should be allowed only after rape or incest, to save a woman's life, or not at all. Only 28 percent said abortion should be generally available, and 70 percent want more restrictions on abortion.

Another sign of slippage in support for abortion shows up in UCLA's annual national survey of the attitudes of college freshmen. Support for legal abortion dropped for the sixth year in a row. In 1990 it was 64.9 percent. Now it's a bare majority, 50.9 percent. Last year Yankelovich Partners, Inc., reported a six-point drop in approval (down to 42 percent) for the statement that "the right of a woman to have an abortion is acceptable in today's society." The National Opinion Research Center found declining opposition to legalized abortion from 1988 to 1996, but opposition climbed again in 1998 and is now in the 55 percent range.

Declining support for abortion owes something to the gruesome details that emerged in the debate over partial-birth abortion. Improvements in ultrasound imaging also tend to undermine abortion, cutting through the abstractions of "choice" and "reproductive rights" and showing pregnant women how much a fetus resembles a newborn. When ultrasound video becomes routine and the fetus is seen in motion and in 3-D, support for abortion could drop further.

But support for abortion may be eroding primarily because sexual attitudes in general have been moving in a conservative direction throughout the 1990s. Wattleton's poll shows that 44 percent of women think divorce should be harder to get, and 52 percent oppose distribution of condoms in schools. Yankelovich reports that three decades after the sexual revolution only 37 percent of Americans think premarital sex is "acceptable in today's society" (32 percent of women, 43 percent of men). In the UCLA survey, a record low of 39.6 percent of students (down from 51.9 percent in 1987) agreed that "If two people really like each other, it's all right for them to have sex even if they've know each other for a very short time."

Two factors driving the conservative trend are religion and the costs of the sexual revolution (AIDS and other sexually transmitted diseases, the effects of divorce, dissatisfaction with promiscuous sex). The Wattleton survey found that 75 percent of the women polled said religion is very important in their lives, up from 69 percent two years ago. A study of young urban males by the Urban Institute found that the growing trend toward less permissive sexual attitudes in the 1990s is associated with religious beliefs. The number of religious teens didn't rise, but the teens who were religious developed more conservative values. Teen pregnancies are down and so are teen sexual activity and approval of it. Support for premarital sex remains high but it dropped from 80 percent in 1988 to 71 percent in 1988. Over the same period, the percentage of males aged 17 to 19 who have ever had sex fell 7 points to 68 percent.

In a hypothetical case of pregnancy involving an unmarried couple, the percentage of males who endorsed having the baby and supporting it rose steadily from 19 percent in 1979 to 59 percent in 1995. The report says these striking changes, found among whites and blacks alike, are "broadly consistent" with the sexual values reflected in the rise of the Promise Keepers and the Million Man March. The two lessons of the study, said its authors, are that values matter and AIDS education makes a difference.

The high divorce rate and liberated lifestyles of the Boomer generation may now be producing more cautious, conservative attitudes among their children. "Generation Xers basically believe the Baby Boomers went too far with their lifestyle, taking it to the brink," says Ann Clurman of Yankelovich Partners. "Children of divorce are 50 percent of Gen Xers. They think they are victims of divorce and want to pull back from a precipice. Down the road we will definitely see less divorce." Her colleague and fellow analyst at Yankelovich, J. Walker Smith, adds this: "Xers don't want to return to Ozzie and Harriet, but they want to recapture the traditional satisfactions. The family unit is on the decline, but the desire for family satisfaction is on the rise." Smith says Boomers, too, as they age, are developing more traditional attitudes: Gen Xers are 10 to 25 points more likely in surveys to prefer a return to traditional standards than Boomers were when they were young. And Boomers today are just as likely as Gen Xers to differ with the attitudes reported by the Boomer generation in the 1970s.

Smith says some researchers are picking up a rising reaction against the practice of "hooking up" instead of dating—teens or college students going out in groups, maybe drinking a lot, then pairing off for sex. Amy Holmes, now of the Women's Independent Forum, and women at many colleges, are pushing a "Take Back the Date" movement to stamp out the aimless sex of "hooking up." Maybe the tanker is turning around.

PROMOTING NO-DAD FAMILIES

David Blankenhorn has a question: why isn't there some debate about the fact that American sperm banks sell sperm to single women?

As usual, the elite culture in America will hear this question in one way; the rest of the country will hear it differently.

Elite response: here comes another attack on privacy and individual rights, particularly the right of women to control their own bodies. Besides, it insults women to imply that they need a man around to raise a healthy child.

Rest of the country: why is it so obvious that a wide-open commercial market in the production of fatherless children is a social good? The consensus of studies is that no-father children, as a group, are at risk in all races and at all income levels. If so, doesn't society have a stake in discouraging the intentional creation of fatherless children, in suburbs as much as in the inner-city?

Blankenhorn is head of the Institute for Family Values in Manhattan. While researching his new book, *Fatherless* America, he fielded many queries from journalists about the practice of selling sperm to single women. He said virtually every question came from Japanese or European reporters who were shocked that the United States is so casual about a free market in sperm.

Other nations have indeed taken the issue more seriously. France banned the sale of sperm to single women. Britain allows it. Japan makes if difficult, but not impossible, for single women to acquire donor sperm. Italy has no law, but last month its national association of doctors voted to deny artificial insemination to single women. European guidelines, produced by the Council of Europe in 1989, say sperm should be made available only to heterosexual couples.

Somewhere between 3,000 and 6,500 fatherless babies are produced each year through artificial insemination. Why has serious moral debate occurred in other developed nations, but not here, where most of the world's sperm banks are located? Well, for one thing, the United States is the only nation that discusses almost all its social issues in "rights talk," a language with a built-in tendency to grant individuals untrumpable rights against even the most sensible social policy. The American "rights" dialect is so pervasive that even its opponents are usually required to speak it (in this case by arguing that children have a "right" to have a father around).

The abortion wars played a part, too. The sharp focus on women's rights and choice was inevitable, but part of the psychic fallout has been a tendency to downplay the role of the male, as if the father had no stake at all in the fate of the fetus or reproductive issues in general. Feminists, some strongly hostile to men, have been prone to portray all procreative issues as principally a female concern. Fathers and fatherhood have virtually dropped out of the literature and the discussion of reproductive matters. In an age of antagonism between the sexes, it's a short step here to the view of fathers as troublesome, marginal, and essentially irrelevant inseminators.

Alas, the American open market in sperm, virtually unquestioned and undiscussed, institutionalizes this view of the irrelevant male. Men can spawn children with no responsibility. Women can raise them without putting up with a male. Writing in the *Utah Law Review*, Daniel Callahan, bioethicist and former head of the Hastings Center, sees "an acceptance of the systematic downgrading of fatherhood brought about by the introduction of anonymous sperm donors. [It is] symbolic of the devaluation of fatherhood."

People on the other side of this non-debate understand what's at stake. Here is John Edwards, a sociologist at VPI, writing in the *Journal of Marriage and the Family*: sperm donation "purposely makes paternity problematic....In theory, the new reproductive technologies signal the obsolescence of marriage and the family...implicitly the innovations suggest that the family of the future may merely consist of one socialized adult and an offspring."

Biological fatherhood was once understood by society to carry with it permanent moral obligations to the child. Now it can involve nothing more than a financially strapped college student masturbating into a cup for $50 and writing a vaguely caring letter to an offspring he will never see or care about.

Edwards and Callahan are basically saying the same thing: artificial insemination of single women is not just about ticking biological clocks and the urgent desire to have a child; it is, in effect, an expression of a whole new social policy that turns away from the ideal of an intact family toward what we used to call a non-intact or broken one.

This is the most glaring example of what Daniel Patrick Moynihan calls "defining deviancy down." Take a devastating social problem—fatherlessness—and redefine it as an acceptable and even inevitable model for the future. In this new model, the father is either infantilized, absent, or simply dropped out of decision-making and nurturance. In any of these cases, male irresponsibility is basically licensed and legitimated. Before this model gets more firmly established, let's have a real national debate.

DEVALUING THE FAMILY

If you go to a panel discussion in Washington, D.C., on "Reframing Family Values," do not expect much attention either to family or values. Instead you will be flooded with charts and graphs about heads of household and income distribution. The point of this exercise is to show that behavior and values have nothing to do with the crisis of the American family. Everything is economic. If the awkward term "family values" comes up, it will be discussed gingerly as some sort of mysterious and optional product that some households have, while others do not. Then back to the charts.

This was true last week on a panel at the Woodrow Wilson Center. When my turn came, I attempted a few chart-free comments: to bolster the family, we certainly have to come to terms with '90's economics but also with '60's values, particularly the core value that self-fulfillment is a trump card over all obligations and expectations. By breaking the taboos against unwed motherhood and casual divorce, we have created the world's most dangerous environment for children—a new fatherless America filling up with kids who are so emotionally damaged by their parents' behavior that they may have a lot of trouble making commitments and forming families themselves.

The Murphy Brown argument is now over, and Dan Quayle has won—an avalanche of evidence shows that single-parent kids are way more vulnerable than two-parent kids to all sorts of damage, in all races and at all income levels, under all kinds of conditions. The mountain of evidence is just too high to keep arguing that different family forms are equally valuable or that "the quality of the home is the important thing, not the number of parents in it."

Barbara Dafoe Whitehead, who wrote the "Dan Quayle Was Right" article in the *Atlantic Monthly*, says that as she travels around the country to colleges, she is struck by the number of angry, emotionally scarred children of divorce she runs into. They can function and often get high marks, so researchers may not pick up the social cost, but it is being paid. And these are the privileged ones.

Since the obvious tends to come as a thunderbolt on Washington panels, much umbrage was taken at my comments. In closing the panel, the co-moderator, a well-known economist, said that a woman's right to have a baby without having the father around is what feminism is all about. In shaking her hand afterward, I remarked, perhaps a bit ungraciously, that intentionally planning to have a fatherless family was like setting out intentionally to build a Yugo.

It's impossible to overestimate how deeply our intellectual and cultural elite is implicated in the continuing decline of the American nuclear family. It's not just the constant jeering at the intact family as an Ozzie-and-Harriet relic of the Eisenhower era. It's the constant broadening of the definition of what a family is (a New Jersey judge said that six college kids on summer vacation constituted a family), and the equally constant attempt to undermine policies that might help the intact family survive.

Maggie Gallagher, in her forthcoming book, *The Abolition of Marriage*, says that marriage "has been ruthlessly dismantled, piece by piece, under the influence of those who...believed that the abolition of marriage was necessary to advance human freedom." Demoted to one lifestyle among many, marriage is no longer viewed by the elite as a crucial social institution but as a purely private and temporary act.

There are many ways to show this worldview in action. At the 1992 annual convention of the American Association for Marriage and Family Therapy, the word marriage appeared only twice among the 200-plus topics and subtopics to be discussed. In 1993, the word didn't come up at all, and in 1994, the convention gave a major press award to a magazine article arguing that fathers weren't necessary in the home. At last November's 1995 convention, the status was still quo: two mentions for "marital" on the entire program, none for "marriage."

This is an odd business. The therapeutic custodians of marriage don't believe in it any more and seem determined not to bolster, promote, or even talk about it much. The M-word seems to have disappeared from the association's basic vocabulary. Why? Probably because the association is committed to a non-judgmental culture in which all relationships are equally valuable, endlessly negotiable and disposable. So talking about marriage as a long-term serious commitment that must be shored up or preferred over other "lifestyles" becomes dicey and embarrassing.

The next skirmish in this continuing war between the elite and non-elite worldviews will be divorce reform. The elite will depict it as a punitive, backward, and religious attempt to lock people into bad marriages. But that's not it. The point is that wide-open anything-goes no-fault divorce has unexpectedly created its own accelerating culture of non-commitment. Under no-fault divorce, marriage increasingly carries no more inherent social weight than a weekend fling in the Bahamas. The goal is not to halt divorce but to make it rarer by trying to restore gravity to both marriage and separation. But given the attitudes of our elite, the battle will be uphill all the way.

THINGS THAT GO BUMP IN THE HOME

A page one headline in the *Los Angeles Times* announces "A New Side to Domestic Violence." This "new side," apparently quite puzzling to the reporter, is that under mandatory arrest laws, a large number of women are now being arrested after domestic battles. In Los Angeles, arrests of women in such cases have almost quadrupled in eight years. In Wisconsin, the number of abusive men referred by the courts for counseling has doubled since 1989, while the number of abusive women referred for counseling increased twelvefold.

You could sense that the reporter was grappling with a baffling question: how is it that laws intended to protect women are producing so many arrests of women themselves? Luckily, he was able to come up with three explanations: a backlash against women, spiteful action by cops who resent mandatory arrest laws, and outright male trickery.

Under the heading of trickery came the tales of a man who smashed himself over the head with a brick and blamed his wife, a man who bloodied himself by scratching his own ear, and a man, born with an odd bump on his head, who repeatedly showed the bump to police and got his wife arrested three times.

There is another explanation, one that has nothing to do with lucky head bumps or rogue cops. The explanation is this: if mandatory arrest laws are fairly applied, we will see roughly equal numbers of men and women arrested, because the amount of domestic violence initiated and conducted by men and women is roughly equal. In fact, women may be ahead.

You haven't read this in your local newspaper, and certainly not in elite papers like the *L.A. Times*. The reason is that publishing this news would create a severe political problem in the newsroom. To their credit, feminists made domestic violence a political issue. But they shaped the issue around a theory: this violence is an expression of patriarchy as a social force and marriage as a patriarchal institution. It is something men do to women because of the way society is organized.

An enormous amount of evidence from thirty or more studies now shows that this paradigm is quite wrongheaded. But feminists are unwilling to adapt it to reality, and since the modern newsroom is very supportive of feminism, news stories on domestic violence are very carefully crafted, consistently unreliable, and often just plain wrong.

Follow the work of the National Family Violence Survey. The original 1975 survey showed rather high rates of female-on-male domestic violence, but these were fitted to the paradigm and explained as understandable reactions to male violence. But the second National Family Violence survey in 1985 clearly showed equality in turning to violence: in both low-level assaults and severe assaults, only the wife was violent in a quarter of cases, so was the husband, and in half of the cases both were violent. These findings came from self-reports.

This signaled a split in research: feminist researchers keep churning out work that fits feminist theory, while independent researchers keep finding equality in the use of violence. Men are more dangerous—ahead by two to one in the domestic murder sweepstakes—and more likely to inflict serious damage. But women are just as inclined to be violent with their partners as men are. (The rather high rates of violence in lesbian homes echoes this finding.)

The equality findings undercut the feminist theory of partner violence as patriarchy-in-action, with its dark view of men and marriage. Instead they supported the commonsense view that violence between partners has more to do with problems of individuals in a difficult culture rather than with any vast ideological scheme.

The feminist insistence on using theory to mug facts has had many unfortunate results. One is that a generalized view of men as uniquely violent and dangerous to women ("men batter because they can," "the most dangerous place for a woman to be is in the home") has leeched deep into the popular culture. It turns up everywhere. In a recent TV ad for girls' athletics, a young girl says if she plays sports, she will be more likely to leave an abusive relationship. A recent survey of what children want actually included the wish that daddies would stop hitting mommies.

In fact, children are now more likely to see Mommy hit Dad. The rate of severe assaults by men on women in the home fell by 50 percent between the first National Family Violence Survey and the most recent update of data in 1992. It dropped from 38 per 100,000 couples per year to 19. Give the feminists credit for this. They did it mostly by themselves. But the rate of dangerous female assaults on males in the home stayed essentially static over that period—43 per 100,000 couples—and is now twice as high as the male rate. Give feminists some responsibility for this, too. By defining partner violence as a male problem, they missed the chance to bring about the same decline in violence among women.

Feminist studies of partner violence rarely ask about assaults by women, and when they do, they ask only about self-defense. Journalists, in turn, stick quite close to the feminist-approved studies for fear of being considered "soft" on male violence. The result is badly skewed reporting of domestic violence as purely a gender issue. It isn't.

DEFENDING THE INDEFENSIBLE

"Partial birth" abortions are unsettling even to read about—the only version of abortion in which fetuses, either viable or near viability, are partly visible outside the body while alive and inches away from birth before being dispatched.

They are typically performed at 20 to 24 weeks, but sometimes later. The fetus is manipulated so that its feet and sometimes part of its body are outside the mother. The head is left in the uterus. Then the skull is pierced and the brain is suctioned out, causing skull collapse and death.

Why is the head of the fetus left inside the uterus when the removal of the brain takes place? "Avoiding trauma to the cervix" is usually cited as the reason, but the bottom line is legal. Stopping the head just short of birth is a legal fig leaf for a procedure that doesn't look like abortion at all. It looks like infanticide.

Brenda Shafer, a pro-choice registered nurse with 13 years experience, says she witnessed three of these operations during a brief assignment to assist Dr. Martin Haskell at an Ohio abortion clinic in 1993. She says the three fetuses, two normal and one with Down's syndrome, all three 25 or more weeks along, were alive when Dr. Haskell inserted scissors in their skulls. "I still have nightmares about what I saw," she said in a letter to a pro-life congressman urging passage of the "Partial Birth Abortion Act."

Pro-choicers have greeted the "partial birth" issue as the beginning of a new crusade to undermine Roe v. Wade. For some pro-lifers, it obviously is. But it's also true that a great many Americans, on both sides and in the middle, are deeply troubled by the brutality and questionable morality of this particular procedure.

In the House vote, a dozen pro-choice congressmen, including Ted Kennedy's son Patrick, joined the lopsided majority and voted to ban "partial birth" procedures. They did this knowing they face some aggressive retribution from the abortion lobby without gaining any support from the anti-abortion side. "It was a costly vote," said pro-choicer Jim Moran (D., Va.). "I'm not going to vote in such a way that I have to put my conscience on the shelf."

It should be noted that the abortion lobby is having trouble getting its facts straight. After Brenda Shafer made her statement, Dr. Haskell said he didn't recall any such person working at his clinic. An employment card was produced. Then Congresswoman Pat Schroeder and others extracted a non-denial denial from Dr. Haskell's head nurse, saying that Brenda Shafer "would not" have been present at the three abortions she said she saw.

Kate Michelman and other pro-choice lobbyists insisted that "partial birth" abortion is confined to "extraordinary medical circumstances" and that anesthesia "causes fetal demise—the death of the fetus—prior to the procedure." But a 1993 interview with Dr. Haskell in an American Medical Association newspaper quotes him as saying that 80 percent of these procedures are elective, and two-thirds occur while the fetus is alive. Dr. Haskell wrote a letter strongly implying he was misquoted. But an audio tape was produced showing that he wasn't.

And Kate Michelman said, "It's not only a myth, it's a lie," that "partial birth" abortions are used to eliminate fetuses for minor defects such as cleft palates. But abortion practitioner Dr. James McMahon had already told Congress he had personally performed at least 9 of these procedures solely because of cleft palates. Compared with the pro-choice lobby, the O.J. defense looks obsessively ethical and tightly focused on verifiable truth.

In the *New Republic*, pro-choice feminist Naomi Wolfe wrote that "with the pro-choice rhetoric we use now, we incur three destructive consequences...hardness of heart, lying and political failure." She wrote: "By refusing to look at abortion within a moral framework, we lose the millions of Americans who want to support abortion as a legal right but still need to condemn it as a moral iniquity."

The "partial birth" issue is a good time for pro-choicers to reclaim the moral framework that Wolfe says they have relinquished. This repellent procedure goes way too far. No other Western nation, to my knowledge, allows it. It was unanimously condemned by the American Medical Association's council on legislation. (The full Association later decided to duck the issue and take no position.)

Pro-choicers who defend it reflexively because it may lead to other legislation are in the exact position of gun lobbyists who shoot down bans on assault weapons because those bans may one day lead to a round-up of everybody's handguns. It a refusal, on tactical grounds, to confront the moral issue involved. More of the abstract hardness that Wolfe writes about.

Killing a 5-month or 6-month fetus that's halfway down the birth canal raises a moral issue way beyond that of ordinary abortion. It's perfectly possible to support a woman's right to abort and still think that the anything-goes ethic of this horrific procedure has no place in a culture with any reverence left for life.

FAIRNESS? PROMISES, PROMISES

The *Los Angeles Times* has a problem with the Promise Keepers, the Christian men's movement. It suggests that by waiving admission fees to rallies for some minority men, "the organization is trying to engineer diversity that is not happening naturally." Wow. A newspaper which has never met a quota it didn't like is lecturing religious people about the evils of engineering diversity.

The Promise Keepers' commitment to racial reconciliation irritates the *Village Voice* too. A *Voice* article attacked "the sanitized multiculturalism" of the movement and called its "policy of racial diversity so overt that it reeks of insincerity." Apparently either covert diversity or overt exclusion of minorities would have been better.

The cultural left has worked up a lot of bile over the Promise Keepers. In a long and mocking piece, *GQ* magazine called Promise Keepers" founder, Bill McCartney, a "lop-eyed loon" and a "raving lunatic," and repeatedly used Nazi imagery to describe the movement. Even *GQ*'s headline, "Triumph of His Will," is a reference to a famous Nazi movie, *Triumph of the Will.*

The *Voice* article dismissed the movement's "Jesus-goes-to-Sears aesthetic." These were apparently not the writer's sort of people: They go to church and they go to Sears. Somehow the *Voice* writer found a "message of hate" in a rally at New York's Shea Stadium but didn't report that Promise Keepers' founder Bill McCartney had told the crowd that a "spirit of white racial superiority" is deepening "insensitivity to people of color."

New York Times' columnist Frank Rich, also ignoring the anti-racism theme and the heavily integrated crowd, sneered at the Promise Keepers' "Robert Blyesque hunger to overcome macho inhibitions." After Louis Farrakhan's million-man march, Rich had counseled his readers to look beyond Farrakhan and concentrate on the yearnings of the men who attended. Journalist Jim Sleeper writes: "There were similar yearnings at Shea, but Rich didn't mention them."

The same sort of double standard is showing up in the current crusade against the Promise Keepers by the National Organization for Women. By any normal expectation, NOW would express at least some guarded praise for any program that urges men to be honest, loyal, and respectful to their wives and families. The Promise Keepers are urged to show their emotions, let go of their anger, never to cheat on wives, or become violent.

No good words about this came from NOW, however, mostly because the Promise Keepers are working within a religious tradition that takes seriously St. Paul's statements about male leadership in the church and in the home. The starkest formulation of this view in the Promise Keeper literature is by Tony Evans, a black pastor in Dallas, who once urged men to tell their wives, "I gave up leading this family, and I forced you to take my place. Now I must reclaim that role." He tells wives: "let your man be a man if he's willing...if your husband tells you he wants to reclaim his role, let him! God never meant for you to bear the load you're carrying."

These are hardly the tones and accents one would hear at a NOW meeting, or even in many Christian traditions, including my own. But at least they can be heard in context. The Promise Keepers appear to be a response to the alienation of men from the Evangelical churches, and the physical or emotional absence of men from their families. It's a males-only movement because it is based on the perception of male failure, abdicating adult roles, and forcing women to fill the vacuum in church and at home. In this sense "reclaiming the male role" isn't nostalgia for patriarchy, but an attempt to re-energize men and get them functioning well.

Lacking any feel for religion, the cultural left misses all this, defining the males-only rules as a nasty form of "exclusion," overlooking the movement's therapeutic trappings and insisting that the Promise Keepers are a purely political battalion disguised as a religious one. Always tone deaf in these matters, NOW president Patricia Ireland calls the Promise Keepers "a stealth political group formed by people who think the former Christian Coalition leader Ralph Reed is too liberal."

Even MS. magazine was more nearly correct than Ireland. Disguised as a male, Donna Minkowitz attended a Promise Keepers event and came to the conclusion, unsurprising for MS., that "the fantasy of benevolent domination moves the Promise Keepers." But she also reported the heavy emphasis on conscience, forgiveness, humility, and the willingness to change. "Six of the eight major speakers emphasize that men's fear of being seen as weak or unimportant—in effect their fear of being equated with women—can become a terrible obstacle in all their relationships. I'm struck by how close it all sounds to feminism."

She should have read some of this aloud at the NOW convention. NOW might have adopted a more adult and nuanced resolution instead of just denouncing the movement as a great danger to women's progress. The demonization continues.

PART FOUR

RACE AND MINORITIES

A DUBIOUS DIVERSITY REPORT

While clicking from channel to channel in search of the basketball game last week, I came across a bit of "diversity" reporting on CNN. "Diversity" reporting is similar to ordinary reporting, except that facts are usually avoided and the central message is that life in America is essentially a racial struggle between whites and non-whites, which the non-whites, or people of color, will win by becoming the majority in the year 2050.

The point of the CNN report—a dubious one supported by no evidence—was that young blacks and Latinos are starting to form a strong racial alliance. The correspondent said, "The once deep divisions between these groups are now blurring, as little by little, consciously or not, young African Americans and Latinos are creating a common culture, one that will be in the majority by the year 2050." This emerging black-Latino culture isn't discussed much, though one youth worker says that blacks and Latinos now dress alike, listen to each other's music and both came from "the same slave ship."

All suspense as to what the two groups are uniting against disappeared when CNN's correspondent said they "are beginning to realize they're not fighting each other for jobs. Instead they share a far greater challenge." This undefined challenge was immediately defined by a teenage student. She said: "I don't think there's competition between the blacks and the Latinos. I think it's us against the whites."

Oddly, the report introduced two rather impressive young men, one black and one Latino, who talked about getting ahead by perseverance and hard work. But they apparently didn't much interest the correspondent, who seemed more interested in racial politics.

The basic question raised by "diversity" reporting is this: is it really news, evidence of something actually happening in the outside world, or is it the expression of a reporter's or editor's wish, in this case that blacks and Latinos ought to unify themselves by hostility to whites? A real news account of a dawning black-Hispanic culture or alliance should presumably include some facts indicating that it actually exists. And the reporting would have to take into account how the "deep divisions" between the groups are supposedly fading. Relations in prisons between Latinos and blacks are so bad that the ACLU supports segregated cells and cellblocks.

Also, journalism has its familiar 2050 problem. Some projections indicate that by the middle of the next century, the United States will be about 53 percent non-Hispanic white, 47 percent minority, with the white plurality supplied mostly by older citizens. The fastest growing segment of the population, Hispanics, will be about 25 percent of the national total, and when added to the black and Asian-American totals, will produce enough political power to neutralize or overthrow the existing order.

Maybe. But this assumes that people always vote their skin color, not their interests or beliefs. A lot of very different peoples come under the general heading of "Hispanic," but if you look at surveys of Hispanic attitudes, they seem very close to traditional American values. Family solidarity, the work ethic, religion and patriotism rank very high. Polls repeatedly show that 90 percent of Hispanics think anyone living here should learn English as quickly as possible. About 75 percent think we have way too many immigrants and that continued immigration depresses wages. Professor Rodolfo de la Garza at the University of Texas held a focus group in which all 14 Hispanics in the room supported California's Prop. 187, which limited benefits for immigrants.

In De la Garza's Latino National Political Survey, people of Mexican, Cuban, and Puerto Rican origins didn't acknowledge having much in common and each group said it was fonder of Great Britain than of Latin America. Only a few called themselves Latino or Hispanic. Most wanted to be called "American." About 90 percent said they were "proud" or "extremely proud" of the United States.

It's certainly true that Hispanics will have a lot to say about America's future. But what they apparently intend to say does not seem out of line with what earlier Americans of all races have believed. The other problem with the picture of a non-white majority coalition is that three-quarters of Hispanics identify themselves as white and intermarriage is bound to raise that percentage. Hispanics are blending into the general population at least as fast as earlier white ethnic groups. Forty percent of Americans of Puerto Rican ancestry who were born here are married to Anglos. About a third of all young American-born Hispanics are marrying non-Hispanic whites. Will their children identify themselves as Hispanic, or as generic whites, like the Italian Irish or the Polish Swedes?

It's a fluid situation that can't be summed up by the simple math of the 2050 demographics. Many newcomers seem trapped in communities with few jobs, no education, and segregated schools. Many more are moving up the ladder, into the middle class and out to well-off suburbs. On the evidence so far, it's hard to believe that Hispanics will become frozen into a victim stance or help organize an anti-white coalition. Diversity reporters take note.

A WASPISH, NIGGARDLY SLUR

The non-impeachment story of the last week of January was the controversy over the word "niggardly." David Howard, a white mayoral aide in Washington, D.C., used the word in conversation with a black official, who took offense because he felt that "niggardly," which means miserly or cheap, was a racist term. Mr. Howard offered his resignation, which was accepted by Mayor Anthony Williams. The mayor explained that although Mr. Howard didn't say "anything that was in itself racist," using a word that could be misunderstood was like "getting caught smoking in a refinery with a resulting explosion."

The resignation of Mr. Howard was, of course, a shock and a tragedy, but it had a good result too. It sensitized us all to the hidden and hurtful ethnic slurs that darken—oops, sorry—that afflict American life and allow the wily perpetrators to get off Scot free—er, without any punishment at all.

That's why in February and March of 1999, America's alert press corps turned up a staggering number of coded insults. For example, at a fancy dinner in Washington, the British ambassador called the Japanese ambassador a "jolly good chap," exactly the kind of sly detraction that no one would have noticed before the consciousness-raising Howard case. Luckily a savvy columnist pointed out that "chap" is unmistakably close to the insulting word "Jap," so the British ambassador was recalled and is now serving as second assistant to the operations director of the Liverpool sewage works.

A similar verbal crisis arose in Chicago. While presenting a bill to a Jewish patient, a dentist said "Don't be afraid of chewing down on it." At his two-day hearing before the city human rights committee, the dentist lamely kept trying to argue that he was talking about his patient's new filling, not about a bargaining trait often attributed to Jewish people by their detractors.

In Manhattan, irate Polish-Americans rallied outside the Museum of Modern Art, convincing most fair-minded onlookers that the museum's current show on Jackson Pollock was intended as a punning attempt to revive the demeaning term "Polack."

Religious controversy erupted in Lincoln, Nebraska, when a diet instructor said to her class, "I think some of you are natural snackers." Catholics in the group caught on immediately, identifying this apparently innocent remark as a coy version of "mackerel snappers." A fair-minded local priest spoke out. Although "natural snackers" is not literally an anti-Catholic slur, he declared, the plain fact is that mentioning natural snackers in the presence of mackerel snappers was like "hurling a grenade into a munitions dump."

In Cincinnati, the manager of an art theater was fired for showing the old Fred Astaire and Ginger Rogers movie, *The Gay Divorcee*. The manager pretended to be bewildered, but an astute activist explained that the screening was a subtle homophobic slur insinuating that any gay or lesbian marriages were bound to end in divorce.

White Anglo-Saxon Protestant Americans joined the debate. They held a low-key rally in Bangor, Maine, to express controlled but sincere grievance over such hurtful language as the scotching of rumors, welching on bets, the use of "waspish" as a negative word and the inexplicable refusal of most musicians to remove the word "honky" from "honky-tonk" music.

The most serious of the covert slurs stirred emotions in Utica, New York. Italian-Americans rioted for three days after a local disk jockey blithely played a song containing the phrase "as each day goes by." "I can't believe they're calling us dagos again," said Giuseppe Abondanza, president of the Italian-American Alliance Against Hate, Discourtesy and Ambiguous but Perfectly Actionable Affronts. Labeling the incident "just another musical hate crime," he managed to get the slur-prone disk jockey fired. Then Mr. Abondanza rushed off to North Bergen, New Jersey, where other members of his anti-hate group were protesting Burger King's insensitive decision to sell a large burger called "the Whopper" right in the middle of a proud Italian-American community. "Next they'll be starting a radio station with the call letters WOP, or suggesting that Italian-Americans refresh themselves with a vacation in New Guinea," quipped Mr. Abondanza.

By April, every ethnic group in America was in full cry. German-Americans wanted the term "kraut" removed from the word sauerkraut. Asian-Americans resented the bigoted word "slope" embedded in the name of Park Slope, Brooklyn. Hispanic activists shredded thousands of copies of a newspaper that had dared to use the toxic phrase "spick and span." Some also demanded that the offensive title of Sigourney Weaver's movie, *Alien* be changed to "Undocumented Worker."

But in May, everything began calming down. A columnist who specializes in ethnic bias said, "Maybe we're finding bigotry where it doesn't actually exist." Shocking at first, this novel idea caught on. By June angry discoverers of artfully hidden bias were out of fashion. So people went back to the impeachment trial. The crisis was over.

JELLY BEAN: THE SEQUEL

The headline in the *Wall Street Journal* said, "Racist E-Mail Messages at Donnelley Show Pattern of Bias, Attorneys Claim." The reference was to jokes and insults said to show "a long-term pattern of racial discrimination and harassment" at R.R. Donnelley & Sons, the huge printing company.

Journalists are a bit wary about sensational charges like this because of the dismal performance of the *New York Times* in the discrimination suit against Texaco. The *Times* hammered away at Texaco executives for slurring blacks as "n———rs" and "black jelly beans." It turned out that the *Times*, and the transcript of a tape of a conversation at Texaco cited by plaintiffs in court papers, were quite wrong. The jelly-bean remark referred to language used by a black diversity instructor and was not a slur. The reference to "n———rs" turned out to be a garbled mention of "St. Nicholas." The *Times* didn't verify the transcript, or even insert the word "alleged" in front the word "slurs." Because of the *Times'* immense authority, the factoid of these "slurs" was endlessly repeated in the media, turning up as true on one network show two months after it had been proved false.

It's hard to shed tears for Texaco. The tape has one irritated executive complaining about Kwaanza and Hannukah for horning in on Christmas (narrow-minded but minor) and talking about the destruction of documents in the discrimination case (very serious). Still, Texaco was forced to settle the case quickly for a very large sum, $176 million, not on the legal merits, but because of the worldwide furor aroused by the bad transcript and the *Times'* awful screw-up.

Is the Donnelley case a re-run of the Texaco disaster, "Jelly Bean, part 2"? Donnelley has explicitly charged that plaintiffs are trying to turn the case into another Texaco. In the Donnelley case the slurs appear to be real, though we don't know how much the company knew about them or whether they created or reflected a pattern of bias.

A "Blacktionary," allegedly found on at least one site of the Donnelley computer system in Lancaster, Pennsylvania, is a crude dictionary making fun of the diction and intelligence of black people. The list of "165 racist, ethnic and sexual jokes" turns out to be a collection of what used to be called "Polish jokes" or "Aggie jokes," one-liners about nearly all sexual and ethnic groups.

Obviously, the dictionary and the stupid jokes shouldn't be allowed in the workplace. But yes, it is starting to look like another Texaco. What the Texaco case proved is that if you can create enough bad publicity, depicting a company as hopelessly racist, you can win without ever proving your case or going to trial. Though the media are predictably bored by the dry facts of employment discrimination, they will almost always bite on colorful news about slurs and jokes (the Donnelley slurs and jokes were not part of the original suit, which got little publicity).

After the first slur or joke story hits, you will flush out a few other complaints, which will appear to be part of a strong pattern of bias, whether they are or not. (In the Texaco case, it was a birthday cake with an apparently well-meaning but racist message, helpfully shown in a large photo in the Sunday *New York Times*.) Before long, the target company will hire a prominent black protector (Judge A. Leon Higginbotham, Jr. by Texaco; ex-Secretary of the Army Clifford Alexander by Donnelley).

Feeling cornered, and rightly fearing that the corporate name will never be cleared, the company will contribute to Jesse Jackson when he appears on the scene and it will redouble its commitment to "managing diversity." This can mean hiring a new level of executives with no known function. It often means forcing employees to endure "diversity training," the only function of which is to ward off lawsuits. "Diversity training is generally nonsense," Secretary Alexander said in an unexpected burst of candor which preceded his hiring by the beleaguered folks at Donnelley. "Many managers who go to them think they're laughable." Many columnists think so too.

The loss of face can be great enough that the company will lurch toward a quota system. Check out the statement by the obviously wounded Texaco chairman and CEO Peter Bijur talking about the "goals—they are not quotas" which have now been "set by determining what the demographics of Texaco's workforce are likely to be in the year 2000." Promising to meet demographic-based goals which are not quotas is familiar diversity-speak for the common English phrase, "We are going to have quotas."

Corporate America has not adapted to the new era of huge settlements which are drawing more high-rolling litigators and revenue-hungry diversity entrepreneurs into the field. The Donnelley case shows that three years worth of diversity programs is no protection. The Texaco case shows that a huge company can be brought to its knees quickly, even by questionable evidence. Somehow sensible policies have to be framed around the right message: diversity is not a goal; it is the natural byproduct of a genuinely open company that hires and promotes by energy and talent.

THE OPPRESSION SWEEPSTAKES

Many readers thumbing through the April 20th issue of the *Herald* of Randolph, Vermont, stopped in surprise when they read the big ad on page B-12.

It was a notice for a farm sale by the federal government's Farmers Home Administration. A 245-acre parcel in Braintree with "tremendous views of the Green Mountains" was up for sale by sealed bids.

One paragraph caused all the eyeball-rolling. It said that offers would be given priority in the following order:

1. Socially disadvantaged beginning farmers or ranchers

2. Beginning farmers or ranchers

3. Socially disadvantaged operators of not larger than a family-size farm.

4. Operators of not larger than family-size farms.

"Socially disadvantaged" is a government euphemism for blacks, Hispanics, Indians, Asians, natives of Alaska, Pacific Islanders and white females. The news was that race and gender preferences had come to Vermont farm sales.

The ad listed Gary Braman as FmHA county supervisor, so I phoned him. Yes, women and non-whites get first crack at this government-owned farmland, acquired from a bankrupt dairy farmer who defaulted on his loans. Who had won the property? Braman wouldn't say, even though the bids closed on May 1st and this was May 4th. A legal appeal had been filed that he couldn't talk about.

He referred me to his boss at the state level, who referred me to *his* boss in Washington, Marlin Aycock. How does a race-and-gender auction work, I asked. Is a $90,000 socially disadvantaged offer weighted to make it worth as much as a $100,000 socially advantaged bid?

It's not an auction, he said, at least in the first year. The government lists its appraised market value. If a sole bidder in category one offers to meet the price, he or she will win. If there's a tie—say, if a black man and white woman both meet the price—they flip a coin. (If Brooke Astor wants the Vermont farm, does a black farmer have to flip her for it?)

When there are no takers, the government moves to category two and three, and eventually to category four, where non-beginning white male farmers get their first shot at the property. After a year, if nobody meets the price, the parcel is declared surplus property and auctioned off to the highest bidder, with no preferences and no commitment to farm the land. It can be developed or put to any non-farm use.

The racial preferences, copied from the Small Business Administration, became law in the Agricultural Credit Act of 1987. Congress added the gender preference in 1992. Almost everyone who discussed this addition seems to use the phrase "tacked on" or "slipped in" to express how casually this was done. It is highly questionable and unusually open to abuse. Male farmers sometimes enter bids in their wives' names and win out over other farmers who don't know the system of preferences. At the local level, this puts power in the hands of FmHA officials, who can whisper advice to friends and withhold it from rival bidders.

The winning bidder of the Vermont farm was Bob Simpson, a successful, high-tech dairy farmer with a nearby spread of 611 acres. Without naming Simpson, Supervisor Braman said he had won out over five other bidders including two white women who had submitted lowball bids. Under the regulations, this is all wrong—bids lower than the appraised value are not allowed in the first offering, when race and gender preferences are applied. To add to the confusion, Bramam seemed to think that Simpson's appeal in the case might be an attempt to have himself declared an American Indian. Could be, said M. Dickey Drysdale, editor of the *Herald*, "Everybody in Vermont claims to have some Indian blood."

But no, Simpson said he isn't an Indian and has made no attempt to become one. His appeal, apparently moot now, was a pre-emptive strike against any rival farmer who might have tried to get an edge by bidding in his wife's name.

Simpson, a category four applicant, said he could have moved to category three by using his wife's name, or to category two by filing under the name of his son, who just graduated from high school. And if he had a daughter around the same age, she might have carried the Simpson family's bid into category one.

This raises the question of whether it is good social policy for the government to create four different levels of legal preference for four members of a single farm family. Answer: no, not really. Just another rococo flourish in our system of race and gender preferences.

Most of us would say that farm wives and farm daughters are approximately as "socially advantaged" as their husbands or fathers, but according to the FmHA system they belong in a higher legal category of oppression and protection. Most of us would say that any historic moral debt owed to black farmers hardly applies to Samoan or Inuit farmers too, but the FmHA doesn't see it that way. Samoans and Inuits and the Hmong are legally protected, and Palestinians and Pakistanis and Russian Jews are not, for no very sensible reason. It's just the way things have always been done by the race-and-gender alliance. And it will be that way until the whole thing goes under.

A SUNNY SIDE ON RACE

Suppose you polled liberals and conservatives on whether unemployed blacks deserve government support. Suppose further that you use a computer to scramble the questions so that in each interview the identity of the out-of-work person seeking benefits changed randomly by race, sex, family status, and work habits. Wouldn't the bulk of conservatives take the opportunity to deny aid to blacks labeled as "single parents" or "undependable" at work?

Answer: no. Although conservatives are predictably more opposed to government intervention than liberals, they don't single blacks out. They are more willing to vote support for blacks than for whites, and single motherhood and work habits make no difference. In fact, they are just as willing to vote support for blacks described as "undependable" as for whites called "dependable."

This kind of finding, reported in the book, *The Scar of Race*, by two California social scientists, is usually called "counter-intuitive," which is campus jargon for "really surprising." The question was designed by the authors, Paul Sniderman and Thomas Piazza, to smoke out covert racism. Conservative whites were given a chance to deny benefits to blacks without appearing to be racist. They could have hidden behind "traditional values" while penalizing blacks. But they didn't.

The point of this is not that conservatives are all wonderful citizens. (The authors picked up signs of patronizing bias among conservatives who wanted to extend benefits to blacks.) The point is that responses to race issues often depend much more on principles and feelings about government's role than on feelings about blacks.

And this in turn calls into question the fashionable theory that seems dominant among older black leaders and mostly white academics: that America is inherently a racist nation, with a strong hidden stream of racism flowing beneath apparently improving racial attitudes.

The "racism" theory of America, explicitly set forth in Andrew Hacker's book, *Two Nations*, tends toward a very pessimistic view of race relations, with whites depicted as so bigoted and dug in on race that little progress is possible. This naturally leads to more adamant attitudes among whites and defeatism among blacks.

The Scar of Race, on the other hand, is an optimistic book. It finds plenty of prejudiced views and shows whites deeply dug in on busing, affirmative action, and quotas. But elsewhere it sees openness and very fluid political opportunities.

Here's one demonstration of how pliable racial attitudes are in America. The authors' survey asks whether the government should spend more to help blacks, or whether blacks should rely only on themselves. Whichever way the question was answered, the interviewer immediately challenged the interviewee in a follow-up question, either "Doesn't this mean special treatment for blacks?" or "Wouldn't this mean that blacks will continue to be poorer and more often out of work than whites?" (The questions are shortened here.) More than 40 percent of those polled instantly changed their opinion when confronted with a different consideration.

There's an asterisk. People are more easily dislodged from "pro-black" than from "anti-black" positions, by 52 to 40 percent. And when the question is preferential treatment for blacks in colleges, the percentage of Americans willing to change their opinions drops down to 20 percent.

The authors report that white Americans, far from having their feet set in cement on race, "are open to persuasion to a striking degree on issues on the social welfare agenda, resistant to a striking degree on issues on the race-conscious agenda." They conclude that a great many white Americans can shed their opinions instantly because they have no consistent worked-out theory on racial matters. Many seem to pick their racial positions almost randomly.

From this point of view, opposition to racial preferences is not evidence of racism, just evidence that one kind of plan—affirmative action—has almost no takers, so something else should be tried. Around the world, affirmative action plans almost always draw great resistance. The authors point out that such plans favoring women are massively unpopular in Western nations, even among women themselves, so "the reactions of white Americans to affirmative action are in no way unique."

The depth of resistance to affirmative action shows up in an intriguing experiment in the authors' survey. It demonstrates that the mere mention of affirmative action significantly increases the likelihood that whites will perceive blacks as lazy and irresponsible—evidence that affirmative action is having a highly toxic effect.

The thrust of the book is that race is not a single moral issue, as it was in the 1960s. There are many issues, and a swirl of constantly shifting attitudes and principles. "The politics of race belongs to ordinary politics," the authors write. With very few hard-core bigots and a large majority open to persuasion, those who want racial justice can rally the electorate. Despite all the pessimism, the chance for change is there.

FEEL ABUSED? GET IN LINE

Consider how far we have wandered since the civil rights movement focused national attention on one undeniably victimized group: American-born blacks.

Armenian-Americans are a protected class in Pasadena, California. Massachusetts includes its large Portuguese immigrant population in its programs. Italian-Americans qualify for affirmative action treatment at the City University of New York. And people of "Appalachian regional origin" are a protected class in Cincinnati, safe now—within the city limits, anyhow—from "hillbilly" jokes and anti-Appalachian bias.

Transsexuals are a protected class in at least four cities (Minneapolis, Seattle, San Francisco, and Santa Cruz, California). The Department of Housing and Urban Development (HUD) wants its contractors to pay special attention to "Hasidic Jewish Americans." Drug addicts and alcoholics are protected under disability laws. And the Amish, or Pennsylvania Dutch, probably should be included in affirmative action programs, according to a *New Republic* article, on the basis of their low income and a history of religious and civil harassment.

Many people think Arab Americans belong on the list of the oppressed. Are they any better off than Samoans, Inuit, or the "Spanish surnamed," listed in some programs, who presumably include many rich, white Euro-immigrants coming direct from Madrid or Barcelona? The problem here is that any Middle Eastern category would logically have to include Jews, who are widely regarded among the protected as just another segment of the dominant white establishment.

Even successful bankers can qualify as victims. Columnist Linda Chavez points out that 19 separate federal regulations benefit "economically disadvantaged" bankers, since the top five affirmative action groups (women, blacks, Hispanics, Asians, American Indians) are "presumed to be socially and economically disadvantaged" under some bank programs, no matter how much money they actually have.

Though most of us are totally oblivious to the possibilities of anti-Canadian-American bias, Tama Starr knows better. She is the head of a New York City neon-sign company. Writing in the *Washington Post*, she said the New York State Division of Human Rights ordered an intense examination of her company's payroll "by age, race, color, sex, creed/religion, martial status, and disability, with special emphasis on Canadian Americans."

Here's one sign of the times: white guys may be in trouble within the gay-rights movement. A complicated system of race and gender preferences at the Gay and Lesbian Alliance Against Discrimination (GLAAD) made it hard for any white males to rise in the organization. Though the quota system was altered, the New York chapter of GLAAD currently has no white males on staff.

White-guy victimization is in the news now, but not because of backlash. It's because white males are the only growth area for the modern victim movement. Everybody else is already covered.

Tama Starr wrote: "Everybody in my employ is a member of a 'protected minority.' Every one is female, gay, foreign-born or of foreign ancestry, religious or atheistic, dark-skinned or melanin-impaired, single or married, old or young. They are physically, mentally or culturally disabled....It is impossible to find anyone not entitled to a group entitlement."

One reason for universal entitlement is that America's racial classifications are mostly self-administered. Nobody really knows whether the protected Armenian-Americans of Pasadena actually include some unprotected ethnic Lebanese or Syrians.

Anthony Falcone, an Italian-American born and raised in New Jersey, described himself as a Hispanic minority and won $17.3 million in construction contracts at the new Denver airport. "I've known Tony Falcone for the last 10 or 15 years," said the head of a local contractors association. "He was always Italian—never Hispanic."

The 1990 census listed the American Indian population as 1.8 million, but 8 percent of that total identified themselves as members of these tribes: Haitian, Polish, African-Americans, Hispanic, or Arab-Americans.

Some of the jockeying for racial classification in the next census may have affirmative action implications. Many Hawaiians want to be shifted from the Asian-Pacific Islander category to the Native American classification. While there are sensible ethnic reasons for the shift, it would also mean that indigenous Hawaiians would no longer have to compete for federal benefits in the same racial category as Chinese-Americans and Japanese-Americans.

The breakup of large affirmative action categories is on the horizon. The general success of the Asian-American category masks the problems of some lagging groups, such as the Hmong. The same is true among Hispanics. But do we really need more and more subdivisions of victim categories? Only if we are determined to look at all our social problems through the lenses of race and gender. Any time we want, we can skip all the racialism and oppression theology and just address social problems directly on the basis of need and fairness. Just a thought.

WAR AGAINST WARRIORS

Asheville, North Carolina, is the site of a brand new legal question, never raised before in the annals of political correctness: should the federal government be involved in determining the mascot or nickname of your local high school sports teams?

Erwin High School in Asheville is being investigated by the Justice Department's civil rights division for using the nicknames "warriors" and "squaws" and for having students dressed as Indians at games and pep rallies.

The investigation will center on whether the Indian theme creates a racially hostile environment that violates the civil rights of Indian students, according to a letter sent to the school system by Bill Lann Lee, acting head of the civil rights division, and Lawrence Baca, a department trial attorney. The letter was a response to a complaint from an Asheville nurse, Pat Merzlak, a Lakota Sioux Indian.

Some Indian activists and their allies have campaigned against Indian nicknames for years. Some 600 schools have dropped these names. More than 2,500 have not. But so far, the Justice Department has never tried to intervene. This is a first. It is also a fresh example of how broad concepts like "hostile environment" and "racial harassment" are constantly being extended from serious issues to minor and symbolic ones.

On the nickname issue, a reasonable case can be made on either side. Indian activists say that it's wrong to use living people as mascots. But on the college level alone, teams are named for Gaels, Scots, Norsemen, Dutch, and the Fighting Irish, as well as Seminoles, Chippewa, Aztecs, and the Fighting Sioux. Some nicknames certainly sound like slurs—redskins and redmen—but most Americans don't think that braves, chiefs, warriors, or famous tribal names fit into this category.

Most Indian names were adopted to indicate that the teams using them have a fierce fighting spirit. This may help promote a stereotype of Indians as savage or hopelessly primitive, particularly when war whoops and tomahawk chops are part of the act at sports events. But many nicknames seem harmless or positive. Some were clearly intended to honor Indian nations or heroes—the Chicago Blackhawks celebrate the Sauk chief Blackhawk and the Cleveland Indians were named, by a vote of fans, to honor the first native American major league star, Lou Sokalexis. And if Indian nicknames are inherently oppressive, why do many Indian and Indian-dominated schools use them?

Debatable issues like this are the proper concern of schools and local communities. When the feds intervened, Asheville had already spent two years and a good deal of money to prepare students at Erwin to make their own decision on a possible change of nicknames and mascots. Students had many discussions and met with the chief of the large Cherokee village in western North Carolina. Student support for a name change, which had reached 44 percent, dropped to 24 percent after the federal intervention.

The civil rights division says it was bound to act after receiving the Merzlak letter, but Asheville was an odd choice for its first nickname intervention. The local community was already addressing the issue. The school usually has only one or two Indian students at a time, and local Indian opinion at Cherokee village seemed indifferent. The damage claimed in the case was allegedly inflicted on a single Indian student, Rayne Merzlak, who never filed a complaint with the school district and had long since graduated when the feds moved in.

A letter like the one sent by the Justice Department carries the implied threat of spending the school board into submission. The board chairman says it might cost $500,000 in legal fees to fight back. About $8 million in federal school funding is also at risk, but the justice department lacks jurisdiction and would have to go to the department of education to cut funds. Or it could go to civil court, seeking damages and an injunction against the school board.

The civil rights division has a reputation of using the threat of costly litigation to get what it wants. In 1993 the division targeted the city of Torrance, California, for allegedly discriminating against minorities in written tests for police and firefighting jobs. The city said the tests were fair and widely used so it dared the division to sue. It did, and last year federal judge Mariane Pfaelzer found the suit so unfounded and frivolous that she ordered the government to cover Torrance's legal costs, about $2 million.

In the Asheville case, the Justice Department asked for so much paperwork that the school district says will take staff 12 full working days to provide it. One of the requests is for the names and racial identifications of all students who have performed as Indian mascots. This wretched excess seems to ask board to violate the Federal Educational Rights Privacy Act. Lawyers for the board say they will refuse to comply.

The division has short-circuited normal democratic debate, intervened clumsily and attempted to manufacture a grave civil rights violation out of a nickname. Apart from that, it's behaved professionally.

A SECOND LOOK AT LANI GUINIER

The Tyranny of the Majority, Lani Guinier's book of essays is out, and the first line of the introduction sounds a familiar note of complaint: that she was unfairly done in by her critics. In it, Yale Law Professor Stephen Carter compares her with George Washington's first Supreme Court nominee, who was heavily attacked as a crazy person.

My view is different. Guinier took some unfair shots for her hair and appearance, and the "Quota Queen" headline was an ugly epithet.

But the debate did turn, after all, on ideas. Her intellectual work—her academic writing—was circulated widely (not snippets, the full texts) and taken seriously. The alarm came from the right, but her ideas seemed so radical that doubts about her quickly arose on the left and in the center (the *New York Times*, the *New Republic*, moderates in think tanks, and the Senate). The president analyzed her ideas, said those ideas were difficult to defend, and pulled her nomination. Isn't this how the system is supposed to work?

Not according to Professor Guinier and her supporters. A story line has emerged about her downfall: that she was ushered to defeat by a shallow and incompetent press corps that either didn't read her work, or couldn't understand it. The press has widely accepted this anti-press indictment and Guinier herself has pushed it hard. "I was dismissed without the usual journalistic intervention of primary reporting," she told a convention of black journalists. She spoke of her "silencing" at the hands of the press and said, "very few journalists apparently were interested in the facts."

Is this true? Certainly the press had to struggle to put her ideas in plain English. Her style is unusually difficult, even for an academic. In Guinier's articles, it's hard to figure out whether Guinier is speaking in her own voice or somebody else's. Sometimes, as in her discussion of what an "authentic" black is, she seems to hold herself apart from other people's views, then doubles back to endorse them herself. Even a sympathetic article in the *Columbia Journalism Review* concluded that "Guinier's views on authenticity are so convoluted that the best solution probably would have been to avoid the issue entirely." But could the press do that, particularly when the name of Virginia Governor Douglas Wilder popped up in a Guinier footnote on authenticity?

It's wrong to blame the press for this. Guinier has a real problem with clarity and directness. For example, does she want to mandate equal voting outcomes, or just equal opportunities? In one article she says her purpose "is not to guarantee 'equal legislative outcomes'; equal opportunity to INFLUENCE legislative outcomes regardless of race is more like it." But in a footnote in another essay, she says civil rights enforcement should be "a result-oriented inquiry, in which roughly equal outcomes, not merely an apparently fair process, are the goal."

Guinier and her supporters say that the next line in the essay eliminates the confusion. But does it? Here it is: "Accordingly, substantive equality should be measured by equality in fact; the process must be equal but the results must also reflect the effort to remedy the effects of a century of official discrimination." Say what? In reprinting the essay, Guinier just drops the footnote. That's in chapter 2, a chapter labeled as containing some ideas "not necessarily representative of my current thinking."

Here's another example of how hard it is to pin Guinier down. In her works, she repeatedly depicts black Americans as helpless in the face of hostile and united white power. As Stuart Taylor wrote in *Legal Times*, it's a vision of America as "a land in which a pervasively racist white majority continues to oppress 'subjugated minorities.'

Yet when I phoned Guinier about this last week, she gave a very different vision. I asked about this line in chapter 2—"Blacks are still the pariah group: systematic losers in the political marketplace." She said, "I probably wouldn't make that statement today."

She said, "I don't believe that there is a monolithic white majority. If I've been construed this way, I've been misrepresented, or I haven't been sufficiently clear in my writing." She repeatedly denied that she views whites as a permanent homogeneous majority. But on page 70 (outside the chapter with some discarded ideas), she questions "the fundamental fairness of permanent majority hegemony in a political system whose legitimacy is based solely on the consent of a simple, racially homogeneous majority."

It's unusual for an author, in an interview, to disavow an opinion she is just about to bring out in book form. And this isn't just any old idea. It's the cornerstone of her argument that courts have to step into the electoral system to give blacks a fair amount of power. If there's no "permanent majority hegemony" to fight, we don't need her exotic remedies, except in isolated cases of gross electoral abuse.

It's not an easy task to figure out what Professor Guinier really thinks. The book gave her a chance to clarify her ideas. It's a chance she missed.

The Junking of History

Time Warner's Home Box Office, joined by PepsiCo, is having a bit of trouble celebrating Black History Month in a truthful way. An HBO-Pepsi poster and advertisement honoring black achievement features a large picture of the pyramids, and many smaller images, including one of the Sphinx.

This means that two of America's best-known corporations have officially bought into the historical howler believed by many

Afrocentrists: that blacks built the pyramids, and have been robbed of credit for it. Quoting the lyrics of a song, the poster says: "We are the builders of the pyramids, look what you did...so much to tell the world, the truth no longer hid..."

Worse, this stuff is being injected into the schools. HBO and Pepsi sent the posters, and other materials, to 20,000 predominantly black schools and community groups. So honest teachers in these schools now have to explain the corporate seal of approval given to a historical claim that isn't true. ("Sounds like we need a history lesson," the chairman of HBO said when his Black History poster was described to him.)

This is no isolated example. The culture is now seriously plagued with deeply felt assertions that aren't true, but are slowly sliding toward respectability anyway. Think back over the assertions that have won a measure of acceptance in the past year or two: the denial of the Holocaust; Oliver Stone's notion that a vast conspiracy to kill President Kennedy involved the Mafia, the military-industrial complex, and many government officials; the idea, depicted in a TV documentary, that a black U.S. Army regiment liberated Dachau and Buchenwald (tough-minded, honest veterans of the regiment stood up and said it wasn't true); and the supposedly strong influence of Iroquois thought on the U.S. constitution, now taught in many schools.

Behind the rise of rhetoric and pure assertion is a growing contempt for facts. "What we are witnessing is the transformation of facts into opinion," wrote the editors of The New Criterion. Note the number of times that commentators argue that the facts don't really matter. When the Tawana Brawley hoax was revealed, the Nation ran an article saying that "In cultural perspective, if not in fact, it doesn't matter whether the crime occurred or not." The facts were irrelevant, it seems, because Brawley's story line reflected the broader reality that whites have abused blacks over centuries. In other words, forget about facts. Just tell stories that convey emotional truth.

This is the climate HBO and Pepsi responded to, probably without much thought. Under different conditions, the corporations might have been just as willing to assert that the Irish invented jazz and the Cherokee developed Styrofoam.

"We're in a day and age in which I can make any claim I want," says Deborah Lipstadt, a professor at Emory University. "I can say I believe the Buffalo Bills won the Super Bowl. Then I say that it's my opinion and I have a right to it, and you're supposed to back off." Lipstadt should know. She is the author of Denying the Holocaust: The Growing Assault on Truth and Memory.

The Nazi slaughter of six million Jews is exhaustively documented. Many of the killers, survivors, and soldiers who liberated the camps are still alive. Yet the people who deny that the Holocaust occurred have made great headway, simply by stating their claim loudly and often. A Gallup poll last month showed that 33 percent of Americans think it seems possible that the Nazi extermination of Jews never happened.

"Good students come in and ask, 'How do we know there were gas chambers?'" Lipstadt says. "Not that they become deniers, but what happens is that in a subtle way, the attackers put history on the defensive." Denial slowly becomes just one more familiar and alternate way of thinking about Jews and Nazis. In a talk-show culture, all talkers have equal status, flat-earthers and round-earthers, Holocaust deniers and Holocaust historians, people who speak regularly to interplanetary aliens and people who don't.

Holocaust denial is only the most spectacular example of a broader assault on knowledge, facts, and memory that is sweeping through the culture. A lot of it comes from some disastrous intellectual trends on campus. Deconstruction and its allied movements say that knowledge is constructed, texts are biased. Values and truth are nothing more than arbitrary products of a particular group. History is not true, merely a story imposed by the powerful on the weak. (Time Warner managed to pick up this theme in a Warner Bros. Records' ad celebrating Black History month. "History is written by the winners," the ad said, a quote from Alex Haley.)

At the extreme, some of these theories say there is no external reality at all, merely consciousness, and some say that personal experience or stories are the only source of truth. This is all intellectual junk, but it's having a profound effect in the real world. Everything is up for grabs now. Like the black veterans who blew the whistle on the false TV documentary, it's important for honest people to take a stand and not let lies slide by. Otherwise reasoned discussion in America will descend further into a fact-free opinion fest.

OUR ADDICTION TO BAD NEWS

The economist Peter Drucker says no other group in world history has ever made so much economic progress so fast as American blacks have since World War II. Three-fifths of African-Americans rose into middle-class incomes, he wrote in the *Atlantic Monthly*. Before the Second World War the figure was one-twentieth.

Nobody would call this picture totally rosy, of course. College-educated black men still make only 72 percent of what their white counterparts earn. And we can certainly quibble about what a middle-class income really is. But a lot of the news is upbeat. The black dropout rate from high school has come way down and is now 5 percent, versus 4 percent for whites. There are almost seven times as many black college students today—1,410,000—as in 1960. Among college-educated full-time workers, 28 percent of blacks have executive, administrative, or managerial jobs, versus 30 percent for whites—a dramatic improvement. Doors are opening every day. America is changing.

Now here is the well-known sociologist, Seymour Martin Lipset, commenting in *The New Democrat* magazine on all this: "Awareness of such gains is not widespread, however. This is partly because the leadership of blacks, women, and Hispanics generally does not admit to significant progress."

Ah, yes. Here is a problem nobody talks about—the mandatory doom and gloom of race and gender spokespeople. Never is heard an encouraging word. No matter how much progress is being made, it is always brushed aside and fresh evidence of oppression is detected. Refusing to acknowledge any good news keeps the pressure on for more concessions. It keeps constituencies resentful and loyal, and it keeps the lines of the new balkanized America nice and sharp.

We pay a high price for this strategic negativism. Progress is made to seem hopeless. Blacks come to think whites will never let them in, even as the doors swing open. With so much money spent, whites come to think that blacks must be at fault for an impasse that doesn't really exist.

The same problem distorts the immigration debate. Some natives seem to regard Hispanics as an unassimilable horde. But the statistics tell a different story—Hispanic immigrants are succeeding, assimilating, and intermarrying with native stock at about the same rates as the white ethnic immigrants of a century ago. The wages of second generation Mexican-Americans are nearly identical to those of similarly educated non-Hispanic whites—quite an accomplishment. My own Irish and Italian immigrant ancestors took much longer to reach parity, under far better economic conditions. But don't breathe a word of this. It's good news.

The recent report by the Glass Ceiling Commission is a wonderful example of desperately rooting around for bad news. To bolster female support for affirmative action, the commission was determined to high-light some allegedly impenetrable barrier placed before white women. (It is, after all, by its very title, in the business of finding invisible, unbreakable obstacles. Thanks a lot, Bob Dole.)

The trouble is that women are rapidly running out of barriers. In a single generation, women have gone from low-level sex-typed jobs to a point where they account for roughly 40 percent of medical and law students, executives, administrators, managers, and Ph.D. candidates. Women are now 44 percent of economists and 59 percent of public officials. It's a spectacular and ongoing transformation, accomplished with amazing speed.

Scanning this sunshine-soaked weather map for a bit of drizzle was hard work indeed, but the invisible-barrier commission finally spotted some: women account for only 3 to 5 percent of senior managers—vice president or higher—in Fortune 1000 companies.

Well, sure, it's an issue. The most elite jobs at the most elite companies are always the last to open up to new workers. It's partly a pipeline problem, too. Many women just haven't been with their companies long enough to challenge for top jobs. Even the 3 to 5 percent represents real progress—a tripling of the number of women holding those jobs in the 1980s. And women are already doing much better as entrepreneurs and in companies outside the Fortune 1000. A recent *New York Times* article featured a fairly long list of women who run billion-dollar companies or billion-dollar divisions of companies. Does anybody really think this progress will slow or stop?

When Sylvia Nasar, the talented economics reporter for the *New York Times*, did her round-up of what working women accomplished during the 1980s (when the war against women was allegedly being waged), she contrasted the professional downbeat comments of the feminist establishment ("All we got was a few little crumbs," said Pat Reuss of the NOW Legal Defense Fund) with the stunning gains women were actually ringing up.

There's a serious disconnect between the official race-and-gender rhetoric and the progress that's being made. Next year, with a presidential election and affirmative action on the ballot in California, the Glass Ceiling people will go into overdrive and find even more undiscovered horror in the workplace. Count on it.

YOU ARE WHAT YOU EAT

John Concordia got in trouble with his teacher for bringing a hamburger to class. He's in high school in Los Angeles, and he was told to bring a favorite family dish to school. So he brought a hamburger, apparently because his family likes burgers.

What a mistake. His teacher was very disappointed. "This is not your food," John was told. John's parents are Filipino immigrants so their favorite food should have been some tasty and authentic Filipino dish. Hamburgers are mainstream American food, hardly a choice that affirms ethnic roots. Stopping in at McDonald's or Wendy's may seem harmless, but it clearly can be one of those subtle ways of denying tribal identity.

Older and wiser veterans of diversity training could have told John the correct answer to the food-choice question. For instance, I am half Italian and half Irish, so I would have known enough to bring in a favorite family meal of half a boiled potato and half a can of Chef Boyardee. The ethnic food police would surely have been satisfied. After school, in case a diversity monitor was watching, I would have made a point of seeking out other half-Italian half-Irish people so we could explore our ethnic halfness together.

It gets trickier, of course, as Americans keep intermarrying. Many of us think this is a good thing, that we are becoming one people. But to identity politicians it's a nightmare. Tribal lines blur. And who can bring in a favorite family meal of souvlaki, chitlins, roast buffalo, and borscht?

This is not the first time that John Concordia has flunked a school identity test. When he filled out an emergency notification card, he was asked to state his ethnicity. So he jotted down "American" in the ethnicity box. Another mistake. "No, you're Filipino," he was told.

It's a rock-bottom idea among the diversity people that people who check off "American" are in denial about their own tribal identity. "Assimilation" is a dirty word these days. Some diversity people think it's a way of identifying with the oppressor—white America. So John was urged to think again. Now he seems to be getting with the program. At least he was quoted as saying the right things, like "People kept telling me I was a Filipino, but I really didn't know what one was, so I had to search for it."

Luckily, John Concordia fell into the hands of a diversity-minded reporter at the *Los Angeles Times*, who told his tale on the front page of the newspaper. The reporter saw nothing out-of-line or amusing about John's rejected hamburger, or his two school-vetoed attempts to declare himself a mainstream American.

Instead, as diversity reporting usually does, the article recounted lots of bias stories (crude anti-Filipino jokes on radio, vague charges that Filipinos are dog-eaters whose women were mail-order brides, the cruel "model minority" myth that all Asians are bright and successful). It also depicted the attempt to find oneself, tribally, as a harrowing struggle: "Some experts believe that stress associated with the search for identity is a key factor in suicidal thought and rising cases of juvenile delinquency among Asian American youth."

Maybe so, but a lot of stress, too, comes from the diversity movement's all-out effort to make sure that minorities stand apart from the mainstream. The Ford Foundation, which is the Vatican of diversity ethics, is clear about its great respect for this apartness. Edgar Beckham, vice president of the foundation, said that "Students now enter college with their group identities intact, and they expect the institution to respond accordingly."

One of the reasons that freshmen arrive at college that way is that high school teachers, like John Concordia's, work so hard to keep ethnic and other tribal divisions sharp. That's why many colleges have different dorms, yearbooks and even different graduations for various racial and ethnic groups. Brown University, always ahead of the curve on such matters, has a separate freshman orientation program for non-white students. This reduces the danger that freshmen of Asian, Hispanic, and African heritage will bond with white classmates.

Of course, if the diversity movement really believed in diversity, it would let Asian-American students pick hamburgers as a favorite food and encourage all students to think of themselves as fellow Americans, not mutual aliens. But don't expect this soon.

LET'S NOT CALL IT A QUOTA

Serious people probably shouldn't use the word "underrepresented." It's a word with an argument embedded in it, that proportional representation by group, not ability or effort, should determine who gets what in America.

Still, most group complaints are framed in the language of "representation." Many blacks argue that they are overrepresented among prison inmates and underrepresented in most jobs worth having. Recent complaints from women's groups focused on underrepresention in symphony orchestras and the art collection at the U.S. Capitol building. Hispanics, who account for 56 percent of the population of Compton, California, argue that blacks are wildly overrepresented among city jobholders. Asian-American students are said to be overrepresented at elite public high schools, such as Stuyvesant in New York and Lowell in San Francisco. (Maybe they should try for lower marks to achieve a lower group representation.)

Even the National Park Service is fretting about overrepresentation of white visitors to the parks, said to be at least 85 percent of the total, well above the 73 percent of the population accounted for by Caucasians. Plans are afoot to divert minorities from their non-park vacations until the proper ethnic representation is achieved at Yellowstone and other sites.

The recent flap over the lack of a black law clerk at the Supreme Court was a representation argument. Can it be that all nine justices are biased against blacks? Well, no. Chief Justice Renquist basically said that he looks forward to the arrival of blacks into the top one-tenth of one percent of young clerks able to compete successfully for these jobs. It was the right answer. Courts should look hard for clerks from all sorts of backgrounds. But at the level of the Supreme Court, justices have to pick the best, and not worry about appearances or representation.

In Marietta, Georgia, a black school board member complained that blacks are only about 45 percent of the student population, but close to 90 percent of those sent to the district's center for students with behavioral problems. The implication here is that the numbers alone prove bias, since overrepresentation in any negative category is automatically presumed to be unjust.

A blizzard of overrepresentation arguments greeted New York state statistics showing that more minorities than whites are in special education programs, even though the numbers seemed fairly close. Whites, with 58 percent of the school population, accounted for 54.3 percent of the special ed students. The apparent assumption that only exact representation is acceptable led one bureaucrat to say "We just don't want to jump the gun and go with an emotional response. There may be some reasons for this."

The same assumption is being made in some gifted programs too, though various ethnic groups view the importance of education differently and therefore produce different results. Under pressure from the Department of Education's Office for Civil Rights, the Palm Beach County school district in Florida passed a new rule: all teachers with ten or more poor or minority students in a class are required to nominate three of them as gifted. Those chosen still have to be evaluated by higher-ups and it's possible the program will work fairly. But gifted programs are under political pressure. If they follow demands for representation, they will cease to be gifted programs.

The main problem with "representation" arguments is that they clash with the norms and standards set up to reward merit. So it's no surprise that supporters of representation have produced a series of arguments attacking merit. One helpful professor wrote about the "illegitimacy of mainstream judgments of merit" and said qualifications for a job depend on "meeting ever-shifting social needs."

Another problem is that demands for representation can't easily be confined to the protected groups established by the federal government. For instance, Italian-Americans have started to complain that they are seriously underrepresented in elite universities. (The Italians are after us, said Harvard's admissions director. "I'm sure the Irish may be too.) White males may make a group argument as well. Since Jews and Asian-American make up almost half of the Harvard student body, non-Jewish, non-Episcopalian white males (about 36 percent of the population) wind up with only 19 or 20 percent of admissions to Harvard.

The American Society of Newspaper Editors has a new diversity director, who probably intends to concentrate only on the usual protected groups. But she is bound to hear from Moslems, Evangelicals, Appalachian whites, and other groups that are much less visible in the newsroom than blacks or Hispanics. Arthur Hu, an Internet pamphleteer and gadfly on diversity issues, calls the Christian right "the most underrepresented group in America." He says, "It's only a matter of time until the least represented begin sounding the mantra of diversity." A universal spoils system is the logical outcome of "representation." Do we really want to play it out this way, or can we just go back to merit?

PART FIVE

POLITICS AND LAW

Avoid "climate" control

Here come the "climate" arguments implicating conservative religious and political leaders in the murders of Barnett Slepian, the Buffalo doctor who performed abortions, and Matthew Shepard, the gay student in Wyoming. The contention is that the leaders are morally responsible for the murders because they created an atmosphere that produced and incited the killers.

A good example is the comment by Polly Rothstein of the Westchester (N.Y.) Coalition for Legal Abortion. She said that the pope, the bishops, and conservative Protestant clergymen "didn't pull the trigger," but the blood of Dr. Slepian and Matthew Shepard "is on the hands of religious leaders who have, with vitriolic language, incited zealous followers to murder abortion doctors and gays and lesbians."

Herblock, the political cartoonist, made his own climate argument in the *Washington Post* by showing a shooter standing behind a suit-and-tie abortion protestor. The protestor, carrying an "Abortions are murders" sign, says "What me, an accomplice?" Well, yes. I don't think we should call women and doctors "murderers" for coming to different moral conclusions about abortion. On the other hand, a CBS-New York Times poll reports that 50 percent of Americans think that abortion is murder. This raises the interesting question of whether it is incitement, climate-wise, to use a word that half the country says is accurate.

The *Nation* magazine published the most overwrought of all "climate" editorials. Written by gay playwright Tony Kushner, it said that Pope John Paul II "endorses murder" of gays. He went on to say that the pope and orthodox rabbis are "homicidal liars," and the Republican Party, by endorsing discrimination "endorses the ritual slaughter of homosexuals."

Similar arguments, a bit more coherent, are everywhere in the media. Katie Couric focussed on "climate" arguments twice on the *Today Show*. On ABC's *Politically Incorrect*, host Bill Maher said the Republi-

can Party has created an anti-sexual atmosphere that unstable borderline personalities hear and pick up on. Gloria Feldt of Planned Parenthood said the "anti-choice" movement has created a "social climate in
which those who are extreme and violent feel they have permission to do
what they are doing." Gay activists and letters to the editor in newspapers
say they see a climate of hatred and fear pushing fanatics to shoot.

The first thing to note is that the "climate" argument is a familiar
political device. Newt Gingrich's anti-Washington rhetoric was blamed
for the Oklahoma City bombing. Columnist Carl Rowan once wrote
that "a lot of the blood of race war victims" will be on the hands of
Rush Limbaugh and Howard Stern.

Jesse Jackson said it wasn't just a few individuals who were responsible for the church burnings in the South in 1995 and the murders of
twenty-three black people in Atlanta in the early 1980s. No, in each
case it was "a cultural conspiracy" that created an atmosphere condu-
cive to violence, Jackson said. (Later we learned that the vast majority
of the church burnings weren't racially inspired, and the killer of the
twenty-three blacks turned out to be black himself.)

Professor and author Marvin Olasky once said that the "climate"
argument reminded him of the days when newspaper tycoon William
Randolph Hearst urged his reporters to jump on any disaster and tie it
as closely as possible to his political enemies.

It's useful to remember that "climate" arguments were once commonly used against the left. During the 1960s, the most crazed and
violent anti-war radicals were depicted as representing all anti-war sen-
timent, just as the wildest anti-abortion zealots are depicted as representative of a broad mainstream movement that opposes all killing.

Now, of course, "climate" arguments are used almost exclusively by
the left. In different form, these arguments show up in speech codes,
sexual harassment doctrine and some of the loonier politically correct
rules on campus. (The ban on "inappropriately directed laughter" at
the University of Connecticut, for example, reflects the idea that apparently innocent laughing can create a climate that results in real
harm to minorities. People who draw a straight line from *Seinfeld* jokes
at the water cooler to persecution of women in the office are essentially making the same argument.)

The political advantage of using "climate" arguments is that you
can discredit principled opposition without bothering to engage it.
All you have to do is connect the pope, your local rabbi, or any other
adversary to a gruesome murder and your work is done. Seen though
the lens of "bias" (often no more than disagreement with the value
system of the cultural left), the pope and the shooters start to merge

in the minds of rational people, just as they do in the minds of Tony Kushner and editors of the *Nation*.

Beware of arguments based on climates or atmospheres. Most of them are simply attempts to disparage opponents and squelch legitimate debate.

WHEN I WAS BILL'S GUY

Three year's ago on New Year's Eve, I suddenly acquired two unexpected dinner partners—Bill and Hillary. The scene was Renaissance Weekend in Hilton Head, South Carolina. I was sitting down with friends in the distant reaches of an enormous ballroom when two large men in suits came by and asked me to follow them. They took me to Table Number One, where I was seated next to the First Lady and three chairs down from the President.

The first thing I noticed were the irritated stares of well-known Washington reporters at nearby tables. The stares meant, "Why is he at the power table and we aren't?" Good question. I had met the Clintons a few times and been invited to the Clinton White House once, mostly because of my wife's connections. I couldn't recall writing anything favorable about the president, though I once chided the Republicans for demonizing Hillary.

None of this qualified me for the deluxe Clinton treatment. I had my suspicions, though, and later they proved correct: Clinton's staff was foraging for ideas among all known social conservatives who were not completely identified with the Republican party. Clinton was starting to recover from a terrible year. The Republicans had been riding high in the wake of the 1994 elections, and since Clinton had not yet been discovered having sex with any interns, his poll numbers were still unimpressive. Bending to the prevailing wind, Clinton was eager to look conservative, particularly in his upcoming big-government-is-over State of the Union speech.

Two days after I got back from Renaissance, Don Baer called from the White House. Baer, a former colleague at *U. S. News & World Report*, was then communications director for Clinton. "You really made an impression on the president, John," he said. "You're his guy." Being the president's guy was a brand-new role for me. "Don," I said, "I don't understand how he could be impressed. It was noisy at the table and I shouted only three comments in his direction." "Four," said Baer. My estimate of Clinton's operation started to rise. He not only invites you to his table. He has someone who counts the number of comments you make and corrects you if your total is wrong.

A second phone call from Baer asked if I would fax ten or twelve of my recent columns down to the White House, and three copies of my book, *Two Steps Ahead of the Thought Police*—one each, I was told, for Bill, Hillary, and Don himself. The next day a White House aide called several times complaining that the books hadn't arrived. At 3 p.m., I checked and found that the plane carrying the books was still on the tarmac at Newark Airport, but the package would definitely arrive by 5 p.m. The White House aide was frantic. "The president has to have the book NOW!" she screamed. A copy was located in Washington and sent quickly by messenger so that Clinton could begin reading the book at 4 p.m. instead of waiting until 5.

A couple of days later, Baer called again, and said the president wanted to phone me the following Monday for a chat. But it would have to be private—I couldn't write about the conversation. I said O.K. In the last in my series of White House phone calls, Baer asked me, "So what should the president say in his State of the Union message?" "Beats me, Don," I said. "I write columns. I don't advise politicians." Everybody does it, he said. Apparently not, I replied, and that was the end of the stroking. No presidential calls came, and no White House invitations either. I am no longer the president's guy.

Oddly, Mrs. Clinton made no effort to extract any useable conservative ideas during our conversation at the dinner. Perhaps that is not her department. While we talked about our teenaged daughters and her views of children's rights, I noticed, or thought I noticed, that some irritation or anger seemed to be flashing back and forth between the Clintons. Other journalists said they had noticed it, too.

It carried over into the after-dinner speeches. The normal routine at this dinner is that President Clinton gives the main talk, after Mrs. Clinton introduces him with a few brief remarks. But that night Mrs. Clinton's remarks went on and on. They must have lasted 45 minutes, ranging widely from women's rights to Afghanistan. At one point she said, "What can you say when you introduce your husband. There are a lot of things I could say about MY husband." This had an ominous ring to it, and by the time she finally sat down, the president had time for only a short speech before the midnight celebration of the new year.

Later, I wondered if the tension between the Clintons had anything to do with Monica Lewinsky. Could be. According to the Starr Report, Lewinsky testified that her third sexual encounter with the President took place at the White House in the early afternoon of December 31, 1995, a few hours before the Clintons' flight to Hilton Head for the dinner. So Mrs. Clinton's comment that "There are a lot of things I could say about my husband" may indeed have been a serious warning shot about the Lewinsky affair. Or it could have been a semi-coded expression of her fury. I think it was both.

WHAT RHYMES WITH CARTER?

Ex-presidents probably deserve some degree of automatic deference, so reviewers and reporters have politely tip-toed around the issue of whether Jimmy Carter's new book of poetry, *Always a Reckoning*, is any good.

Mr. Carter says he worked very hard to learn how to write poetry, as hard, apparently as he worked to learn carpentry. The bad news is that his poetry is what most of us would call prose. It's just that his prose comes in small doses that run down the page erratically, just like poetry.

The good news is that the book is no worse than Reagan's memoirs, and a good deal lighter and cheaper as well—at $18 plus tax, it's only about forty cents per poem, a bargain. People who buy it are essentially buying a presidential souvenir. Those who buy it and get Mr. Carter to autograph it (he signs 3,700 copies per hour) are getting a somewhat more valuable souvenir. Unlike the $4.5 million advance offered to Newt Gingrich, Mr. Carter got only "a modest amount of money."

Another bit of good news for the author (not to be too cynical about it) is that English is the third language for many of the folks who vote on the Nobel Peace Prize, and many of these voters may have no glimmer that this isn't actually poetry. Instead they will home in on the sentiments, which are high-minded and partly geared, it seems, to catch the judges' eyes.

In the poems, Mr. Carter laments racism and political corruption in his hometown, and claims some credit for getting Westminster Abbey to accept a memorial to the poet Dylan Thomas. He writes about nature, including a flight of geese that thrilled him when it flew over the White House. He complains that some people call Japaense "Japs" and Italians "Wops." Some nice humorous touches appear. After he introduced a bill to keep dead people from showing up as voters, "I lost the next campaign, and failed to carry/ A single precinct with a cemetery." Still, the politician-poet might loosen up a bit more, so here are some suggestions for poems in his next collection:

I Went Canoeing

(Note: In 1979, President Carter used a paddle to beat back a rabbit which he said was swimming toward his canoe in Plains. He said it was a fairly robust-looking rabbit that would have created an unpleasant situation, had it been successful in boarding his canoe.)

I went canoeing one sparkling day in Plains
Or rather, I should say I went fishing in a canoe
On a sparkling Plains day
The sky was blue, the sun orange-yellow
birds chirped
frogs burped
Trees stood there, green and brown
I was at peace with nature
at least until the rabbit came
it swam toward me, heedless and aggressive
so I just clubbed it senseless
(In general I hold pro-environmental views,
but rabbits shouldn't swim toward presidents' canoes)

Two Carpenters

Okay, I wasn't great at White House residency
But that was just the path to my ex-presidency
Instead of playing golf like Gerry Ford
or clearing brush to keep from getting bored
I've run around the globe and helped the sick
and built some homes and shown I'm not a hick
and though I do so much for this great nation
I shun all moral self-congratulation
the tide of honors heaped on me displeases
I'm just a simple carpenter, like Jesus.

Dictators and Me

Kim Il sung was pretty good
Ceacescu was misunderstood
Brezhnev I found kissable
Assad's wit unmissable
The Shah and Tito fought for rights
Cedras simply lit my lights

Tyrants rarely cause me pain
the last who did was Tamerlaine

Dictators' Wives and Me

How come the military guys who rule with guns and knives
tend to have such luscious looking wives?
Just go to Ethiopia or Haiti
The thug in charge will introduce some lovely lady
Take Mrs. Cedras—she's so slim and strong!
Can anyone so stunning be so wrong?
It's so distracting—I should be acting
tough, like everybody said
but wives of military monsters always get inside my head
When I'm beside each military moll I see
I tend to feel ashamed of U.S. policy
Instead of getting rid of each Caligula or Borgia
I ask them all to come and visit me in Georgia
Perhaps it's dumb to say all this out loud
Too bad I burbled it in front of Maureen Dowd
But gosh, not all my interviews go well
I hope this doesn't cost me my Nobel.

Yes, I Sing

I sing of America, two hundred million strong
a free and democratic people, so rarely in the wrong
No foolish fullness flaunts the common good
How come I lost to Reagan? Am I wood?
Each ballot like an arrow, left its quiver.
Why did they vote me out? Am I chopped liver?
Was it Bert Lance, "lust in my heart" or Billy?
Was it "malaise" or something just as silly?
The rescue choppers rotting in the sun?
The fact that I could rarely ever get things done?

THE SHRINE AT YORBA LINDA

One of Richard Nixon's poker hands—a pair of deuces—is framed, under glass, just inside the entrance to the Nixon Library and birthplace in Yorba Linda.

This is an odd thing to frame, but then the Nixon Library is a very odd, very interesting place.

"Why are these cards here?," I asked a guard. "Read it," he said. The inscription just says that Nixon won a $1,500 pot with the deuces, bluffing out a lieutenant commander. This happened during his boring, no-action, poker-filled nights in the Pacific during World War II.

It doesn't say why this pot, one of Nixon's many lucrative poker hauls, was so important. Many of us win nice pots without wishing to frame the cards for public inspection 45 years later. But I think I know why. It's one of Nixon's parables about his life: the fellow who was dealt the bad hand triumphs by guile and will over privileged people who have all the luck.

The people who created the Nixon complex seem to have given some thought to parables, mood, and non-verbal persuasion. When I visited the place two years ago, one display showed Nixon campaigning for the Senate in 1950 alongside a wood-paneled Mercury station wagon. Nixon was shown in a photographic cutout, but the wagon was real.

At the time, I thought this display was a dreadful mistake. Nobody was concentrating on Nixon and his breakthrough campaign. Everyone was ooh-ing and ah-ing over the elegant old station wagon. In retrospect, though, it seems that the museum-makers knew what they were doing. They were stressing his connection with a bit of lost Americana. Instead of Nixon, the smearer of his 1950 opponent, Helen Gahagan Douglas, we get Nixon, custodian of Fifties nostalgia.

The creators of the library did the same thing in showcasing Nixon on television. Around a TV set, they created an old-fashioned living room, thus associating Nixon with family warmth and middle-class values. A Princeton professor of architectural history, M. Christine Boyer, once wrote that recreated historic sites like New York's South Street Seaport and, for that matter, San Francisco's Fisherman's Wharf are "self-conscious attempts to regain a centered world, to re-establish a mythical base" for American traditions. Parts of the Nixon library too, I think. At the gift shop, rock-and-roll nostalgia is available in many items, including T-shirts and postcards, showing Nixon with Elvis Presley.

But the nostalgia strategy, if that's what it is, is certainly ruined by the Richard Milhous Nixon interactive television forum. Here you select a question from a Jeopardy-like electronic board, and Nixon jumps on screen to answer it.

Most of the answers seemed too bitter and paranoid for such an image-enhancing institution. As I approached, Nixon was saying, "My lawyer told me I would never get a fair trial in Washington." So I hit the button for "Are you sorry for Watergate?" Nixon told me that resigning the presidency exceeds any possible apology, and that he wasn't going to say anything more on the subject.

Since there was no button for "You didn't answer my question," I pressed the one for "Why is the media so tough on you?" and Nixon said, somewhat ruefully, "They like fashion, and I'm not a fashion person..." Well, then, "Were the media ever fair in the treatment of your presidency?" Nixon replied, "I would say some people say that I got fair treatment on the China issue." But he didn't tell us whether he agreed with the people who say this, or whether they (and he) believe all six years of non-China coverage of the Nixon presidency was unfair.

After grilling Nixon so relentlessly, I decided to lob him a soft question, so I pushed the button for "What was the most memorable meal you've ever eaten?" Here Nixon surprised me. No smiling memories of discovering an out-of-the-way bistro while strolling with DeGaulle or Adenauer. Instead, he grimly discussed a long and excruciating meal in Hong Kong that he had to eat while suffering from a virus infection and diarrhea.

Soon I was out the door and into the famous birthplace, a spartan four-room bungalow built from a mail-order kit by his father. Nixon and his brothers slept in the attic, a room carved out of the cramped space at the peak of the building.

I asked a guide whether the house was just the way it had been when Nixon was born, and he said yes. "Then the Nixons must have been one of the first families in California to have recessed lighting," I said, pointing to the ceiling. Well, no, said the guide. The recessed lights were new.

I asked about the chimney. "Frank Nixon was a wonderful mason," the guide said. "He did it himself." "It looks newer than that," I said. This prompted another confession from the guide. Frank's wonderful masonry was gone. The chimney work was new.

Much seems new and gleaming at the homestead. Ed Nixon, the president's younger brother, once said their mother wouldn't have been happy to see the place so gussied up. Heavily renovated, the house is somewhat Disneyfied, just like South Street Seaport and Fisherman's Wharf. Now it's a shrine, performing its mythic duty.

A FABLE: "PRO-CHOICE" IN 1860

Odd as it may seem today, tent-size was the biggest pre-convention issue for the Republican Party in 1860. Unfortunately, the party was divided by a vexing issue of slavery, which most party leaders fervently wished would simply go away.

The "small-tent" people, as they came to be called, thought slavery was a great evil and wanted the party to say so plainly in a convention plank. But making a moral issue out of something as private and personal as slave-owning was widely regarded as controversial, and pointlessly so. Enlightened opinion was offended.

This was particularly true among the many rights-oriented Republicans who had no slaves themselves, but wished to defend the human rights of those who happened to own a few here and there. As they tirelessly explained, they were not "pro-slaveholding." Not at all. They were merely "slaveholder-rights advocates" defending the right to choose.

Shaking their heads in disbelief, the "large-tent" people argued that a moralistic, intolerant plank would drive away the slaveholder vote and bore the socks off the many mainstream Republicans who believe that issues such as slavery have nothing at all to do with life's central tasks of making a buck, getting taxes reduced, and holding conventions in large tents.

Still others admired the fervor of the abolitionists, but insisted that a national political convention is hardly the place to discuss ideas, let alone principles. "Why insert a plank into the platform that divides the party?" asked one exasperated Senator from Maine. Instead, he favored a unity platform dedicated to peace, justice, and the American way, but he swiftly added that he was willing to bargain those phrases down if anyone felt they were too insensitive or non-inclusive.

The same big-tent advice came from major newspapers in New York, Los Angeles, and Washington, all of which liked to counsel Republicans in the spring and summer of election years before endorsing Democrats in the fall.

As it turned out, however, this expansive big-tent advice applied only to one political party. The Democrats had long since shrunk tent-size by kicking out all known anti-slavery delegates and then screening to make sure that none would ever show up again. The key enforcement was provided by a women's group called "Enemies List," which made certain that no anti-slavery Democrat got a nickel from its list of wealthy contributors, even if he or she had won the Nobel Peace Prize or achieved sainthood on the side.

In fact, nobody had even uttered the word "slavery" at a Democratic convention since 1832. The entire discussion was conducted in a clever code built around the secret word "choice." Abolitionists were "anti-choice." Those who criticized anti-choicers were "anti-anti-choice," while those inclined to rebut such criticism were "anti-anti-anti-choice," and so on.

The public and the government were not to stick their noses into these private matters, unless, of course, there were people who wished to own slaves but couldn't afford them, in which case (the Democratic platform insisted) it was the public and government's job to stick their noses in and provide subsidies. The only other approved government role was to fund slaveholder missionaries as they fanned out to places like Cairo and Beijing seeking converts.

Just before the Republican convention, the issue heated up when an unusually bizarre plantation practice came to light. Some slaveowners were killing babies as they were being born, seizing the feet and driving an ice pick up through the birth canal and into the infant's head. The Democratic nominee said this was all right with him, since he understood that it was well within the privacy and property rights of owners, though probably not too good for the babies involved.

Yet this operation, apparently adapted from a terror tactic used for generations in the Balkans, was so horrific that the media had to react swiftly. They thought up and installed a soothing new term: Certain Late Term Procedures, or CLTP. All reporters agreed that this term was easier to take than the obvious alternative: the Baby and Ice Pick Procedure, or BIPP.

Despite this timely linguistic intervention, many Americans remained greatly troubled, perhaps for once beyond the reach of euphemism. As one prominent Democrat admitted, off the record, "This is just the sort of thing that gives slavery a bad name."

Against this ominous backdrop, the Republicans gathered for their convention, eager to increase tent-size by coming down firmly on both sides of the slavery issue. Luckily their front-runner (not Abe Lincoln, who, at the time, was well behind) was a man of deep convictions about slavery, half of them pro, half con. Perhaps anticipating what the party expected of him at the convention, he had been coming down on both sides again and again, quite sincerely. He had never met a slavery opinion he didn't respect and agree with.

In the end, of course, they threw him out and picked Lincoln. A good thing too. Otherwise we would probably still have slavery and the Democrats would be holding their 36th straight convention calling it a fundamental human right.

IN THE MATTER OF THE COURT VS. US

Robert Bork's new book, *Slouching Toward Gomorrah*, contains a surprising suggestion: a constitutional amendment allowing Congress to override any Supreme Court decision by a simple majority vote of both houses.

Bork is brilliant, conservative, pessimistic, and angry. He calls the court "despotic," which is not the right word for the giant shadow that the court now casts over normal democratic politics. Much of his language is so rough that he sometimes seems to be preaching only to the converted.

Yet his idea is not a wacky one. Canada's constitution allows legislative overrides of the judiciary. Britain, with no written constitution, has the same principle built right in. Any democracy can do it. Chances of getting an override established here by amendment are currently around zero. But Bork believes that frustration is building steadily, so he is putting the idea on the table now.

Bork thinks the court is basically an instrument of the intellectual class: the law schools, the academy, the foundations, the media, the arts community, the left activists. Judges come and go. Sometimes mavericks, such as Antonin Scalia, get through and resist pressures to "grow" on the bench. Sometimes the court strays from the script, as in the current waffling over affirmative action and racial gerrymandering. But in general, it can be relied on to enact the agenda of its class, finding whatever principles it wishes to in the constitution, imposing its own cultural and political values on large and unwilling majorities. "What matters," Bork writes, "is that the result be consonant with the modern liberal mood."

He is hardly the only important social or legal critic who thinks this way. Mary Ann Glendon, a moderate liberal who teaches at Harvard Law School, refers to the intellectual elite as "the semi-skilled knowledge class" and has this to say about it in her book *Rights Talk*: "Their common attitude that the educated are better equipped to govern the masses finds its institutional expression in a disdain for ordinary politics and the legislative process, and a preference for extending the authority of the courts, the branch of government to which they have the easiest access."

The elements which Glendon sees at work—elitism, corner-cutting, righteousness, love of the quick fix, contempt for democratic politics—are a combustible mix. And as the country has grown more conservative, the elite has relied more heavily on the courts. It doesn't organize or seek consensus by going to the American people; it litigates and goes around them. Major social policies don't arise from the democratic consensus-making clash in the political arena. They appear out of the blue, unsupported by any semblance of a social consensus. The result is a growing crisis of legitimacy.

This whole system works so well for the class that runs it that Bork thinks the British have learned the lesson. In Britain, the primary advocates of a U.S.-style written constitution with judicial review are the Labor Party and intellectuals. That development, Bork writes, "would shift a great deal of power from the British electorate to judges who would better reflect the leftist agenda."

The elite pressure on justices who vote the wrong way is enormous. Opinion at the law schools, which are increasingly devoted to freewheeling judicial activism, matters a lot to the court. Lino Graglia, law professor at the University of Texas, says: "The approval of the law schools means as much to a justice as a *New York Times* review of a new play means to a playwright."

Some of this pressure from the schools, the media and the rest of the establishment helps account for the fact that nine straight Republican appointees made such a small dent in the court's ideology. The system is set up to produce converts. Justice Blackmun, widely derided as a lightweight and as Chief Justice Burger's "Minnesota twin," transformed himself into a famous, wildly applauded figure by conjuring up the right to abortion out of penumbras and shadows in Roe v Wade. Similarly, David Souter, severely mocked as a tongue-tied and talentless nerd, unexpectedly voted for abortion rights in Planned Parenthood v Casey, and is now hailed as "a brilliant conversationalist," "one of the court's leading thinkers" and "the conscience of the court," to cite a few compliments recently heaved at him by the *Christian Science Monitor*. The same miraculous transformation presumably awaits Clarence Thomas, should he wish to reinvent himself by embracing the expected values.

"They know they have the power," says Lino Graglia. "Are they going to use it and become famous for some breakthrough decision, or or they going to just trudge along applying the constitution?"

The court has developed the sad habit of creating linguistic sink-holes in its decisions that can be cited later to justify even further out rulings. This amazingly gassy sentence appeared in Casey: "At the heart of liberty is the right to define one's own concept of existence, of meaning, of the universe, and the mystery of human life."

This "mystery passage" can easily be cited the next time to justify suicide clinics, gay marriage, polygamy, inter-species marriage, or what-ever new individual right the court feels like inventing. We are mov-ing firmly into the court's post-constitutional phase. The more you think about this, the less radical Bork's idea seems.

It's a Tort World After All

Ralph Nader is irked that America has 63 museums honoring the field of medicine but none at all honoring the field of law. He particularly wants to celebrate lawsuits dealing with such things as exploding Pin-tos, flammable pajamas, and overly hot McDonald's coffee. So he plans to open a Museum of American Tort Law in his home town of Winsted, Connecticut. It would be something like the baseball Hall of Fame and something like Disney World—a tourist attraction for the whole family.

Nader wants to build a mock courtroom where famous tort cases would be re-enacted. He expects that children will be eager to check out the litigation gift shop. They might plead with mom and dad for toy replicas of faulty products, tiny Pintos, perhaps, cans of beans containing dangerous little pieces of glass, or miniature pajamas with a pair of matches attached. Maybe the kids would collect figurines of the tort all-stars, including Nader himself and all the trial lawyers who have bought major league teams or large chunks of Montana with their share of the litigation bonanza. Famous plaintiffs would be in there, too, including Stella Liebeck, who decided to put the famous container of McDonald's coffee between her knees for a minute while rumbling along a highway, a questionable but historic decision.

For some reason, a lot of people are making fun of Ralph's idea. But why? The litigation explosion has been a boon to us all, particularly those of us who happen to be trial lawyers. It's useful to recall that the baseball Hall of Fame was not built until baseball clearly emerged as the dominant national pastime. Now that litigation has achieved similar status in our time, a similar museum should follow.

One of the museum's dioramas would be a re-creation of the burnt-out Dupont Plaza Hotel in Puerto Rico, torched by unhappy union members. Following the time-honored deep pockets strategy, lawyers for victims did not sue the perpetrators. Nothing so obvious. They sued hundreds of companies that made various hotel items that burned on the scene, from wallpaper and bar stools to the flammable dice used in the hotel casino. (New flame-proof safety dice available in museum gift shop.)

Nader says he wants interactive exhibits. One could be based on the famous talking Lincoln at Disneyland, and might feature a life-sized model of Houston lawyer George Fleming. In a suit over faulty plastic plumbing installed in millions of homes in the sun belt, Fleming won a settlement of $170 million in cash, then demanded nearly two-thirds of it for himself. The talking figure of Fleming might discuss with tourists why he is entitled to $108.8 million for his work and how that computes on an hourly basis.

Surely the exhibit devoted to emotional damages, a profitable frontier in tort law, would be very popular. A Minneapolis bank teller, pressed by her employer to take a lie detector test when she was questioned about missing funds, sued for emotional damage and won $60,000. A pain and suffering display could show the devout Hindu plaintiff who mistakenly bit into a beef burrito at Taco Bell. He sued, claiming he had clearly ordered a bean burrito and suffered emotional damage because beef is forbidden in his religion.

Dog litigation would loom large at the museum, particularly since the recent article in the *American Bar Association Journal* pointing out that dogs and cats represent new areas of practice for attorneys to consider. The dog exhibit could feature Joe Smith, a 56-year-old Texan who wrecked one knee when a small dog scared him by darting in front of his bicycle ($1.7 million, including a million for pain and anguish, plus $50,000 to his wife for loss of household help, companionship, and sexual affection.) Canine litigation can be combined with tobacco litigation, as in the case brought by a Californian charging that her dog was killed by a neighbor's second-hand smoke.

One whole wing of the museum should be devoted to litigation over subway incidents. The New York subways are a prime target for tort lawyers, who usually win between $40 and $50 million a year from the transit authority. One couple sued the New York transit authority for $10 million for injuries received when they were hit by a train while having sex on the tracks. In another celebrated New York case, two homeless men, after splitting a bottle of wine for breakfast, loitered on the tracks and were severely burned by the third rail ($13 million, including $9,000 for loss of income as squeegee men washing car windshields).

Other famous subway cases include a New York drunk who lost an arm when he fell in front of an oncoming train ($3.6 million, set aside by a 3-2 appeals court ruling), a fleeing mugger shot after trying to rob a 71-year-old man ($3 million to the mugger) and a Chicago woman whose late husband, an immigrant from Korea, climbed down on the tracks and urinated directly on the third rail, thus electrocuting himself ($1.5 million because there were no signs in Korean warning against such behavior). (Anti-urination subway warning signs in Korean also available at gift shop.)

Others may giggle over the Ralph museum, but you can look for me there on opening day.

STEAMROLLED AND BULLDOZED

Justice Ruth Bader Ginsburg made a revealing comment recently at the University of Virginia law school. She said she would still like to see the Equal Rights Amendment in the Constitution as "a symbol" for her granddaughter, but it doesn't really matter because "there is no practical difference between what has evolved and the ERA."

In other words, the voters said no, but the courts overrode them and installed the ERA anyway. "How We Got the ERA" is the lead article in the spring issue of *The Women's Quarterly*, a publication of the Independent Women's Forum and an opponent of the feminist establishment. The article's subtitle tells the story: "The people rejected it, but the Supreme Court steamrolled it into the Constitution anyway." The word "steamrolled" echoes Justice Antonin Scalia's complaint that the court is "using the Constitution as a bulldozer of social engineering."

How did this happen? In part, it is the natural result of the interplay between litigating lobbyists and judges who mostly share the same attitudes, social goals, and elite law school training. Justice Ginsburg has sat at both ends of the table in this cozy dialogue, first as a Columbia Law school professor who moonlighted as head of the ACLU's Women's Rights Project, later as the Supreme Court justice who wrote the VMI decision which ratcheted up the existing legal standard for any sex-based state action to a strict ERA level.

More broadly, the modern self-aggrandizing judiciary is the product of many trends—the rise of cynical, postmodern philosophies in the law schools; disgust with an increasingly venal and deadlocked political system; and the endless fallout from Brown v. Board of Education.

The lesson of Brown, alas, is not that an out-of-the-blue precedent-shattering decision is occasionally required, but that all precedents and traditions are suspect and can be overturned at any time by any court. And since nearly everybody agrees that Brown was correctly decided, it is almost impossible to make the case against the troubling legacy of Brown without criticizing Brown itself.

Conservatives and a few moderates tend to agree that the judiciary has vastly inflated its proper role and that a constitutional crisis may be at hand. If so, it is fair to say that conservatives have made a mess of coping with it. The heavily publicized collection of articles in last November's issue of the conservative religious magazine, *First Things*, was serious and well argued. But it was marred by several frustrated suggestions of civil disobedience and one of "morally justified revolution." These ideas dominated news coverage and managed to change the subject. Instead of talking about judges, people began to talk about the mental state of some conservatives.

The campaign by Rep. Tom DeLay (R., Tex.) to impeach activist judges was worse. In three instances, DeLay wanted to impeach a judge on the basis of a single ruling made on the bench. Like the sign-it-or-else pledge against the confirmation of activist judges that is being circulated in the Senate, the DeLay effort has the whiff of the campaign against Communists in government in the Forties and Fifties.

Besides, nobody can clearly define what a "judicial activist" is, and who may be guilty of the charge. As a result, vaguely liberal judges are lumped with judges (some of them conservative) who are willing and eager to vote their biases from the bench. And most of the egregious activists have the wit not to reveal themselves in advance. As Judge Robert Bork says, "We usually discover what we've bought after the candidate is on the bench."

Some in Congress talk as though the main task is to stop the flow of hyper-activists to the bench. But the truth is that the imperial judiciary keeps expanding with ordinary Democratic and Republic nominees doing the work. The new report by the libertarian Institute for Justice concludes that Clinton nominees Ruth Ginsburg and Stephen Breyer are not flamethrowing activists—they were more restrained and less likely to strike down federal and state laws than their Republican colleagues on the court.

The problem is usually not the nominees, but the legal culture they come from. That culture, vastly transformed in the last generation, is eager to solve social problems, addicted to rights-based claims, dismissive of religion, and dubious about the fairness of existing law. As Maryann Glendon of Harvard Law School wrote in *A Nation Under Lawyers*, the free-wheeling impulses unleashed by the Warren Court proved difficult to contain: "Many lawyers and laypeople began to imagine that wise judges in black robes could cure social ills....The flight from politics turned into a stampede, as courts became alternatives to legislatures and judges began acting like executives and administrators."

This is the case that has to be made with the voters. It's not that some abstract "judicial activism" is a threat, but that an elite legal culture has emerged, contemptuous of ordinary democracy and willing to handle things without all that old-fashioned messy involvement of the people. It may take time, but this is a message that can get through.

CHANGING THE RULES OF A DEADLY GAME

To put the sexual predator laws into perspective, consider some of the predators:

- Earl Shriner stabbed, raped, and strangled a 7-year-old boy, then cut off his penis and left him for dead. This crime, which led to the first sexual predator law, in Washington State, capped Shriner's 24-year career of sexual attacks on children and teens, including rape, beatings, and stabbings, various assaults and the probable murder of a 15-year-old girl (he led police to the girl's body). Before his 1987 release from prison, which freed him to attack the 7-year-old boy in 1990, authorities knew he was extremely dangerous and knew he had hatched elaborate plans in prison to maim and kill children.

- Westley Dodd, hanged in Washington at the age of 31 for the rape, torture, and murder of a 4-year-old boy, had a 15-year career as a sexual predator, punctuated by a few months of jail time and repeated misjudgments by psychiatrists and judges who took note of his upbeat, apparently frank attitude and thought him treatable. "I liked molesting children, and did what I had to do to avoid jail so I could continue molesting," he said. He eventually killed three children. In one of his court briefs, he said "If I do escape, I promise you I will kill and rape again, and I will enjoy every minute of it."

- Donald Chapman of Wyckoff, NJ, served 12 years for the rape and grisly torture of a young woman, who somehow survived. After a public uproar at the prospect that Chapman would go free, he was committed to a state mental institution. Some analysts think he would have to be set free if the Supreme Court knocks down Kansas' sexual predator law during the current term. Chapman has promised to rape again and calls himself a failure for letting his previous victims live.

What should society do with predators like this?

David Boerner, author of Washington State's sexual predator law, points out that our current criminal justice system is working exactly as designed. It is designed on the "debt to society" model—each career offender pays his debt with a few years in jail. It basically operates like a game. Once very violent people go free, authorities can't act until another woman or child is attacked and the cycle begins again with a short prison term. No one takes responsibility for looking at the long-term picture—the arc of an increasingly dangerous career.

Charles Krauthammer argues that because of the civil liberties issues involved in sexual predator laws, courts should throw the book at sexual criminals early, locking them up for good after the first or second offense. But this will never happen. Because of crushing caseloads and the unwillingness of many victims to testify, particularly child victims, serious cases are routinely plea-bargained down.

Besides, it isn't easy to identify a dangerous career predator after one offense or even two. With penalties so harsh, more and more first felonies would likely be plea-bargained down to misdemeanors to avoid. And public compassion for an offender jailed for life after a first offense would likely break this plan very quickly.

It makes much more sense for the states, and the Supreme Court, to affirm narrowly drawn predator laws. Yes, there are serious questions of double jeopardy and preventive detention in extending incarceration on grounds of dangerousness. But look at the Shriner case. The state has a obligation to defend the public from dangerous criminals. Is it really helpless to act if a violent inmate with a long record says he plans to mutilate and kill children when released? To say that authorities can't do anything but wait for a child to be murdered is a confession of moral bankruptcy. It's an admission that our criminal justice system is too rigid to meet its real responsibilities.

"Which interest are you more concerned about protecting?" asks Rutgers Law Professor Alexander Brooks. "Keeping dangerous offenders on the street...or protecting women and children by committing the most dangerous offenders with the hope of treating them?"

Treatment, though, should not be used as a fig leaf to cover what is happening here. The test of whether the Earl Shriners should be kept in jail is not whether they can be cured by therapy (very unlikely, on the evidence) but on a judgment of overwhelming dangerousness. What should it take? Well, a clear and credible Shriner-like statement of intent to mutilate or kill again would automatically qualify. (A no-brainer.) So would an unusually long track record for serious violence. Dangerousness is indicated by behavior, not by psychiatric guesswork. Larry McQuay, with 240 attacks on children in Texas, would easily make the cut. So would Reginald Muldrew, linked to more than 200 sexual attacks in California, set free after 16 years in prison, and now in trouble again in Indiana.

The bar should be set very high, but low enough to stop our most violent career predators. If we are serious about crime, we have to do more than just release our sexual monsters every few years and let new victims pay the price for the next brief round of confinement.

Playing any reindeer games?

If this is December, we know for sure that the American Civil Liberties Union is running around snatching nativity scenes and menorahs from public squares, and, in response, some believers are busy arguing that their most sacred symbols are actually secular in some sense and therefore should be allowed.

Various backpedaling Christians have argued, sometimes successfully, that the cross of Jesus is not really a religious image, but merely a traditional cemetery adornment or a historical marker indicating Spanish settlement in America. The Supreme Court famously promoted this effort to secularize Christian symbols with its "plastic reindeer rule" in the Pawtucket, Rhode Island, case in 1984. A city-owned Nativity scene on private property was allowed because images of Santa Claus, reindeer, a clown, a teddy bear, and an elephant somehow detoxified the Christian content of the crèche.

Justice Harry Blackmun applied this line of argument in a two-part Pittsburgh case in which the court disallowed a solo crèche in a court-house (no Rudolph, Frosty, or elves) and allowed a menorah that had been placed next to a Christmas tree outside a city-county building.

Blackmun wrote that when you place a menorah next to a Christmas tree on public property, the religious content fades and the menorah becomes secular enough to pass the Establishment Clause test. "A majority of the court now instructs Jews on the percentage of religious content in their symbols," columnist Nat Hentoff wrote. Even worse, the court seemed to be suggesting that a decorated spruce tree could work something like a cross in a vampire movie, draining away dangerous spiritual power.

In the Pawtucket and Pittsburgh cases, the court unwittingly demonstrated how peculiar it is to allow religion in the public square only if it can demonstrate its own secularity. Justice Sandra Day O'Connor made things worse by inventing a new constitutional test from the rising culture of feelings, sensitivity, and self-esteem: does the religious display make non-adherents feel like outsiders in their own community?

Justice Anthony Kennedy, writing for the minority in the Pittsburgh case, seemed aghast at the spreading mess the court was making of this issue. The court, he wrote, should stop being a national censor and simply let crèches, menorahs and other religious symbols bloom inside and outside public buildings, as long as government is not seen as coercing or proselytizing onlookers.

A case involving Jersey City, New Jersey (ACLU v. Schundler), may one day allow the court to extricate itself from reindeer-mindedness and do what Justice Kennedy so sensibly suggested. When the ACLU sued over the city's crèche and menorah, the city tried the conventional reindeer strategy, adding some trivial secular symbols. A federal court approved the display, but an appeals court reversed, saying the reindeer strategy was not enough to desanctify religious symbols. The city appealed last summer, arguing that the decision ignored the menorah decision in Pittsburgh. No decision yet.

What makes the Jersey City case distinctive is its multicultural argument. The City's display includes a sign saying that the crèche and menorah are part of a broad policy acknowledging diversity. The City population is 41 percent foreign born, with immigrants from everywhere. The city celebrates Ramadan Remembrance Day, and important Hindu, Buddhist, and Jewish holy days as well as Christmas, Hannukah, and Kwaanza. Mayor Bret Schundler argues that residents have a right to live in a city that does not actively discriminate against religion in its celebrations of the community's cultural diversity throughout the year.

The city's diversity carries no weight judicially, but it may function as a political counterweight to the traditional ACLU belief system—that the no-establishment clause must be read as a mandate to cleanse the public square of religion. That belief system is based mostly on the notion that religion is divisive and toxic, something that lawyers and enlightened judges must work to protect the people from.

The ACLU belief system, which comes close to being a secular religion, has been dominant in the courts for forty years, though its support among the populace has always been minimal. It's probably just a matter of time before the American people rebel against the long effort to suppress religion in the public square. "Everything else gets expressed on public property—why not religion?" says Kevin Hasson, president of the Becket Fund, which defends Jersey City and other cities, free of charge, against ACLU-type crèche-and-menorah suits.

Religious displays that make government look like the civil arm of muscular Christianity are rightly challenged and mostly gone. But what's wrong with a city acting to reflect civil society by acknowledging, neutrally and equally, the religious and other cultural heritages of its people? Eventually, the Supreme Court has to forget the reindeer and give a coherent answer to this question. Jersey City may be forcing the issue.

ARE PROTESTERS RACKETEERS?

Congress wrote an intentionally vague and loosely worded law in 1970 as a tool to combat organized crime—the Racketeer Influenced and Corrupt Organizations Act (RICO). The American legal system being what it is, RICO was soon put to more imaginative uses. It's civil provisions—triple damages and the opportunity to smear somebody as a racketeer—made it a favorite among plaintiffs' lawyers. Soon tenants were suing "racketeer" landlords under RICO, and divorcing wives were suing their "racketeer" husbands. And a chorus of voices, left and right, warned that it was just a matter of time before someone managed to use RICO against political protestors.

That has now happened, but because the target group—anti-abortion demonstrators—is very much out of favor with civil liberties groups and the chattering classes, the chorus has been mostly silent. One who did speak up, Harvard law professor Charles Ogletree, said this use of RICO "is unprecedented and raises serious questions about chilling important opportunities for political protest. This stretches the law beyond its logical limits."

The political stretching was accomplished by the National Organization for Women (NOW) and two abortion clinics in a 12-year civil suit against anti-abortion activists. Last week a U.S. district court jury in Chicago decided that two anti-abortion groups and their leaders had engaged in a conspiracy to commit extortion and threats of violence against those operating or patronizing abortion clinics.

Lethal violence, such as arson and bombing, was not an issue in this suit. The anti-abortion activists were accused of making threats, blocking clinic doorways, putting glue in door locks, occasional grabbing and pushing, and pulling the hair of doctors or patients and "creating an atmosphere" that made arson and bombing possible.

All lawbreaking deserves punishment, but RICO allowed these mostly low-level offenses to be lumped together and seen as a nationwide conspiracy to intimidate abortion doctors and patients. Congress specifically intended to make conspiracy easy to demonstrate in mob cases—under RICO two violations over a period of ten years, even relatively trivial offenses—can be defined as a pattern of racketeering activity. But using this easy standard against political protestors should raise eyebrows. When combined with the severe threat of triple damages, it invites the use of the courts as arenas to punish political enemies.

One of the drafters of RICO, Notre Dame law professor G. Robert Blakely, warns that under RICO, a minor illegality—a bit of pushing and shoving or a rock thrown through a window—can transform a constitutionally protected demonstration into an attempt at "extortion."

The concepts of "extortion" and "obtaining property" used in RICO cases comes from another law, the Hobbs Act, and courts have constantly broadened their meaning. "Property" now means anything of value, such as the right of a store or clinic to solicit business or an individual's right of access to a clinic, so even momentary interference such as blocking a doorway, can be deprivation of property or extortion.

RICO could easily have been used to quell the anti-war protests in the 1960s, as the American Civil Liberties Union noted years ago. But thanks to the ever-broadening language of RICO decisions, it could also be used against non-violent protests and simple sit-ins. If RICO had been written a decade earlier, segregationists would surely have used it to cut the legs out from under the civil rights movement. In the 1960 Woolworth lunch counter sit-in in Greensboro, North Carolina, the "property rights" of Woolworth to attract paying customers would have been seen as violated by conspirators who tied up the counter seats for months. The black football players who stood around protecting the demonstrators would have been depicted as an illegal intimidating force.

In the Chicago anti-abortion case, the judge's instructions to the jury stressed that property rights included the right of women to use the clinics and the right of clinic operators to provide services free of fear, including "fear of wrongful economic injury." Surely Woolworth customers and owners would have qualified for the same property rights, and the "fear of wrongful economic injury" was beyond dispute. Woolworth lost $200,000 during the sit-ins. That's why it capitulated.

It takes little imagination to see how almost any protest group could be hammered by RICO, from Greenpeace and nuclear protestors to Caesar Chavez's" grape boycott (which certainly induced the growers' fear of wrongful economic injury). This has been clear for years. In 1970, the ACLU opposed RICO as being "one of the most potent, and potentially abusive, weapons for silencing dissent." Since then, the ACLU's voice has been more muted and ambivalent, mostly because the group's feminist allies argued hard that RICO was an ideal weapon to use in the abortion wars. The ACLU really ought to make an effort to recapture the clarity and principled position it staked out in 1970. Either you believe in First Amendment rights or you don't.

WHEN JUDGES FEEL ROMANTIC

Mary Ann Glendon, a professor at Harvard Law School, has a nice image of what much modern judging has come to: a baseball game in which the umpire abandons neutrality and decides to play for one team.

Peter Edelman is surely an example of what she means. Edelman, a former Georgetown University law professor and husband of Marian Wright Edelman of the Childrens' Defense Fund, is reported to be President Clinton's choice to fill a vacancy on the U.S. Court of Appeals for the District of Columbia. Because of the dark cloud over the White House since the November elections, the controversial Edelman may not, in fact, be named. Even if he isn't, he will certainly do as a horrible example of what is decending upon our judiciary.

Edelman thinks the poor have a right not to be poor—America is rich enough to give every needy person cash payments equal to two-thirds of the poverty line, plus housing subsidies, food stamps, Medicaid and other subsidies. There's nothing wrong, of course, with holding such views. A lot of people think cash is better than welfare, and a lot of people are unconcerned about the increased dependency and alienation from the work force that such handouts might bring.

The problem is that Edelman doesn't really think these views are the normal, debatable stuff of democratic politics. He thinks they should be imposed by judges because not giving substantial cash payments to the poor is unconstitutional, a violation of due process. Nobody else seems to have noticed this in the Constitution. As an appeals judge, he would be an umpire who knows, before the first pitch is thrown, how this particular game should turn out.

In her new book, *A Nation Under Lawyers*, Glendon calls this "romantic judging," an adventurous, free-wheeling approach by reformers who passionately wish to do good, and who do not intend to let tradition, law, precedents or non-romantic readings of the Constitution get in the way.

She writes that the classical ideal of modesty, impartiality, and restraint "has been rivaled by an image of the good judge as bold, creative, compassionate, result-oriented, and liberated from legal technicalities."

Glendon thinks Brown v. Board of Education ushered in the great modern age of romantic judging. This is a hard argument to make, since Glendon, like almost everyone else, thinks Brown was correctly decided—segregated schools were a massive injustice. But Brown changed our legal culture. It got law students excited about using the clean and quick route of litigation to get social change. Many lawyers and non-lawyers came to believe that judges could cure our social ills.

"Many unwise judges down the line began to believe they had the magic touch," Glendon writes. "Interest groups of many sorts seized the opportunity to advance their causes by taking them to the courts rather than to the people. The litigating branch of the legal profession was off to the races."

Romantics learned to cite "due process" and "equal protection" to justify almost any preconceived result. State supreme courts followed the trend, multiplying rights-based decisions and pushing legislatures aside. Glendon notes that federal and state judges now oversee 500 school districts and supervise prisons in forty states.

Instead of being accepted as a justified exception, Brown came to be seen as the model of how judges should operate to impose progressive solutions that legislatures were afraid of, or hadn't gotten around to.

Again, Edelman is a wonderful example of this mentality. He says that the courts' power to make law stems from Brown v. Board of Education in which the Supreme Court undertook the "affirmative duty" vacated by legislators. In the Brown case, this was true, but to romantics such as Edelman, it is a wide-open door that invites judges to impose their own social agendas.

Roe v. Wade is the most prominent romantic decision of the post-Brown era, conjured up out of penumbras and shadows, and sternly criticized by the pro-choice but non-romantic Ruth Bader Ginsburg before she ascended to the Supreme Court.

The most celebrated judges of our time have been romantics—William O. Douglas, Earl Warren, William Brennan. How could it be otherwise? Today judges don't get to be famous through restraint and modesty. They get there by producing unexpected, breathtaking decisions admired by the media. We have created the conditions under which a judge's place in history will likely hinge on some startling lurch away from critical but humdrum decision-making.

It is the rise of post-Brown romanticism—not the usual liberal-conservative split—that has made hearings on Supreme Court nominees so important. The arrogance and utter contempt for democracy shown by some romantic judges is stunning. Given the current law-school culture, the problem is likely to get worse. If some judges are determined to rule like philosopher kings, the only proper democratic response is to knock them down at nomination hearings, or just vote out the officeholders who tend to nominate romantics.

JUDGES 1, PEOPLE 0

Judge Stephen Reinhardt is pleased with himself, and no wonder. Discovering a new constitutional right is no longer quite so rare as finding an El Greco in your attic, but a lot of judges obviously yearn to do it and Reinhardt succeeded. Peering deep into the Constitution with his colleagues on the Ninth Circuit Court of Appeals, he discovered something nobody had known was lying around in there for 200-plus years: a constitutional right to physician-assisted suicide.

"I think this may be my best ever," the proud inventor of this brand new right told the *Wall Street Journal*. The *Journal* described him as someone known on all sides as "a crafty advocate for his left-leaning views" who once wrote a blistering letter to the Clinton administration complaining that it wasn't appointing enough judges as ideologically firm as himself. (He's a Carter appointee.)

Once appointed to the bench, crafty advocates like Reinhardt have a strong track record for craftily trying to settle political and moral debates by imposing their opinions on the populace. That's how we got Roe v. Wade, which many pro-choicers, including Justice Ruth Bader Ginsburg, now acknowledge was a sorry bit of judicial overreaching that short-circuited the political process and gave us thirty years of social warfare.

Unable to resist telling us the correct answer to our political-moral problem, Reinhardt and his colleagues have essentially taken the issue out of the legislative process, just as Justice Blackman and the Supreme Court majority did with Roe. But the political process is crucial. On one side, we have the classic libertarian argument: what right does the state have to intervene between a dying patient and his doctor, or to force a suffering terminal patient to stay alive?

On the other side, we have society's interest in protecting human life and discouraging suicide, in not converting doctors into healer-killers, and in avoiding the moral disasters that have occurred in Holland's de facto program of physician-assisted suicide.

In one recent case the Dutch supreme court held that a patient need not be suffering physical pain, let alone terminal illness. In another, the court said it could be lawful to assist killing a woman depressed at losing her two sons. And last year a doctor in Holland was acquitted after euthanizing a spina bifida infant at the request of its parents.

Richard Doerflinger of the Catholic Bishops' Secretariat for Pro-Life Activities thinks the Ninth Circuit decision has pushed us as far down the slippery slope in one day as the Dutch have traveled in 20 years. The court found a "liberty interest in determining the time and manner of one's death" and unsurprisingly pointed to the abortion decision, particularly the finding in Casey that "these matters, involving the most intimate and personal choices a person may make in a lifetime, choices central to personal dignity and autonomy, are central to the liberty protected by the 14th Amendment."

In all, this is a more peculiar and alarming decision than media accounts have yet indicated. It includes a series of language games apparently intended to rid us of words such as "suicide" and replace them with happy euphemisms like "hastening (death) by medical means." ("We are doubtful that deaths resulting from terminally ill patients taking medication prescribed by their doctors should be classified as 'suicide.'")

The court blurs the line between pulling the plug on a respirator that artificially keeps someone alive and actively intervening on a request to kill a terminal patient. It also casually opens the door to direct lethal injections: "We consider it less important who administers the medication than who determines whether the terminally ill person's life shall end."

Just as casually, the court allows the killing to be ordered by a court-appointed or patient-appointed surrogate ("a decision of a duly appointed surrogate decision maker is for all legal purposes the decision of the patient himself"). It does this by extending the law on ordinary medical treatment, but in doing so, it crosses over into approving what most of us would call euthanasia.

But the gravest legacy of this decision is that a crucial and gradually unfolding debate has been suddenly constitutionalized into yet another constricted and specialized legal argument about rights. Not much room here for the issue many of us think of as central: what kind of society, with what values, do we want America to become?

Daniel Callahan of the Hastings Center writes that "legalization of physician-assisted suicide/euthanasia requires a fundamental and drastic realignment of all codes of bioethics since Hippocrates." Anything that grand should depend on the will of the people, not on a court-invented right. In dissent, the Ninth Circuit's Judge Kleinfeld wrote: "The Founding Fathers did not establish the United States as a democratic republic so that elected officials would decide trivia, while all great questions would be decided by the judiciary." That comment should rattle around during the presidential campaign and beyond.

BUST THOSE CANDY CANE FELONS

Can an event marked by about 90 percent of Americans become unmentionable? Sure. School bus drivers in Fayette County, Kentucky, were warned not to say Merry Christmas to any of the children. Presumably they should say "happy holidays," "merry solstice," "hail to winter," or something of the sort. In Pittsburgh, they might say "Happy Sparkle Days," the city's weird euphemism for the Christmas season.

A high school dean in West Orange, New Jersey, reprimanded a student for singing "God Rest Ye Merry, Gentlemen" on school property. The student probably could have avoided criticism more easily by singing a song about overthrowing the government.

The nervous principal of Loudoun High School in Virginia told student editors to keep the newspaper as secular as possible and "to be careful that they don't associate the upcoming holiday with any particular religion." No, I guess not. You wouldn't want people to go around thinking that a Christian holy day is somehow associated with the Christian religion.

Why all these neurotic mental gymnastics? Christmas is the second most important feast on the Christian calendar (after Easter) and possibly now the second most important feast (after Thanksgiving) on the American civil, secular calendar. Though increasingly regarded as vaguely unmentionable, it is also a national public holiday like Independence Day and Memorial Day. Instead of acknowledging all this (along with the religious significance of Hannukah and Ramadan), our schools and other public institutions make their grim annual effort to pretend that Christmas isn't occurring.

The evasiveness seems to grow worse each year. Some schools allow only instrumental versions of traditional carols—no words. Others allow carols at school concerts as long as they are mixed in with, and presumably disinfected by, songs about Frosty and Rudolph. But schools in Scarsdale, New York, forbade "Jingle Bells" and "Frosty." (Is Frosty a serious violation of church-state separation?) They also banned candy canes from schools. The only remotely possible explanation for this is that they dimly recall the shepherd's crook or staff in Christian symbolism.

Trees are acceptable in some schools if they are sanitized as "the giving trees," "mitten trees," or multicultural "unity trees." Jittery about criticism, a few other schools banned wreaths and poinsettias. One Nebraska school went so far as to invent a seasonal Santa-like traveler from outer space known as Leon (Noel spelled backwards, which proves that Christmas can be discussed in schools, if it is French, backwards, and involves non-religious space travel).

Many schools now ban Santa Claus, guilty by association with Christianity because he is remotely based on the fourth-century saint. Not to worry. Santa is about as relevant to the religious feast of Christmas as Bugs Bunny is to Easter. But we are dealing here with an obsession, not rational school policy.

In some cases, schools have more or less consciously swept away discussion of living traditions (Christianity, Judaism) while conjuring up silly new seasonal liturgies out of "unity trees," Leon the space traveler, and the various trappings of a vague new pagan nature cult.

This avoidance of religion makes no social sense. Nobody wants the government to become the propaganda arm of Christianity or any other religion. But children should be taught about one another's religious traditions and what those traditions mean. The supreme court has let stand a lower court ruling that schools may recognize religious holidays "if the purpose is to provide secular instruction about religious traditions rather than to promote the particular religion involved."

Part of that teaching may occasionally involve posting pictures and symbols of various religions, and it certainly can involve the songs and music of different faiths. No court has ever held that singing carols in school or at school concerts is unconstitutional.

Schools do more damage than good when they address only the secular elements of religious holidays. This trivializes religion, withholding important learning, while blinking the message that religion is dangerous and divisive.

The public schools don't exist to promote religion, but they don't exist to marginalize it either, or to promote secularism as a dominant religion. "The public schools have lurched light years to the left on this issue; it's time to level the playing field," says Kevin Hasson of the Becket Fund, which litigates many church-state issues on the non-ACLU side.

Part of the problem with religion and the schools is that school officials are so sensitive to pressure that they cave into almost any protest or any threat to sue. The usual result is that policy is geared to a veto by the most sensitive person in the community, whose feelings are hurt when any religion is brought up or given any attention. Too bad. Religion is an important social force. Marginalizing it or banning neutral instruction about it from the schools is not a neutral act.

Merry C———s. Happy H———h.

Praying for sanity in schools

There are two ways of looking at the call for a school-prayer amendment to the constitution.

1. The radical religious right, angry at the modern world and contemptuous of the constitution, is trying to subvert church-state separation

and take over the public schools. This is the conventional view of the American Civil Liberties Union and its easily alarmed ally, People for the American Way.

2. It is a predictable, explosive reaction to the vast hostility toward religion that has steadily permeated the schools since the Supreme Court struck down school prayer in 1962. Egged on by the ACLU, with its "customary crabbed view of religious speech," (Nat Hentoff's memorable phrase), the school establishment has refused to make any reasonable and constitutional accommodation to the feelings of religious parents.

My vote is for explanation two.

The establishment clause does not require government, or public schools, to become adversaries of religion. But the need to avoid any endorsement of religion has mutated into an unmistakable antagonism.

The almost obsessive attempt to stamp out any religious utterance in or around public schools is now routine. Principals try to make an alarming church-state issue out of teachers who discuss religion with one another on their lunch hours, students who gather at the flag pole for voluntary pre-school prayer, and children's drawings or show-and-tell items that contain religious references.

A suit against a St. Louis public school alleged that a fourth-grader was ridiculed and placed in three-day detention for bowing his head and whispering a private prayer before lunch in the school cafeteria. Another suit charged that school officials ordered an 11-year-old Oklahoma girl not to use her recess time to pray and discuss religion with classmates.

The senior class president at a Douglasville, GA, high school, was ordered not to give the traditional farewell address to classmates because he could not be relied on to leave religion out of his speech. He presumably could have turned the occasion into a rally for Jeffrey Dahmer or called for the violent overthrow of the state of Georgia without attracting any censors, but a suspected reference to God was enough to shut him up. Where is the ACLU when you need it? Answer: in its usual place, on the wrong side. Ultimately, sanity prevailed and he was allowed to give his speech.

Fearing ACLU litigation, even soft secularists in the school bureaucracy have been converted into grim zealots determined to root out anything that looks faintly religious. They have done everything but arrest kindergartners for bringing in coins saying "In God We Trust." Christmas trees, an ancient pre-Christian Teutonic custom, are being banned in some schools, and so is Santa Claus, who is approximately as religious as Frosty and Rudolph and just about as threatening to church-state separation.

A clear indicator of the pointless hostility is the long shameful battle to prohibit students from forming after-class religious discussion groups. As columnist Jeff Greenfield writes, "It took years of litigation and political pressure before young Christians were given the same legal rights as the 4-H Club, the glee club, the stamp collectors club, and the gay youth of America."

The campaign against a moment of silence is even more debased. So far the ACLU is the best-known organization willing to insist that sixty seconds of silence establishes a religion, perhaps its most tortured reading of the constitution. Behind it, of course, is the fear that not all students will use the quiet minute for praiseworthy secular thought or salacious musings. Some may actually pray!

Though the growing hostility to religion in schools is clear, the need for a school-prayer amendment is not. Official school prayer would dishonor our tradition of church-state separation. As a practical matter, it would tie up energies for many years that are desperately needed on other fronts. And even success would look bleak: a watered-down generic set of prayers that would be litigated over for a decade and have little impact on the social and moral decline they are supposed to arrest.

A better goal would be to push for the moment of silence and relief from the day-to-day anti-religious pressures on the schools. A minute of reflection before the school day is perfectly appropriate in a culture that has always believed in the moral, character-forming aspect of schooling. Nobody outside the ACLU should feel threatened that students are invited to take stock of their lives and think about where they are going, even if this results in some ethical or (gasp!) religious thoughts not shared by all.

And we should note that the school-prayer issue is surely a symbolic struggle as well as a literal one. A lot of parents have lost confidence in the school system and the new values that have overtaken it. Gil Sewall, head of the American Textbook Council, says: "They see the schools accommodating a lax secular age and they don't like it. They want something with more soul and character." Instead of railing against these parents, the elite in this country might take time to find out what alarms them about the culture of our schools, and how these concerns might be met.

A MAN'S GOT A RIGHT TO RIGHTS

Freshly minted "rights" are so common these days that they even pop out of cereal boxes. At least through last fall, Post Honeycomb boxes contained a 7-point "Kids Bill of Rights," including one on world citizenship ("You have the right to be seen, heard and respected as a citizen of the world") and one entitling each cereal-buyer to world peace ("You have the right to a world that's peaceful and an environment that's not spoiled").

Expressing every goal, need, wish or itch as a "right"—either fundamental or inalienable—is almost mandatory. Here are some newly discovered rights:

The right not to be mugged. California Governor Pete Wilson said every state resident "has a fundamental right not to become a crime victim...and not to live in fear."

The right to rubber sex toys. Citing Roe v. Wade, an Alabama court ruled that a man had a constitutional right to sexual devices made of rubber.

The right to have one's breasts touched by strangers in Massachusetts bars. As part of her act at Alex's Lounge in Stoughton, Massachusetts, Chesty Morgan invited patrons to come up and touch her bosom, claiming a constitutional right to be touched. The judge said no.

The fundamental rights of trees and rocks. "Trees and rocks have rights to their own freedom," said Michael McCloskey, chairman of the Sierra Club.

The right to rape. In California, Ramiro Espinosa used a butter knife to pry open the locked bedroom door of his wife of 30 years, then tried to have sex with her against her will. Convicted of spousal rape, Espinosa appealed on grounds that he has a constitutional and a religious right to have sex with his wife at any time. He lost.

Women's right to use men's rest rooms. In Santa Monica, California, men were selling drugs in women's rest rooms. So the City passed an ordinance prohibiting men and women from using the opposite sex's facilities unless a line of three of more people kept them from using their own. Gloria Allred, a lawyer and activist, declared that this violates women's right to urinate in any facility at any time, calling it "the first step down a long dark road of restricting women's rights..."

The right to food. The World Food Summit in Rome, sponsored by the United Nations, proposed the "fundamental right to be free from hunger." The United States delegation balked, calling the elimination of hunger a goal or aspiration, not a right to be fed.

The right to a satisfying career. The newsletter *Family Affairs* noted a clash between "parents rights" and women's "right to satisfying careers outside the home."

Every writer's right to get published. This right was asserted by *Publishers Weekly* in an editorial deploring Simon & Schuster's decision not to publish Bret Easton Ellis' hyperviolent novel, *American Psycho.*

Prisoners' right to die with barbiturates. Psychiatrist Thomas Szasz suggests "the right to a bottle of barbiturates for every prisoner who requests it (or perhaps only for those sentenced to life)."

Prisoners' right to procreate before being executed. Fourteen prisoners on death row in California claimed "the right to reproduce" through artificial insemination.

The right of gays to be affirmed by government. Gay Activist Jeff Levi claimed that homosexuals "have a right—as heterosexual Americans already have—to see government and society affirm our lives."

The right to steal or burn bundles of newspapers so that others can't read them. Also the right to deface bulletin boards or to pull down any posted material one doesn't like. Both have been asserted on many campuses as First Amendment rights, including the Washington and Lee School of Law (bulletin boards) and the University of Pennsylvania (newspaper thefts).

The right to commit perjury. A federal court in Richmond, Virginia, said the Constitution bars additional jail time for a convict's "disbelieved denial of guilt under oath." Overturning this decision, Supreme Court Justice Anthony Kennedy said a defendant's right to testify does not include the right to commit perjury."

The fundamental right to a Ph.D. or other long-term schooling. The first draft of a proposed amendment to the Illinois constitution declared that "a fundamental right of the people of the state is the educational development of all persons to the limits of their capacities."

The constitutional right to backpack. When a New Jersey school banned backpacks from classrooms and hallways as a hazard, 14-year-old Elyse Meredith didn't just protest the ban as many other students did. She claimed a constitutional right to carry her backpack anywhere.

The fundamental right to proportional representation on television. Discussing a study that found too many white males featured on TV shows, Professor George Gerbner of the Annenberg School of Communication announced "a new civil right" for all people, including minorities, the poor and the disabled, "to be represented fairly and equally in the cultural environment in which we grow."

Still to come: the fundamental social right to be free of the manufacture and mining of any more new fundamental rights.

PART SIX

CULTURE AND LANGUAGE

OF FAMINE AND GREEN BEER

This week's St. Patrick's Day parades commemorate the 150th anniversary of "Black '47," the worst year of the Irish potato famine. "The Great Hunger" was the most searing event in Ireland's long and sad history. It killed a million Irish and drove a million and half more to America. Among them were Ellen Burke and Thomas Leo, my great grandparents.

It was the last big famine in western Europe and the greatest loss of life in the century between the Napoleonic wars and World War I. When a wind-borne fungus wiped out the potato crop, the Irish began to die of yellow fever, dysentery, typhus, and starvation. They ate dogs and rats, often dogs and rats that had already eaten human corpses. When one English traveler spat out some gooseberry skins from a passing carriage, a mother raced to pick up the skins and place them in the mouth of her starving infant. The roadways were littered with bodies of people with green stains around the mouth, from eating grass as a desperate last meal.

In the beginning, the British made many honest attempts to help, some of them heroic. Later, politics and what we would today call "compassion fatigue" sealed the fate of the Irish. New York State has just passed a law requiring public schools to teach about the famine, and some of those who lobbied for it wanted teachers to say that the British intentionally tried to kill off as many Irish as possible. It's fairer to say that rescue efforts, often halting and grudging, were colored by a hands-off free-market philosophy and the fact that the Irish were a despised people in a captive society, semi-enslaved for 600 years, and therefore regarded as primitive, stupid, and hopeless.

The voyages that brought the dazed and starving Irish to America were a cross between the scramble of the Haitian boat people and the middle passage of African slaves. Fever broke out, but there were no medicines. The stench of excrement filled the holds. The Irish were jammed in like cordwood, gaining a bit more room as dead bodies were heaved overboard. During one storm, 178 immigrants were shoved down among the cattle, where half of them quickly suffocated. If crosses and tombs could have been placed on the water, one American official said at the time, the Atlantic would have looked like a huge cemetery stretching from Ireland to America.

In America, the Irish ran into the same contemptuous attitudes they had to bear at home, this time centering more on their Catholic religion. The Know-Nothings and other nativists campaigned against the Irish in much the same way that the Klan organized against blacks. A few convents and churches were burned. "No Irish Need Apply" signs appeared in store windows.

The rural Irish, entering an urbanized and industrial culture, arrived in much worse shape than most immigrants and bore the psychic marks of an increasingly sick and violent society back home. They were quickly identified in the public mind with poverty, disease, alcoholism, crime, and violence.

Much of this was an accurate portrait of the Irish at the time. Irish violence was often astounding. Bodies floated in New York City's East River almost every day. At one point, the city jail population was 90 percent Irish. Police vehicles that rounded them up were called "paddywagons," the wagons that carried all the hopeless Paddys to their natural home. Cartoonists drew pictures of the Irish as monkeys, and good citizens wondered about a permanently unfit underclass and the possibility of genetic inferiority. Does any of this sound familiar?

Almost in the blink of an eye, the Irish "erupted" out of allegedly permanent underclass status, as one author put it, pouring into the middle class and taking political control of Boston and New York. Along the way, the St. Patrick's Day parade, once a defiant show of strength against WASP power, gradually declined into a pointless march of aging suburbanites and drunken collegians in funny hats.

The good news is that efforts are under way to reconnect the Irish and their parades with their roots in famine, poverty, and despised immigrant status. Commemorations of the famine, both here and in Ireland, have become fundraisers to combat famine in Africa and Asia. Seminars and conventions on the Irish famine often have surprisingly little material on Ireland and a lot on the problem of world hunger today. "We are allergic to famine," said Mary Robinson, president and national icon of the confident and rapidly changing Irish republic. She is widely known as a "faminist."

Two summers ago my daughter and I climbed halfway up a mountain in the raw and empty west of Ireland to inspect a large Celtic cross, placed strategically in the middle of nowhere. We thought it would be a monument to the famine, but we didn't expect the inscription: "to all those who walked this way in the great famine, and to all those who walk this way now in the Third World." A very nice touch. Congratulations, Ireland.

THE TWO SINATRAS

The gold plaque that once hung on Frank Sinatra's desert home in California had it right. It said "Never mind the dog. Beware of the Owner."

That was bravado, but good advice, too. Frank was a dangerous man. The comedian Jackie Mason, savagely beaten by a group of thugs after making fun of Sinatra, turned the event into a comic routine. "Frank Sinatra saved my life," he would tell audiences. "A bunch of guys were beating me up and Frank came along and said, 'That's enough, boys.'" Later he announced that everybody says Sinatra is the greatest singer in the world, because if they don't say that, they get killed.

A well-known writer who mocked Sinatra several times in print once told me he was sure that Sinatra was actually going to have him killed. The cloud lifted when the singer attacked him verbally during one of his concerts. The writer figured he was safe at last: Sinatra wouldn't do him in after demonstrating his anger so clearly in public.

I asked Jonathan Schwartz, who is probably our best living expert on Sinatra, what he thought of the man. "The greatest musician of his age," he replied. No, I said, as a person. "Oh, he's a monster," Schwartz said.

Right on both counts, I think. He was an astonishing, sensitive artist and an unusually crude, violent jerk. No popular singer has ever gotten inside a lyric and put a song across like Sinatra. By day he surrounded himself with the best jazz and pop musicians of his day, and the clear respect they had for Sinatra shines out of all the studio photographs of the period. By night he was surrounded by a wall of his personal goons, ready to rough up gossip columnists and the public at large.

The gap between the artist and the jerk was so wide that it often seemed as though two people were sharing the same body. Just when you have him pegged as a touchy whiner, he shocks you with an astonishing album like "In the Wee Small Hours," one of the greatest popular albums ever recorded.

If you haven't heard it, go get it now. It's a "concept" album about loss and romantic defeat. The album, writes Jonathan Schwartz, is "nakedly honest, unmushy dignified...on CD it's a miracle." It's pure grief, not a false note or a hint of self-pity anywhere. Nobody had ever sung these songs that way. Professional musicians were astounded. How did a singer with Sinatra's dismal, self-absorbed character handle emotions like this?

The same huge gap appears in the way Sinatra treated women in song and in real life. The romantic longing in his music is unmistakable, and three generations of women responded. But in real life, it would be hard to find a star who treated women worse. He had some sane relationships. But in general, women were lower beings to be used sexually, then passed along to friends. Once he famously ate a meal served to him on a woman's body. There were violent scenes, too, all while he kept turning out the most powerful and convincing love songs of the day.

Pete Hamill reports a remark that may shed some light on Sinatra's woman problem. Hamill was driving across the desert one night with Sinatra, and Sinatra was talking about his mother, Dolly, who was loyal and protective, but strict and fierce, too. "When she came close," Sinatra said, "I never knew if I was going to get hugged or hit." Let the Freudians push that one around.

I grew up in Sinatra territory in northern New Jersey, where his music was all around us and talking about Sinatra was almost as routine as discussing the weather. As kids we would drive past his home in Hasbrouck Heights (Nancy's home actually. Frank had left to chase Ava Gardner). If our summer jobs took us anywhere near Englewood Cliffs, we would take our brown-bag lunches to the steps of the Rustic Cabin, the roadhouse where he was "discovered" by Harry James. On my first job as a reporter, covering the county courthouse in Hackensack, the old-timers talked endlessly about Sinatra, his escapades and his colorful mob ties. All the time his music was working its way into our lives. Nothing that happened to us, no adventure or date or defeat, seemed complete without Sinatra's music. His emotions were our emotions.

In the background was Sinatra's social triumph—the working-class Italian kid who crossed the great divide, the Hudson River, and made it in Manhattan. But that faded as north Jersey became more suburban, less ethnic. What remained was the problem of how we would think about Sinatra, the social phenomenon.

It bothered me (and still does) to have my emotions stirred by such an appalling jerk. I stopped going to Sinatra concerts. I would listen to his records at home, but not be part of any organized group adulation. This is a distinction lost on all my friends, most of whom would have sacrificed an arm to hear Sinatra in person. They would lecture me about the distinction between artists and art. I would say I feel as uncomfortable at a Sinatra concert as they would at a concert by Gieseking, the Nazi pianist. They would roll their eyes.

"He was our Amadeus," said the writer Nick Pileggi, referring to the crude and goofy character of Mozart in the Broadway play *Amadeus*. Yes, he was. He was also an outstanding thug, and I mourn his passing.

THE OFFICIAL COLUMN OF CHAMPIONS

Shortly before Pope John Paul II arrived in New York City, a friend in public relations phoned—did I want to interview a spokesman for the official bottled water of the pope's visit? Only a churlish fellow with no news judgment at all could have refused a ripe journalistic opportunity like this, so I said no.

Later, with the pope long gone, I had second thoughts and checked the story out. To cover costs of the papal visit (the one-day rental of Camden Yard in Baltimore for a papal mass was $105,000), church officials in New York, New Jersey, and Baltimore arranged to sell a lot of t-shirts and papal memorabilia.

Along the way, the Catholic Archdiocese of New York named Castle Springs water the official bottled water of the pope's visit. Naturally, no penalty for consumption of unofficial water during the pope's stay was mentioned, or even implied. Those wishing to call attention to the pontiff's ethnicity were perfectly free to drink Poland Spring as the popemobile rolled proudly past, just as affluent Episcopalian onlookers, always eager to show their independence from Rome, could sip their Perrier quite openly, even in front of all those Irish Catholic cops surrounding the pope.

As it happened, the designation of this water as official was somewhat limited in scope. It extended west across the Hudson River to northern New Jersey, where the pope said mass in Giant Stadium but not east from Manhattan across the East River to the rest of New York City—the bishop of the Brooklyn-Queens diocese took a dim view of the mass marketing of papal trinkets and declined to endorse any papal beverages at all.

Still, just to be the pope's drink in Jersey, Manhattan, the Bronx and Staten Island for two days was quite a coup for Castle Springs. Until then, this three-year-old, flyspeck company in the sprawling Kohlbert Kravis Roberts conglomerate had never sponsored anything grander than a car on the Nascar racing circuit.

Yet here the company was, in obvious partnership with the Vatican, selling its little-known New Hampshire spring water for a pricey $2 a bottle with the gold and white papal insignia right there on the side.

Though analysts believe that the unification of America's third most popular enthusiasm (religion) with the nation's beloved Number One (marketing) is an important breakthrough, the more familiar one-two combination (marketing and sports) is, of course, the richest source of officially designated products.

For instance, the recently concluded New York Marathon had an official bottled water (Vermont Pure Natural Spring Water) and an official pasta (Creamette) which was supposed to be officially served beneath the marathon's official spaghetti sauce (Aunt Millie's).

The marathon also had an official bagel, an official anti-fungal cream, a newspaper whose marathon race results were designated as official, and an official breathing device but, alas, it did not have an official teddy bear. This is because the official teddy of 1994 failed to prove cost effective, and so the 1995 race had to go on without a single cuddly animal or woodland creature being cited as official.

On the other hand, the 1995 marathon did have an official "Erector," a designation which stimulated a good deal of research by this column and which we can proudly announce is a reference to that traditional children's construction toy, the erector set. The reason why an overly long and crowded footrace needs an erector set (official or not) remains obscure.

There's much more you should know—Pepsi is the official soft drink of Air France, and Nestle's was the official (and apparently ineffective) candy bar of the George Bush inaugural.

The first designations are in from the Olympics, the famous quadrennial marketing riot which is run by open-hearted businessman who—at heavy personal cost to themselves—generously operate a few athletic contests on the side.

For instance, Sara Lee has been named the official packaged meat product of the 1996 Olympics. This is nice to know, since nobody really wants to show up in Atlanta on a steamy summer day with the wrong packaged meat product in his pocket. McDonald's is more or less the official unpackaged meat product of the Olympics. McDonald's and the Olympic people are still steamed at Wendy's. This is because

Wendy's ran a TV hamburger ad featuring skater Kristy Yamaguchi during the 1992 games, thus implying (or so McDonald's believes) that Wendy's was the official Olympic burger, when it really wasn't at all.

Nissan is the official sport utility vehicle of the 1996 Olympics, while BMW is the "official provider of mobility" for the Olympic torch relay. And as you probably know, *Jeopardy* and *Wheel of Fortune* are the official Olympic game shows.

I was secretly hoping to get myself named the official weekly columnist for the Atlanta Olympics, but Time, Inc. is "the official publishing sponsor" and they probably will want to pick one of their own. Maybe I'll just settle for naming some obscure bottled water as the official drink of the John Leo column. You can do worse than imitating a pope.

CHEERS, CIRCA 1968

In his wonderful new memoir, *A Drinking Life*, Pete Hamill talks about the late 1960s in the Lion's Head, our neighborhood saloon in Greenwich Village. "In the growing chaos of the sixties, the Head became one of the metronomes of my life," Hamill writes. "It was as if we'd all been looking for the same Great Good Place and created it here."

Drugs had just hit the Village like a tidal wave. But we were a little older than the grunt-and-point druggies and the befuddled flowerpersons beginning to gather over on St. Mark's Place. We were into beer and argument. It was a talker's bar, and you could get into an argument on any subject, from the merits of Virginia Woolf's novels to the bench strength of the 1944 St. Louis Browns.

One night you would be hotly debating the Warren Court with Norman Mailer and the district attorney of Boston. The next night it might be a hilarious rolling monologue on Texas by Linda Ellerbee, a debate with Wilfrid Sheed about Ira Gershwin's lyrics, or a disquisition on Meyer Lansky and other famous Jewish criminals from my fellow *New York Times* reporter, Sid Zion. Vic Ziegel, the sportswriter, missed the place so much when he was out of town that he once phoned from Ohio and asked the bartender to hold the phone up for a minute so he could hear some Lion's Head conversation.

Vine Deloria, the author and a founder of the modern Indian Rights movement, was a regular. So was Father Peter Jacobs, baptizer of my second daughter, and the gentle poet Joel Oppenheimer, who wrote a long, touching (and faintly misogynistic) poem about the birth of my firstborn. We had old lefties like Doug Ireland and Victor Navasky, now editor of the *Nation*, and new righties like Dick Walton, who ran for president one year on the Libertarian ticket. (He lost.) Jose Torres, the light-heavyweight champ, showed up with Hamill occasionally, and Jessica Lange, then in her pre-King Kong days, was a waitress in the back.

The *Village Voice* was next door, and *Voice* staffers used to bring touring politicians. When Jack Newfield brought Bobby Kennedy in, two regular drinkers made a dash for the men's room to erase some anti-Jackie graffiti. "Don't worry about it," said writer Joe Flaherty. "When Bobby has to pee, he sends somebody." Our graffiti, in fact, were famous. Some sociologist from the New School announced one night that the greatest graffiti locations in New York State were the old train station in Albany and the men's room of the Lion's Head.

One of the regulars was George Kimball, now a fine sportswriter at the *Boston Herald* but at the time a quirky candidate for sheriff of Douglas County, Kansas. George had only one eye. He was running against an incumbent who had one withered arm. So he ran on the slogan: "What this county needs is a two-fisted sheriff who will keep an eye on crime."

Everybody seemed to be an expert on something or other. Alice Mayhew, New York's best book editor, was the house Francophile with an encyclopedic knowledge of World War I. Tom Quinn could sing any song from any musical that had lasted more than one night on Broadway. Doug Ireland knew all the old labor and socialist songs. Doug was campaign manager for Bella Abzug. In the heat of arguing with Bella, he once warned her to shape up, or people would dismiss her as "just another pretty face."

The Clancy Brothers and Tommy Makem occasionally sang Irish songs at the big table in the back room, and one night Bob Dylan came in and sang along with them. This was before the birth of the horrendous celebrity culture. Now Dylan would move around with a 40-person entourage of hangers-on, bodyguards, and a bunch of alleged reporters and hair stylists from *Hard Copy*. But that night he was just a local guy stopping by.

The only celeb I regretted missing was Peter O'Toole, said to be one of the great barroom talkers of his era. We waited until 4 a.m. one day, but he didn't show. I think it was Dennis Duggan, the *Newsday* columnist, who told me that O'Toole arrived grandly the next night in a large limo with a case of his own champagne, so he wouldn't have to swill the house brand.

It was a Great Good Place, as Hamill says, with some overtones of family. When one of my out-of-state relatives died, Al, the co-owner of the bar, flipped me his car keys and said he didn't need the car for at least a week. They took all your messages, too, and let the struggling writers (most of us) run endless tabs.

Hamill writes, "I don't think many New York bars ever had such a glorious mixture of newspapermen, painters, musicians, seamen, ex-Communists, priests and nuns, athletes, stockbrokers, politicians, and folksingers, bound together in the democracy of drink." For me, it ended in 1972, when they put in a jukebox. I was offended that actual conversation should have to be conducted while loud guitar-owners practiced in the background.

It ended in 1972 for Hamill, too, for a different reason. He was very nearly the heart and soul of the expansive, talky, amazingly civilized Lion's Head culture. But the damage from heavy drinking was ruining his life. This is a familiar downside to the democracy of drink. On December 31, according to his book, he stared into a vodka and tonic and said to himself, "I'm never going to do this again." "I finished my drink," he wrote. "It was the last one I ever had."

GUNNING FOR HOLLYWOOD

Every time a disaster like the Colorado massacre occurs, the Democrats want to focus on guns and the Republicans want to talk about the popular culture. Much of this comes from actual conviction, but economic interest often disguises itself as principle. The Republicans can't say much about the gun lobby, because they accept too much of its money. The Democrats can't talk about Hollywood and the rest of the entertainment industry, because that's where so much of their funding comes from.

The gun and entertainment executives tend to patrol the same familiar borders. Charlton Heston, head of the National Rifle Association, offered some narrow and dubious arguments: An armed guard at Columbine High School would have saved lives; legalizing concealed weapons tends to lower crime rates. Gerald Levin, the equally adamant head of Time Warner, said he feared "a new season of political opportunism and moral arrogance intended to scapegoat the media." He raised the specter of censorship, noting that Oliver Cromwell, "the spiritual forebear of Rev. Falwell," had shut down the theaters of seventeenth-century England on moral grounds.

Surely we can do better than this. We can talk about the importance of gun control, and we can talk about the impact of media violence on behavior without suggesting that censorship is any kind of solution.

This time around a center of sorts seems to be forming. Bill Bennett and Senator Joseph Lieberman, familiar social conservative voices on this issue, have been joined by Senators John McCain and Sam Brownbeck, and, it seems, by the Clintons and the Gores. Tipper Gore said the entertainment media bear some responsibility for the Colorado killings. In a radio address, President Clinton urged parents to "refuse to buy products which glorify violence."

If more Republicans are willing to talk about guns, maybe more Democrats will be willing to ask their favorite media moguls to think harder about the social impact of the many awful products they dump on the market. "We want to appeal to their sense of responsibility and citizenship and ask them to look beyond the bottom line," said Lieberman. There is talk of some sort of "summit meeting" on violence and perhaps yet another national commission of some sort. McCain will plan hearings this week on how violence is marketed to children. Long-term, we need a broad campaign appealing to pride and accountability among media executives. Shame too, says Lieberman.

Pointless violence is an obvious topic. In the dreadful Mel Gibson movie, *Payback*, a nose ring is yanked off, bringing some of the nose with it. A penis is pulled off in the new alleged comedy, *Idle Hands*. Worse are the apparent connections between screen and real-world violence. Michael Carneal's shooting rampage in a Kentucky school was similar to one in a movie he saw, *The Basketball Diaries*. In the film, the main character dreams of breaking down a classroom door and methodically shooting five classmates while other students cheer. One of the men who stomped a parade-watcher to death on St. Patrick's Day uttered a line from a fictional killer in the movie *A Bronx Tale*: "Look at me—I did this to you."

A damaging kind of movie violence is currently on display in a very good new movie, *The Matrix*. Keanu Reeves's slaughter of his enemies is filmed as a beautiful ballet. Thousands of shells fall like snow from his helicopter and bounce in romantic slo-mo off walls and across marble floors. The whole scene makes gunning people down seem like a wonderfully satisfying hobby, as if a brilliant ad agency had just landed the violence account. What you glorify you tend to get more of. Somebody at the studio should have asked, Do we really need more romance attached to blowing people away?

A generation or two ago, movie violence was routinely depicted as a last resort. There were many exceptions, mostly brief and not very graphic. But violence was typically something a hero was forced to do, not something he enjoyed. He had no choice. Now, as the critic Mark Crispin Miller once wrote, screen violence "is used primarily to invite the viewer the enjoy the FEEL of killing, beating, mutilating."

We are inside the mind and emotions of the shooter, experiencing the excitement. This is violence not as a last resort, but as deeply satisfying lifestyle. And those who use films purely to exploit and promote the lifestyle ought to be called on what they do.

Some years ago, Cardinal Roger Mahoney, Roman Catholic archbishop of Los Angeles, was thought to be preparing a speech calling for a tough new film-rating code. Hollywood prepared itself to be appalled. But instead of calling for a code, the cardinal issued a pastoral letter defending artistic freedom and appealed to moviemakers to think more about how to handle screen violence. When violence is portrayed, he wrote, "Do we feel the pain and dehumanization it causes to people on the receiving end, AND to the person who engages in it?...Does the film cater to the aggressive and violent impulses in every human heart? Is there danger its viewers will be desensitized to the horror of violence by seeing it?"

Good questions. Think about it, Hollywood.

HOLD THE CHOCOLATE

Call me perverse, but I spent an evening last week checking out Karen Finley's new act. Trivia buffs will recall Finley as the chocolate-covered nude performer who did colorful things with yams and federal arts money in 1990, thus attracting great attention as either an embattled artist or a national laughing stock, depending on your point of view.

"Return of the Chocolate Smeared Woman" was staged in a tiny theater in lower Manhattan, with the audience sitting quietly in amazing discomfort on empty paint buckets instead of chairs. The warm-up act, the Dancing Furballs, consisted of several chocolate-marked young people dancing with enthusiasm but not much coordination. Other

Furballs distributed free glasses of beer and wine, perhaps to compensate for the theater's version of bucket seating.

Finley then appeared and immediately took off her dress. Wearing only panties and gold high-heeled shoes, she began smearing her body with chocolate and asked if anybody in the audience would like to come up and take a lick for $20.

This is an odd way to begin a show, particularly since the chocolate is supposed to represent excrement and what men like to do to women's bodies. But art is art, and two women in the audience finally were coaxed onstage to lick a bit of chocolate off one thigh and her belly button. The licking apparently concluded the lighthearted section of the program, because Finley quickly launched into her familiar tirade mode.

The *Washington Post* once described Finley as "an impassioned voice in the wilderness, crying out against perceived injustice." Another way of putting this is to say that she thinks heterosexual males are pigs and she is always eager to share this insight at the top of her lungs. Sure enough, we begin to hear about fathers, preachers, and doctors who molest and rape children and policeman who show up eagerly at rape scenes to demand oral sex from the victims. This dark worldview is right out of the radical males-are-evil feminism of Catherine Mackinnon and Andrea Dworkin. But at least Mckinnon and Dworkin know how to write. Finley's tirade is an angry jumble that comes nowhere near the emotional effect she apparently intends to have.

Every time Finley uses the word "love" it is immediately connected to some form of abuse or hatred. The message seems to be that men are incapable of affection and loyalty. The tentacles of the evil patriarchy are everywhere. To enjoy this show, it is clearly best to have the opinion that women are helpless victims of brutish men. The audience seems to be filled with attractive and successful-looking women who have paid $13 to hear Finley's essentially hopeless message of female victimization.

Among other things, Finley's diatribe seems badly dated. If new material has been added since her first chocolate-smeared headlines, it's not really apparent. Complaining about male perfidy may have been the frontier in 1990, but women have moved on and upward. Nobody seems to have told Finley. This may be why the audience, apparently made up mostly of gay women, doesn't seem thrilled by this act.

Only once does Finley seem to be working material with some power: when she speaks of the loss of friends who died of AIDS. But this is a re-run of her 1990 performance, and she neatly undercuts it by delivering the monologue while sitting completely naked in a washtub, scrubbing off the chocolate and assorted sticky things. We are supposed to believe that the scrubbing is symbolically significant (Finley tells us two or three times that it represents "starting over"), but it's hard to believe that the audience is fully engaged in the horror of AIDS while Finley is working so hard on her personal chocolate-removal.

Finley launches into a gross monologue about having sex with Ken Starr, Jesse Helms, Orrin Hatch, Ted Kennedy, and Bill Clinton. She is the star, lusted after by weird and terrible men. Message: Look at me—I'm saying provocative sexual things about well-known politicians! An unusually pointless monologue depicts Bill having sex with Hillary. Yes, it's surely indecent, but the main problem is that her ramble is so lame, scrubbed clean of any humor, cleverness, or insight. How can she miss targets this huge? Her material "is more inflammatory than insightful," the *Washington Post* said delicately, adding that Finley "goads one into heavy ponderings."

The last phrase is true. I myself was goaded into an unusually heavy pondering on why anyone who is not a columnist would want to sit through this stuff. If she is an artist, so is the drunk on the next barstool whimpering about how awful women are. I also experienced a back-up ponder. It focused on why the taxpayers would want to invest in this with public funds that could more defensibly be spent on those $600 Pentagon-designed toilet seats.

The answer, I suppose is obvious. Everything counts as art these days. This is particularly true of art-free politicized rants from the cultural left, which helpfully supplied most of the judges who awarded the dubious "performance art" grants before political pressure cut them off. The Supreme Court now says, in effect, that we don't have to fund craziness described as art. Be grateful.

A TOWER OF POMOBABBLE

A professor once wrote this about Tonya Harding's attack on Nancy Kerrigan: "This melodrama parsed the transgressive hybridity of unnarrativized representative bodies back into recognizable heterovisual codes." Probable English translation: Maybe Tonya had Nancy's leg smashed because she was attracted to her. If so, the media wouldn't tell us.

The professor was writing in "pomobabble." This is the jargon of postmodernism, the intellectual movement that says truth doesn't exist and that all values and knowledge are "socially constructed"—made up to serve the interests of the powerful.

Postmodernism has swept through our universities, doing great damage. But "pomobabble" has emerged as a source of constant mirth. As a hoax, Alan Sokal, a physicist at New York University, wrote an article in dense pomobabble arguing that gravity and physical reality are social constructs. *Social Text* magazine took it as a serious piece and published it. Later, to explain the joke to the magazine's editors, Sokal said that anyone who doubts the law of gravity should come up to his apartment and try walking out the window. He lives on the 21st floor.

Pomobabblers now win most awards in the annual Bad Writing contest, says Denis Dutton, a professor in New Zealand and editor of *Philosophy and Literature*, the scholarly journal which sponsors the competition. Homi Bhabha of the University of Chicago took second place last year for this sentence: "If, for a while, the ruse of desire is calculable for the uses of discipline soon the repetition of guilt, justification, pseudo-scientific theories, superstition, spurious authorities and classifications can be seen as the desperate effort to 'normalize' formally the disturbance of a discourse of splitting that violated the rational, enlightened claim of its enunciatory modality."

Wondering what an enunciatory modality might be, I phoned Bhabha, who explained that it is technical language referring to a network of terms, vocabulary, and language that construct a particular set of meanings. I was pleased he was able to clear that up.

The grand prizewinner of 1998 was a 94-word effort by Judith Butler of the University of California, Berkeley. For a school assignment, my daughter and a classmate worked four hours to untangle and diagram this sentence. Here it comes, at half its length to save space:

"The move from a structuralist account...marked a shift from a form of Althusserian theory that takes structural totalities as theoretical objects to one in which the insights into the contingent possibility of structure inaugurate a renewed conception of hegemony as bound up with the contingent sites and strategies of the rearticulation of power."

Butler is an academic star. But Martha Nussbaum, a scholar at the University of Chicago Law School, recently wrote that when Butler's notions are stated clearly and succinctly, they don't amount to much. The obscurity of Butler's prose, she wrote, "bullies the reader into granting that, since one cannot figure out what is going on, there must be something significant going on."

Many scholars are now busy mocking pomobabble. The *Michigan Law Review* ran a long spoof of postmodern legal gibberish written by law professor Dennis Arrow ("There is the double narrative, the narrative of the vision enclosed in the general narrative carried on by the same narrator.") Australian professors have created a "Postmodern Generator," an internet website that spits out a new essay in pomobabble each time the site is hit (http://www.cs.monash.edu.au/cgi-bin/postmodern). My visit to the site produced deep thoughts about Marxism ("Thus, Marx uses the term 'Marxism' to denote not, in fact, desublimation but predesublimation. The example of dialectic narrative...emerges again in The Last Words of Dutch Schultz, although in a more textual sense.")

Anyone can learn pomobabble. String together words like "hegemonic," "transgressive," "narrativity," and "valorization." Refer often to murky French philosophers. Deprivilege heterosexuality by gluing "hetero" to the front of normal words, creating terms like "heterotextuality." Denis Dutton is so good at this that I asked him to translate three recent quotes from American politics into pomospeak. Here they are, academically transformed:

1. "Gendered non-being in modes of heterolocalized transgressvity negotiates while it articulates an ontology of the sexualized body simultaneously within a contested absentation of narrativity symbolized within a discourse of indiscriminate penetrative phallicism. ("I never had sexual relations with that woman.")

2. "The multivocality of semanticism essentialized in a dialogue of Being instantiates while it interrogates a hermeneutic of self-annihilating discursive spaces which occlude the ontological signifier. ("It depends on what you mean by 'is.'")

3. "The negotiating of sanguinary tumescence structured by a closure of post-coital transgressivity encodes while it marginalizes a physiognomic narrative of frigid aquacity. ("You better put some ice on that.")"

How to be a Rich Genius

Everyone in the intellectual world and the arts would love to get one of the MacArthur Foundation's "genius grants." They are no-strings-attached gifts, usually in the $250,000-$350,000 range.

One of this year's geniuses is Susan McClary of UCLA, cited as "a musicologist who explores the relationship between human experience and music and relates the creation of musical works to their musical context." There's a plainer way to say this. She is the feminist in charge of discovering that classical music is chock full of phallic themes, patriarchal violence, "assaultive pelvic pounding," and "the necesssary purging or containment of the female."

One of McClary's breakthrough ideas is that the pelvic pounding in Beethoven's Ninth Symphony adds up to non-orgasmic rape. She hears "the throttling murderous rage of a rapist incapable of attaining release."

This is a far more serious charge against Ludwig than the one by 1994 MacArthur winner Adrienne Rich, the radical lesbian poet, who believes Beethoven wasn't thinking about rape in the Ninth symphony; he was merely fretting about impotence. One of her poems describes him as "A man in terror of impotence/ or infertility, not knowing the difference."

Not all MacArthur winners write about penile problems in Beethoven symphonies, but in the current intellectual climate, it doesn't seem to hurt. In fact, it probably helps. The truth is that the MacArthur Awards, launched in 1981 to reward high achievement and high promise, are not what they once were. The science awards still seem to be given out fairly, but other selections pretty clearly have much more to do with politics than with achievement or potential. A lot of the award-winners are either ideologues like McClary or low-luster laborers in the traditional vineyards of the left.

One winner is a lawyer-activist who is trying to launch a new progressive political party. Another is a Latina journalist who showed that the Salvadoran government was guilty of a massacre. Others include the editor of a leftish news service, a lawyer who tries to find flaws in the trials of inmates on death-row, and a feminist professor who lobbies for worldwide abortion rights.

Two of the winners are revisionist historians of the American West. One, Patricia Nelson Limerick, is author of *The Legacy of Conquest*, a book arguing that the settling of the West was essentially one long spasm of greed, racism, sexism, and violence that isn't over yet. If any history book has ever argued that Western history is an uninterrupted triumph by totally fair-minded Anglos, Limerick's book is certainly its mirror image.

In its 349 pages, I don't recall reading about anything done right by white males. Even the act of keeping so many journals and diaries seems to have been a flaw of white pioneers and settlers. Limerick calls them "compulsively literate."

Since I don't keep up with experimental theater, I asked Donald Lyons, theater critic of the *Wall Street Journal*, about theater selections by the MacArthur Foundation. He said two of them are "unusually tawdry awards for self-publicizing radicals rather than achievers of any kind. There are many avant-garde people working today who deserve it more."

The best known of this year's winners is Cindy Sherman, whose photographs regularly appear in shows around the world. The citation says "her photographs of herself in different costumes and poses challenge the way we think about identity, social stereotypes and artistic representation"—one way of saying that her work is profitably compatible with the PC-deconstruction philosophy of folks who give out $300,000 prizes.

As *Newsday* reports, a photo in a recent Sherman show "takes on family values. The twisted body parts of a blindfolded woman and a child have apparently been brutalized by the blue-eyed man-doll who is turning his back on them. His fingernails are blood red." Perhaps the murderous guy-doll was just worried about impotence. Or maybe it was a pounding pelvis problem.

The political turn and the heavy emphasis on gender issues (15 of the 24 winners are female), are partly traceable to the leadership of Catharine Stimpson, who became director of the MacArthur Fellows program two years ago. She has complained that "under the guise of defending objectivity and intellectual rigor, which is a lot of mishmash," neo-conservative critics of diversity programs "are trying to preserve the cultural and political supremacy of white heterosexual males." And she once wrote that "men, because they are men, have been false prophets, narcissistic and perjuring witnesses." Stimpson is a former dean at Rutgers University and former head of the hemisphere's looniest PC group, the Modern Language Association.

The MacArthur Foundation is free to finance political activists and gender ideologues who believe in symphonic rape. It's their money. But it's a shame that a program set up to honor achievement and excellence among creative people of all political persuasions has deteriorated so quickly into narrow partisanship. Lay the money on your political cronies, MacArthur, but let's have no more prattle about "geniuses."

NOBEL PRIZE FOR FICTION?

I Rigoberta Menchu, is a famous 1983 book, "the cornerstone of the multicultural canon," as one journal reported, and a book that won its writer the Nobel Peace prize. But in 1999 the book presents us with two problems: (1) huge portions of it are untrue and (2) a lot of professors who teach it on our campuses don't want to hear about objections to the book, or they just say that the truth doesn't matter. "Whether the book is true or not, I don't care," said Marjorie Agosin, head of the Spanish department at Wellesley College.

Menchu's book told the harrowing story of oppression of Mayan Indian peasants by light-skinned landowners in Guatemala. It tells how the author joined the guerrilla movement that flourished in the late 1970s and early 1980s. The book has strong appeal because it stressed indigenous rights, feminism, identity politics, Marxist class analysis—virtually the entire bundle of concerns of the campus left. The Nobel was given in 1992 as a sort of anti-Columbus prize given to an oppressed native of the Americas on the 500th anniversary of Columbus's landing.

But Menchu's version of events has been picked apart in a book by David Stoll, a Middlebury College anthropologist who interviewed 120 people in Menchu's hometown. Menchu says she was an illiterate and monolingual girl whose father refused to send her to school. Stoll found that she had attended two elite boarding schools run by nuns and knew Spanish as well as Mayan. Stoll discovered that Menchu's black-and-white depiction of villainous landowners and virtuous oppressed peasants was too simple—the landowners often cooperated with the peasants. The great land struggle described in the book between Menchu's father and the landowners was actually between her father and his in-laws. Though described as poor and oppressed, her father actually had title to 6,800 acres of land.

According to Stoll's book, *I Rigoberta Menchu and the Story of All Poor Guatemalans,* Menchu was right about the savagery of the Guatemalan military. But people in the village were just as terrified of the guerrillas, who introduced political assassination to the area. One of Menchu's brothers was killed by the army, but villagers said he was not burned alive as she writes in her book. In chapter after chapter, Stoll claims, Menchu describes "experiences she never had herself." Stoll writes that she consistently altered facts and stories and "achieved coherence by omitting features of the situation that contradicted the ideology of her new organization, then substituting appropriate revolutionary themes."

Stoll's account is unusually convincing because, he says, "I'm a lefty myself" and his book often seems to bend over backward to give Menchu the benefit of any doubt or ambiguity. He says he is astounded by the reaction of professors who dismiss his book as a right-wing attack or who insist that truth is irrelevant to emotionally authentic testimony from the oppressed. "When I began to talk about my findings," he wrote, "some of my colleagues regarded them as sacrilegious. I had put myself beyond the pale of decency."

"Sacrilegious" is a good word, because it captures Menchu's current status as a semi-religious political icon. Besides, the oppressed are never supposed to be analyzed or criticized by professors representing the oppressor cultures of the West. (Stoll has an interesting take on this: if the job of Western professors is to listen in silence to the authentic voices from the third world, what happens to the other authentic voices in Menchu's village? They tell very different stories about what happened there.)

Listen to some of the statements coming from the campus. Michael Berube of the University of Illinois, a star professor of the campus left, says he would continue teaching Menchu's autobiography, if it was on his curriculum, just as he will continue teaching the *Autobiography of Benjamin Franklin*. (No explanation. Apparently the two books are equally reliable or unreliable.) Joanne Rappaport, president of the Society for Latin American Anthropology, told a reporter that Stoll's book is "an attempt to discredit one of spokespersons of Guatemala's indigenous movement."

Another school of thought seems to suggest that lies by the oppressed don't matter. John Peeler, a professor of political science at Bucknell, says that "the Latin American tradition of the testimonial has never been bound by the strict rules of veracity that we take for granted in autobiography." And Magdalena Garcia Pinto, director of women's studies at the University of Missouri, says what Menchu is offering "is not mendacity. Rather it is a narrative about how large communities in the region are/have been oppressed."

Why is it not mendacity? Because our campus culture puts more emphasis on voice, narrative, and story than it does on truth. A growing number of professors accept the postmodern notion that there is no such thing as truth, only rhetoric. The result is the blurring of distinctions between history and literature, fact and fiction, honesty and dishonesty. One outraged professor wrote in an Internet message that "The Menchu controversy, like the Clinton controversy, reveals the depth of academic disregard for truth in the postmodern era." Sounds right to me.

How 'bout those clichés?

Another baseball season is under way, and this means that the lingo of the game is back too, after a long, hard winter of normal English. Otherwise stable people now go around saying things like "Good pitching stops good hitting," "A game in April counts as much as a game in September," "Baseball is a game of inches" (although in Toronto and Montreal, it's clearly a game of centimeters) and "It's not over till it's over" (or, alternately, "It's not over until the size-challenged person of gender sings").

In baseballese, contending teams must be "strong up the middle," and players must "give 110 percent" because "it's a long season," played "one game at a time," and "pennants aren't won on paper." The oldest mandatory comment may be "baseball is like life." Rabbi Mark Gellman, who appears frequently on ABC's *Good Morning America* worked a nice riff on this old remark recently, pointing out that "Baseball is like life.... most of the time nothing much seems to happen."

It's also mandatory to talk about the mystic aspects of the game known as "intangibles." As Oriole scout Jim Russo once mystically observed, "You play 162 games and a lot of intangibles come to the surface." Jerry Brown, former New Age governor of California, once said something similar about politics, declaring that the Democratic Party must strive to "tangibilitize" itself. My thoughts exactly.

Knowing baseball lingo has its uses. As it happens, two of my three daughters are deeply bored by baseball and want no part of it. But I gave them six phrases to use whenever baseball comes up in conversation. Now their friends marvel at my daughters' deep knowledge of the game. Here are the six situations in which non-baseball people are called upon to say something sensible in baseballese.

1. A friend says excitedly, "How about those Marlins!" Do NOT ask what a Marlin is, or wonder how Brando managed to get a whole team named after him. Simply echo your friend's exultation and say, "How about em!" This will be taken as a thoughtful assessment of current Marlin achievements.

2. Someone wants your analysis of a baseball trade, for instance the recent exchange of four star players by the Cleveland Indians and

Atlanta Braves. You always answer: "Looks good for both sides." This is almost always considered a satisfying answer. But if your interrogator asks again, it means he thinks his team was snookered. So you say, "You have to give up something to get something." He knows that.

3. The Giants are in town to play the Dodgers. Your friend is greatly excited. He says, "Who do you like in the first game?," meaning "Who is going to win tonight?" You have no idea, but you don't need one. Simply say, "When those two teams get together, anything can happen." The whole office will hear about this judicious appraisal.

4. You are in a sports bar, wishing you were somewhere else. Someone with a beer in each hand names a local player whose name is unfamiliar to you. He wants you to say something appreciative. Do not say, "He's terrific!" The player may not be terrific. He may just be "scrappy," a baseball term meaning mediocre but extremely active and likeable. Confusing scrappiness with greatness could destroy your sports credibility forever. What do you do? Easy. Nod knowingly and say "He can beat you a lot of ways." This is probably true, although getting hits and fielding ground balls are probably not among them.

5. Someone asks: "What do you think of the Mets this year?" This sad question deserves a response, but remember: never be cruel. Do not say that Stevie Wonder and Ray Charles could easily lead the Mets in batting. The right answer is: "They could surprise a lot of people." If you are aware of Met tradition, then you know that the only way they could surprise a lot of people would be to win more than once a week. The beauty of the "surprise" prediction about any team, is that it can never be proved wrong. Whatever happens, some people are bound to be surprised. If anyone asks about the Mets late in the season, when they have won about forty games and lost seventy, a different answer is called for: "Their record speaks for itself."

6. A friend says, "Did you see what Goose did today?" Be careful here. The automatic answer ("Wasn't that great!") may be faulty. Goose may have hit yet another home run with the bases loaded. Or he may have hit another girl friend while HE was loaded. The correct response is sincere, knowing, and perfectly neutral. Tighten your lips, slowly wag your head from side to side in controlled wonderment and say "That was really something, wasn't it?" Later there will be plenty of time to find out whether Goose went five for five or was once again photographed kneeling on the doorstep of the Betty Ford Clinic, demanding his regular room back.

Commentary on baseball should be thoughtful, enthusiastic, and content-free. Remember, baseball is something like life. Baseballese is something like English.

REPACKAGING THE PERPS

Larry Flynt had a big week in Washington. He was the guest of John F. Kennedy, Jr., at the White House Correspondents dinner and he delivered a lecture at Georgetown University.

At the correspondents dinner, calling attention to one's importance by inviting a well-known low-life or indictee to one's table is nearly a mainstream activity. But Flynt's invitation from Kennedy, president and editor in chief of *George* magazine, was too much for columnist Michael Kelly. He reminded readers that Flynt had tried to short-circuit the impeachment process with "a loathsome campaign of sexual blackmail" against congressional Republicans. Kelly noted that Flynt's porno magazine, *Hustler*, is renowned for its racism and its degradation of women, while one of Flynt's daughters accused him of sexually abusing her. (He denied it.)

What exactly in this career made him irresistible to Georgetown? It's possible that he was invited simply to annoy one side in the current cultural war at the decreasingly Catholic university. If so, Flynt certainly obliged. "The church has had its hand on our crotch for 2,000 years," he told the students. To the surprise of no one, Flynt came out in favor of the constitutional amendment most often cited by pornographers, the first.

Allison Tepley, an official of the student lecture fund, defended the Flynt invitation on grounds that it would provoke dialogue and intellectual debate. She said she is personally a very strong opponent of pornography, "but I can't make a value judgment or decision without hearing the other side." Flynt's 30-year career is enough to make most Americans throw up in unison, but Tepley couldn't make a value judgment yet. It was just too soon. She needed to hear him lecture.

Next thing you know, Georgetown will import some surviving Nazi official so baffled students will finally be able to make up their minds about the Holocaust. Or maybe the Unabomber could lecture on environmental progress through postal explosions. Surely we should hear both sides of the mail-bomb issue before making up our minds.

A Catholic bishop suggested that if Georgetown stands for anything, it shouldn't be showcasing someone with Flynt's views on women, morality, and religion. But it's just as well that Georgetown's president refused to cancel the lecture. The modern campus is filled with aspiring censors eager to defend newspapers or shout down or cancel speakers for having the wrong sort of opinions. It's better to endure a gross pornographer with nothing much to say than to encourage all the heresy-hunters currently in training on our campuses.

But what attracted Georgetown and John Kennedy to Flynt in the first place? Likely answer: because his life was made into a movie, much of Flynt's notoriety has been converted into celebrity, and celebrity washes away sins, even large ones like racism, the degrading of women, and allegations of incest. That's why Flynt drew a crowd two or three times larger than that of New York Governor George Pataki, who also spoke on campus that week. An unusually repulsive pornographer played by Woody Harrelson is a far better attraction than a good but bland governor of a major state played by himself.

Alas, we live in a culture dedicated to recycling the infamous as the famous. Short of murder, it's almost impossible for most perpetrators to stay disgraced for long. Dick Morris survived his scandal, returned briefly to the White House as a close adviser and is now a respected TV analyst and columnist offering moral and political judgments on the Clinton presidency. Whatever. Unapologetic figures in Republican-era political scandals like Gordon Liddy (Watergate) and Oliver North (Irangate) are media stars, too.

Marv Albert was in serious trouble with charges of forced oral sex and physical assault, not to mention the sexual threesomes and the cross-dressing, but within a year it was over. He is back doing national telecasts and more fans then ever seem to want his autograph. One of the stars he covers, Lattrell Sprewell, could have been banned from basketball for two violent assaults on his coach. Instead he was traded to New York and given a massive contract.

Mike Milken is on the cover of *Business Week* ("The Reincarnation of Mike Milken"), smiling sweetly and juggling vegetables, his prison term and financial adventures of the 1980s apparently forgotten. Al Sharpton, a racial arsonist and chief perpetrator of the Tawana Brawley hoax, is back as a vaguely respectable civil rights activist leading protests in New York. Sidney Biddle Barrows, the "Mayflower Madam," continues to cash in on her achievements in the sex industry. Before and after photos of her cosmetic surgery appeared in February in the otherwise elegant *Harper's Bazaar*.

Amy Fisher, the "Long Island Lolita" who shot her boyfriend's wife in the face, gets out of jail this week. A friend suggests that after making the rounds of the TV talk shows, she may get a show of her own, aimed at the youth market. Why not? Or maybe she could lecture on ethics at Georgetown. After all, she's already famous.

OPINIONS WERE EXPRESSED

"Mistakes were made," President Clinton said about his colorful fund-raising tactics. Give him credit for a traditional Washington non-apology. The same phrase was used by Ronald Reagan and George Bush on Iran-Contra and John Sununu on his government-paid private travel.

No-fault syntax is crucially important when issuing vague, no-apology regrets. It's best to stick to the passive voice and avoid the risk of mentioning any living or dead person who might come in for some blame. George Stephanopoulos said on ABC that "the system got a little lax" in the White House fund-raising scandals, which is another nice traditional touch. Abstract villains like "the system" and "society" are always available to take the fall.

Similarly, the high number of young black men in jail is a tragedy, but the sad fact is traditionally softened and attributed to society or the system by heavy use of passive verbs: the men have been "criminalized" or "ensnared." This linguistic ploy is used at both ends of the political spectrum. President Bush complained that Iran-Contra prosecutors were "criminalizing policy differences," not the words most of us would use for the felonies committed.

In an age of language wars, political victory often flows from victory in the battles over terminology. The argument embedded in the term "the homeless"—that people on the street are primarily suffering from a lack of shelter—turned out to be wrong. The dominant problems were mental illness and addiction, but the language used kept pointing policy in another direction. Polemics are powerfully embedded in terms like "homophobia," "family values," "people of color," "retention rates" (of affirmative action students), and "female genital mutilation."

Some feminists are now using the term "unwanted sexual encounter" to refer both to rape and to consensual sex that women later came to regret, thus blurring the line between consensual and non-consensual sex for ideological purposes.

The same sort of blurring goes on routinely in the gathering of alarming statistics by advocacy groups. The easiest way to make the statistics go up is to broaden definitions and hope the media won't notice. During the argument about raising the minimum wage, for instance, the Labor Department put out a press release saying that 40 percent of minimum-wage workers "are the sole breadwinners of their family." But this was a word game. The department counted single people living alone as family heads.

Another example: the annual statistics on violence at abortion clinics. The Feminist Majority Foundation, which compiles the numbers, includes the spraying of graffiti at clinics, the picketing of homes, and "objects such as sand, rosaries, and dead animals discarded at clinic doors." These numbers are always published without any media comment, though the average reporter should be able to figure out that home picketing and rosary-dropping aren't really violent acts.

In general, the anti-abortion side has lost the language war. One-day waiting periods for an abortion are always "restrictions," unlike three-day waiting periods for guns, which are merely "regulations."

The campus wars are primarily about language. One example: the radical egalitarianism now dominant on campus holds that nothing is superior to anything else. As a result, a great many words have been thrown down the memory hole, including "primitive," as in primitive peoples. So have almost all animal metaphors (talk turkey, make a pig of yourself, snake in the grass, etc.), which are seen as speciesist attempts to imply that humans are somehow superior to pigs, turkeys, and snakes. Similarly, all references to humans are supposed to avoid all suggestions of superiority or inferiority. At one women's college, the soccer coach was forbidden to refer to non-starting players as "subs," because the term was hierarchical and hurtful to the feelings of benchwarmers everywhere.

"Remedial classes" is the conventional euphemism for catch-up lessons for students who flunk or are way behind their classmates. Now a gassy new euphemism has appeared: "developmental" classes. Harvard, of all places, is one school that uses the term for its way-behind students (Harvard men and women don't need remedies; they just develop.) A broader trend is to eliminate the concept of student failure and poor work through new and vague language. For example, students in Clark County, Nevada, who fail or scrape by with D's are not described as borderline passing or failing, but as "emerging." Those who get A's are "extending," and those doing adequate or mediocre work are "developing." "Develop" and "developmental" are surely among our most squishy terms, used in various forms to refer to failure and retardation.

Prettified language is all around us. A graffiti sprayer is a wall artist, a prostitute is a sexual service provider, and *Business Week* reports that the sixth leading cause of death among young American males is "legal intervention" (i.e., getting shot by cops).

LANGUAGE IN THE DUMPS

At my local recycling center, I always pause in wonderment at the bin marked "commingled containers." Whoever thought up that term could have taken the easy way out and just written "cans and bottles." But the goal apparently was to create a term that nobody would ever use in conversation, then slap it on every can-and-bottle bin in America to create maximum confusion. (The "co" is a nice raised-pinky flourish. Since "mingled" means mixed up, "commingled" means "co-mixed up.")

The gold standard in government-speak is still "ground-mounted confirmatory route markers" (road signs), a traffic-control term used from coast to coast. In Oxford, England, city officials decided to "examine the feasibility of creating a structure in Hinksey Park from indigenous vegetation." They were talking about planting a tree to get some shade. As the poet Joyce Kilmer might have put it, "Versified and rhythmic non-prose verbal structures are made by fools like me, but only God can create a solar-shielding park structure from low-rise indigenous vegetative material."

In Britain, the Plain English campaign came up with these colorful examples of awful writing: "interoperable inter-modal transport systems (bus and train schedules) and a supermarket help-wanted ad for "an ambient replenishment assistant" (someone to stock shelves). One classic award by the Plain English people went to a snack company for a letter replying to a customer who complained that her potato chips were purple. When a chip is discolored, the letter said, "it is difficult to say whether this is due to a process of active migration of the anthocyanin from the periderm and cortex or to the primary protection within the flesh of the tuber." Whatever.

When it comes to co-mangled prose, America need not take a back seat to Britain. Here is Mike McCurry, the wily White House mouthpiece, replying to a reporter's question on whether Bill Clinton's coffees were used to raise campaign funds: "Technically, they were not used for fund-raising, but they became an element of the financial program that we were trying to pursue in connection with the campaign." Bill Lann Lee, rejected by the Senate but still the acting civil rights chief at the Justice Department, used similar gobbledygook in referring to forced busing. "Forced busing is a misnomer," he wrote. "School districts do not force children to ride a bus, but only to arrive on time at their assigned schools."

Political correctness plays a role, too. The scholar Gertrude Himmlefarb once asked a federal agency for up-to-date illegitimacy rates and was told that the agency preferred less judgmental terms such as "non-marital childbearing" or "alternate mode of parenting." In the athletic department at the University of Minnesota, players who steal are dismissed from their teams, not for theft, but for "violating team rules regarding personal property."

Professor William Lutz of Rutgers University, author of *The New Doublespeak*, says that schools are an increasingly rich source of verbal nonsense. Students now "achieve a deficiency" (they flunk tests). They take part in developmental studies (remedial work) or "service learning" (compulsory volunteer work). And they don't learn to write any more—they "generate text" out of "writing elements," "tagmemic invention," "paradigmatic analysis," and "heuristics."

On the modern campus, the word "integration" is so controversial that a Cornell University committee removed it from an official report. So instead of "promoting integration across racial, ethnic, college, and class-year distinctions" the report called for "promoting meaningful interaction and connection across differences." (Good news: the president of Cornell had the wit to put the original wording back.)

The Dialectic Society gave its 1996 award for buzzword of the year to "urban camper," a new term for "the homeless" or people who live on the street. Similar euphemisms have crept into the language: extra-marital sex (adultery), "aggressive coalitionary behavior" (war games), "hypervigilance" (paranoia), and "wall artist" (tagger, graffiti sprayer).

Gyms are now upscale, known as "wellness activities centers." In medicine, patients who die "fail to achieve their wellness potential" and have to be chalked up as "negative patient outcomes." For the U.S. government, political killings conducted by governments we detest are still known as political killings. If they happen in China, however, they are referred to smoothly as "the arbitrary deprivation of life."

Business is pumping a lot of gas into the language, too. We have "the social expression industry" (the greeting card business), "meal replacement" (fast food, junk food), "a new-car alternative" and "an experienced car" (a used car), "creative response conceptions" (damage control by public relations people) and "access controllers" (doormen).

The federal government gave us "grain-consuming animal units" (the agricultural department's term for cows), "single purpose agricultural facilities" (pig pens and chicken coops), and "post-consumer waste materials" (garbage). Better yet, let's make that commingled post-consumer processed units. The kind of stuff you find at a single-purpose non-recycling center, formerly a dump.

Close the Envelope, Please

By the time he won the best-actor Oscar for *Forrest Gump*, Tom Hanks had already won seven other awards for the same role and the movie itself had collected at least thirty-seven awards. In one three-day period Hanks crisscrossed the country to pick up a Screen Actors Guild Award, and American Comedy Award and a National Board of Review award.

The awards season runs roughly from January through November. During this period, somebody has to keep traveling around the country waiting breathlessly for envelopes to be opened and trophies handed over.

If this is Tuesday, it must be the Golden Globe Awards. Or is it the People Choice or the Screen Actor's Guild Awards? Every group with a piece of the industry seems to have its own awards: Directors Guild, American Cinema Editors, Writers Guild, Films Critics, and soon the Blockbuster Awards (you'll have to wait until June), the first by a video-rental chain.

Like the explosion in urban crime, the sudden growth of awards shows has left ordinary citizens helpless to cope. Flick on the television during primetime, and some celebrity or other is reciting the excruciating tell-tale banter of yet another new awards show.

They may be empty of content and purpose, but they are a major national addiction, a central ritual in the culture of celebrity. Lest any children grow up not thinking about celebrities eight hours a days, we have things like Nickelodean's Kids Choice Awards, to give all our young beginners the hang of the broader culture.

Once we made do with the Oscars, Grammys, Emmys and Tonys. Now there are dozens of competing shows giving similar trophies to the same people, usually to high ratings. Michelle Quinn of the *San Francisco Chronicle* counted sixty entertainment awards shows, including at least thirty-one honoring film, nineteen for television and twenty-two for music.

Each new version seeks to justify itself by complaining vaguely that all the existing awards are somehow deficient. Blockbuster, for instance, decided on a fashionable populist spin, arguing that other awards reflected the opinions of small elites, whereas 40 million video renters will stand behind the Blockbuster winners.

The long-established Grammy Awards seem to be organized around the principle that each person in the music industry deserves to win at least once a year. (Four of my friends each won a Grammy once for working separately on the liner notes of the same album.)

But the annual avalanche of Grammys isn't nearly enough to meet demand, so we now have the Billboard Awards, MTV Awards, the Country Music Association Awards, the Blockbuster Music Awards, the Soul Train Awards, the World Music Awards and the People's Choice Awards, plus all the smaller TV awards ceremonies for specialties such as gospel, reggae, and Christian music. Each area is apt to subdivide into more and more shows. Different country music award shows can be watched on NBC in May, TNN in June and CBS in October.

Some of the shows now play off one another and give awards for performances at other awards shows. Ellen DeGeneres, an actress on the TV show *Ellen*, won an American Comedy Award for being a host at the Emmys. She beat out Whoopi Goldberg, nominated for hosting the Oscars, and Roseanne Barr, who hosted the MTV Video Awards. Dick Clark who has produced about 150 of these programs, has proposed an award show for awards shows.

Celebrity worship is the main attraction. Viewers want to see celebs, what they wear and how they behave, even in the most banal and tightly scripted circumstances. The performers get free exposure and publicity, with little effort, and their success gets validated with a trophy. Sponsors get a large and increasingly targeted audience. Networks, at low cost, get ratings almost always higher than those of the programs replaced. The programs are cheap to produce and make big money.

Along the way, some of the glamour of the Oscars rubs off on soap operas and cable programming. Robert Thompson, associate professor of television and film at Syracuse University, seems to view the surge of awards shows as defiant self-celebration by a heavily criticized pop culture: "In a society that publicly disdains its popular culture, somebody has to celebrate this thing and give it awards. If nobody else will do it, they might as well do it themselves."

Thompson thinks one day there will be a 24-hour-a-day cable channel for awards shows. They could probably do it too, with a little time-filling boost from re-runs of old awards shows and supplementary interviews with Joey Buttafuocco and other achievers heading into the Oscars.

An awards show for coverage of the O.J. Simpson case would be wildly popular. "The nominees for best interview with Kato Kaelin's hairdresser are..." People could vote for the one or two most entertaining outburst by members of O.J.'s defense team, or maybe offer Al Cowlings a lifetime achievement award. Great television. Looks like a 40 share, at least.

OUR KINDER, GENTLER ARMY

In the old days—ten years ago—drill sergeants were still as loud and tough as Lou Gossett in the movie *An Officer and a Gentleman*. Now drill sergeants are more like supportive counselors at a summer camp, eager to avoid tension, please recruits, and build self-esteem. "Stress created by physical or verbal abuse is non-productive and prohibited," says an Army manual, casually dismissing five or six generations of training in which stress was considered very productive in turning out combat-ready troops. So niceness is in, discouraging words are out, and drill sergeants can't touch soldiers, even to check their ammunition. "This is a sea change in the way the Army does its basic military training," said Col. Shane Hearn, whose title is head of corporate strategy of the Army Training and Recruitment Agency. "Instead of breaking and testing, we are now in the game of developing and encouraging."

Under the relaxed new standards, trainees wear gym shorts, T-shirts, and sneakers. Instead of running in formation, they run on their own. Sometimes, as explained by reporter Mark Thompson in last week's issue of *Time* magazine, Navy recruits are given "blue cards" to hand to a trainer when they are feeling blue. They are also told it's OK to cry and told that "physically, anybody can get through boot camp."

Apparently so. At Army bases, bayonet practice may be called off if the weather is too hot. On obstacle courses (many of them sensitively renamed "confidence courses") recruits are allowed to run around some walls if climbing them is just too hard. In Marine training at Quantico, a visitor noticed a footstool placed in front of an eight-foot wall so that no trainee would fail to get over it. But if the Marine brass truly wants to be helpful and encouraging, why not supply stairs, or maybe just make it a four-foot wall that anyone can handle?

Military people say some changes are to accommodate the "couch potato" generation. Social change plays a role too. Today's recruits are unaccustomed to discipline and authority, easily shocked by strong words, and deeply concerned with their own feelings and self-esteem. To attract and hold volunteers to an army with a high dropout rate in basic training, that training is being adapted to Generation X expectations.

But the chief reason for the "sea change" is the return of mixed-gender training, which was tried for five years, abandoned as a failure, in 1982 and reinstalled under feminist political pressure in 1994. Trainees wear sneakers instead of combat boots mostly because women were suffering high rates of injuries in boots. Reconfiguring basic training so that "anybody can get through" was largely a response to women's high rates of injury and inability to meet the old standards. A 1988 Army study of 124 men and 186 women during basic training showed that women were almost twice as likely to get injured, and suffered 481 days of limited duty due to injury, compared with 99 days for the men.

The Pentagon responded by lowering standards, installing some double standards, and redefining basic training "success" in terms of what the women did well. Twenty Individual Proficiency Tests used to measure basic training competence include no physical factors at all, but instead measure tasks such as first aid techniques, map-reading, and putting on protective gear. Self-reported "feelings" in focus groups determine successful "soldierization" and proficiency in basic training, according to standards set by the U.S. Army Research Institute for the Behavioral and Social Sciences. Instead of military or combat criteria, unit cohesion was defined in largely emotional, civilian terms, whether trainees "feel very close" or "like and trust one another."

Gender-norming swept in too. Marine climbing ropes have a yellow line partway up where women are allowed to stop. In the army, male soldiers must do twenty push-ups, women just six. Even the throwing of grenades was gender-normed, after the discouraging finding at Parris Island that 45 percent of female Marines were unable to throw grenades far enough to avoid blowing themselves up in the process. Even more discouraging for morale, gender-norming was papered over by the new concept of "comparable effort." Under this concept, a female trainee who does worse than a male at some physical task can get scores just as good, and sometimes better.

All of this eerily echoes the dumbing down, grade inflation, and collapse of belief in fairness that accompanied the arrival of affirmative action on campuses. Fake scores and the degradation of basic training are a disaster for the military. Mixed-gender training has nothing to do with combat readiness. It has to do with politics and the desire to show absolute equality even where it doesn't exist and can't.

Almost no one in the military or in Congress will say so, because their careers are at stake. Better to go along and create endless study commissions. Reversing the practice of mixed-gender training in the military would "have a negative effect on the cohesion and, by extension, the readiness of our forces," a senior Defense Department official said recently. Exactly the opposite is true, of course. Another push in on to kill mixed-gender training once again. For the sake of the military's integrity, it should be supported.

IN THE KEY OF F

A couple of weeks ago, as I sat innocently reading the Sunday paper, the F-word wafted musically through our living room. My 14-year-old daughter was listening to a Tom Petty album at the time, and the singer had just defiantly warbled the F-word in its familiar participle form.

As my daughter explained it, obscenities are rare in Petty's songs—she has located just two—but Petty apparently thinks it's important to drop one in every now and then, possibly to show that he is just as hip and rebellious as the next man.

My own opinion, I told my daughter, is that Petty is a talented and generally harmless fellow who does not engage in musical rants on the glories of suicide, cutting up women, shooting cops, burning out Korean shopowners or other similar topics judged by the American Civil Liberties Union to be crucial to our civic discourse.

However, I said, he is not allowed to use the F-word in our living room. The proper place to use this word is his own house or in some remote outdoor location, preferably right after smashing his thumb once or twice with a hammer.

This goes for other singers who are beginning to test the waters by emitting gratuitous F-words just to gauge public reaction. The sound track to the wonderful new movie version of *Romeo and Juliet* contains one such word, though that lyric is not sung in the movie itself.

Most of the discussion of obscene music has focused on over-the-top gangster rap and nihilistic hard rock. But it's worth focusing on the first, small steps toward the breaking of norms in mainstream music—the casual insertion of a few obscenities, making them seem normal and unobjectionable. "The language of the streets is coming indoors," Letitia Baldridge said on the *Sunday Good Morning America* show last week. Yes, and we are paying to have it happen.

As I sat there thinking about how all the commercial pressures nowadays seem to be on the side of coarseness, my eye caught a news article about a rare commercial pressure on the other side: Wal-Mart says its stores won't carry CDs with degrading, violent or obscene lyrics. It will, however, be happy to sell cleaned-up versions of these discs.

Since Wal-Mart's announcement, the air has been thick with charges of censorship and violations of artistic freedom. But it seems to me that Wal-Mart is simply saying that it won't take part in the continuing debasement of our popular culture. No store is morally or legally bound to sell products it considers harmful or degrading. The more stores take social responsibility for the things they sell, the healthier the society will be. The alternative—throwing up one's hands and simply selling anything that yields a profit—makes stores part of the problem.

Because Wal-Mart sells so many CDs, about 10 percent of the American market, most singers will adapt by putting out a second, or cleaned-up version, of each album. This is all to the good.

Spare us the argument that Petty's lone F-word was of crucial artistic importance. Nobody believes that. It was put in for commercial reasons and it will come out for commercial reasons as well. As a matter of fact, some of us would be willing to pay a dollar more for the F-word-free version so we could play it at parties. At grown-up parties, playing music with F-words in it is a lot like leaving a dead cat in the punch bowl.

The cry of censorship is a tiresome reaction to decisions like the one made by Wal-Mart. It's a form of pressure intended to coerce someone to remain part of the problem. Wal-Mart is not blocking free expression here. Offensive albums are in no danger of disappearing from the market. Besides, in a free-enterprise system, everything is supposed to respond to market forces. If Wal-Mart doesn't wish to be part of the offensive-music market, well that's the way the system works.

The *Sunday Good Morning America* program focused on the growing incivility in America—more crudeness, confrontation, and public anger—and what we can do about it. Four commissions are said to be studying the incivility problem. Whatever the ultimate recommendations may be, it doesn't take a genius to see that the media and the popular arts are both reflecting and reinforcing the ugly, angry side of our culture. They are creating an expectation that any dissatisfaction or dissent will be expressed in obscene, confrontational language. And this won't change until more and more people say no to creeping incivility. Wal-Mart said no, and it was right to do it.

OH, NO, CANADA!

Left-wing censorship is not yet a major issue, but observe the tide rising: campus speech codes and conduct codes monitoring "verbal behavior," the theft and destruction of dissenting college newspapers, government attempts to ban Indian team nicknames, campaigns to cancel or shout down speakers opposed to affirmative action, the increasing use of harassment policies to silence opponents or get them fired.

If you wonder where the slippery slope leads, take a look at Canada, which is a bit ahead of the United States in sensitivity censorship. In Ontario, it's an offense to say or write anything that might incite someone to violate any of fifteen listed grounds of discrimination. And under Canadian human rights legislation, truth is not a defense.

The Canadian Human Rights Commission called for a major review of Canada's human rights laws to see if "social condition" (poverty) should be listed nationally as a protected class. Advocates for the poor say the new listing would stop "poor-bashing" in the media, for example, comments by talk-radio hosts that some women get pregnant just to get on welfare.

A Winnipeg school asked a university to bring a professor up on charges of violating the Manitoba Human Rights Code by distributing a flyer listing "18 myths spread by gay and lesbian activists." In Saskatchewan, a dry-cleaner was fined $400 for saying to an Indian woman, "If you ask me, there shouldn't even be reserves" set aside for natives.

Ted Byfield, editor of the conservative magazine, *Alberta Report*, was charged with violating the Alberta Human Rights, Citizenship and Multiculturalism Act. His offense: publishing an article saying that although some native children were abused at residential schools for Indians, many others enjoyed the schools and were grateful for their education.

Censors like to congratulate themselves on their dedication to free speech, so the Alberta law says "Nothing in this section shall be deemed to interfere with the free expression of opinion any subject." But last month the Calgary Regional Health Authority used the law to get a temporary injunction against publication of further stories by the *Alberta Report* on partial-birth abortions. Quoting unnamed nurses and hospital documents, the magazine stated that some of the babies in such operations at Foothills Hospital were born alive and deliberately allowed to starve to death.

The same doublethink by censors who proudly announce their love of free expression is common in the U.S. too. "I often have to struggle with right and wrong because I am a strong believer in free speech," said Ronni Sanlo, a gay activist at UCLA. "Opinions are protected under the First Amendment, but when negative opinions come out of a person's fist, mouth or pen to intentionally hurt others, that's when their opinions should no longer be protected."

This is a common mindset: "good" speech is protected expression, but "bad" speech ("my opponents") is a form of action that should be punished like criminal acts. The censors have evolved a whole new vocabulary to blur the line between acts and speech: "verbal conduct," "expressive behavior," "non-traditional violence" (criticism) and "anti-feminist intellectual harassment" (rolling one's eyeballs over feminist dogma).

Gloria Allred, a well-known talk-show lawyer, recently made one of the broader censorship claims in a sexual harassment case. A student at the College of the Canyons in Los Angeles complained after her professor allowed a male student to talk graphically about sex during a class discussion. Allred argued that Title IX, which outlaws sex discrimination in higher education, covers discussions in class. In effect, this would mean that colleges are legally bound to censor their professors' lectures in order to protect vulnerable students.

In their book, *The Shadow University*, Alan Charles Kors and Harvey Silverglate analyze the national spread of college censorship. Among the banned comments and actions are "speech that causes loss of self-esteem or a vague sense of danger" (Colby College),"intentionally producing psychological discomfort" (North Dakota State), "insensitivity to the experiences of women" (University of Minnesota), "feelings" about gays which evolve into "attitudes" (University of West Virginia) "inconsiderate jokes" (University of Connecticut), and the telling of stories "experienced by others as harassing" (Bowdoin).

Serious non-verbal offenses include disrespectful facial expressions (Duke), "inappropriate laughter" (Sarah Lawrence), "subtle discrimination" such as "eye contact or the lack of it" (Michigan State) and "licking lips or teeth; holding or eating food provocatively" (University of Maryland). Because federal courts have struck down speech codes, many of these restrictions have been recast in vague language and buried in student codes of conduct, as the columnist Nat Hentoff writes, "in the hope that judges won't find them." But the appetite to control and censor is greater than ever, a high priority for the cultural left.

THIS COLUMN IS MOSTLY TRUE

In his new book, *Leading with My Chin*, Jay Leno tells a mildly embarrassing story about himself on the old Dinah Shore television show. The only problem with the incident is that it didn't happen to Leno. It happened to another comedian, Jeff Altman.

Leno told Josef Adalian of the *New York Post* last week that he liked the story so much he paid Altman a thousand dollars for the right to publish the tale as his own. (In fairness, Leno claimed that something similar happened to him on the same show, but he wished to "meld" his story with Altman's to acquire a better ending.)

This naturally opens up a whole new industry—selling life stories to needy comedians and unexciting public figures. Those who wish to enliven their autobiographies could acquire colorful and meldable incidents from sellers who no longer need them.

Middlemen might set themselves up as anecdote brokers. With an investment of $200,000 or so, Warren Christopher could presumably buy enough exciting life stories to push his memoirs onto the bestseller list and send Bryant Gumbel into knee-slapping paroxysms of laughter. Stone-hearted economic buccaneers would likely buy up stories about kindness to employees or daring rescues of small children in distress. Kato Kaelin could probably purchase, on the cheap, an entire life full of hard work and adult attitudes, though the commercial value of a truly refurbished Kato might well be quite small.

Leno's stretching of the truth is a minor matter, but there is something fitting about it as a reflection of the current cultural moment. The problem isn't lying. That is certainly too strong a word for what Leno did, and at any rate, a great deal of lying can safely be assumed to be a constant in human history. What seems new today is the amazing casualness about whether something is true or not, as if other goals—success, feelings, self-esteem, and self-assertion—are all so overwhelmingly important that truth doesn't matter very much, and often isn't even perceived as a competing value.

Self-esteem was cited as the reason for a peculiar bit of teaching, revealed last week, at two Afrocentric schools in Milwaukee. Both schools have been teaching children that black Egyptians once had wings and flew freely around the pyramids until the Europeans arrived, killing off all the natural flyers.

Pierre Salinger's claim that a Navy missile shot down TWA Flight 800 surely qualifies as a horrible example of evidence-free assertion. His position seemed to be this: I am ∤ 100 percent sure I'm right that a Navy missile shot down Flight 800, but if I'm wrong, well it's the first time in thirty years. For what it's worth, a survey by *George* magazine showed that 41 percent of Americans think the government is conducting a cover-up about Flight 800.

A minor sign of the new casualness is that we are beginning to see movies that explicitly announce on screen that they are real-life non-fiction, but which turn out to be fiction after all. *Fargo*, for instance, said it was real, but wasn't, and *Sleepers'* claim to be non-fiction has been called bogus by many journalists and critics. The real message here is—we say it's true; maybe it's not, but if it plays well, who cares?

This casualness in popular culture is reinforced by trends in the intellectual world which hold that truth is socially constructed and doesn't exist in the real world. Voices, stories, and narratives are important, an idea which drips into the popular culture as a contempt for truth, or a belief that each group must determine its own private truth through experience and assertion.

This is why wacky group history is so rarely challenged. The Afrocentric theory that Africans invented democracy, philosophy, and science, which were then stolen by the Greeks, is clearly false. But almost all Egyptologists and historians stayed silent during the long controversy. The struggle to state and defend the truth was conducted almost solo by Mary Lefkowitz, the classicist from Wellesley College who wrote *Not Out of Africa*. She suffered a lot of abuse and ostracism for stubbornly insisting that the truth mattered. For her silent peers who looked the other way, it obviously didn't.

Alas, we are awash in conspiracy theories: one Clinton or another killed Vince Foster, the Holocaust is a myth, IQ tests are rigged against minorities, the crack epidemic in urban America is a CIA plot, the CIA or maybe the Cubans killed John F. Kennedy. With the glut of information and the rise of talk radio and the Internet, data and factoids are available to suit any theory. Joel Achenbach, writing about all this last week in the *Washington Post*, said: "The danger is that we are reaching a moment where nothing can be said to be objectively true, when consensus about reality disappears. The Information Age could leave us with no information at all, only assertions."

Maybe so, but the best antidote is to care about the truth more than feelings or group rights, and to teach respect for truth in our schools. On the grounds that even tiny fibs matter, one vote here for asking Jay Leno to delete all autobiographical material that actually comes from somebody else's life.

THE LEADING CULTURAL POLLUTER

Which corporation is doing the most to lower standards and further degrade what's left of American culture? When this question came up at a New York dinner party last summer, there was a vote or two for Viacom and Paramount, a lot of talk about Madonna, and strong support for Rupert Murdoch's Fox Network.

After a half-hour or so of wrangling, we had a consensus winner: Time Warner. Here's how to reach this rather obvious conclusion on your own: whenever a new low is reached in the culture, check for the corporate name behind it. With amazing frequency it will be Time Warner.

The schlocky *Jenny Jones Show*, the first show on which a guest who was set up to be humiliated later was charged with murdering his humiliator, is a Time Warner product. The most degrading commercial picture book about human sexuality may be Madonna's $49.95 porn book, which, I am told, pictorially indicates that she is game to have sex with everything but babies and folding chairs. It was published by Time Warner, and (surprise!) chosen as an alternate selection by Time Warner's once respectable Book of the Month Club.

In the movies the all-time low for cynicism and historical lies (Oliver Stone's *JFK*) and for graphic, wholesale serial killing presented as fun (Oliver Stone's *Natural Born Killers*) were both produced by Warner. In the category of movie nihilism for children, my vote goes to Warner's *Batman Returns*, a dark and sadomasochistic film pushed hard to kids through a tie-in with McDonalds.

But it's in the music field that Time Warner does most of its damage. Dr. C. DeLores Tucker, chair of the National Congress of Black Women, says Time Warner is "one of the greatest perpetrators of this cultural garbage." She may be understating the case. From the rise of 2 Live Crew and Metallica, through the national uproar over Ice-T's cop-killing lyrics, down to Snoop Doggy Dogg, Nine Inch Nails and Tupac Shakur, the sprawling Time Warner musical empire has been associated one way or another with most of the high-profile, high-profit acts, black and white, that are pumping nihilism into the culture.

Like a junkie quivering toward a fix, Time Warner simply can't resist cashing in on the relentlessly amoral singers who work tirelessly to tear the culture apart, glorifying brutality, violence, and the most hateful attitudes toward women the public culture has ever seen, ranging from rape to torture and murder.

After the Ice-T fiasco, Time Warner pulled in its horns a bit and turned down a few recordings, including one about a killer stalking President Bush. But those feeble PR-oriented efforts were in areas where the pressure was coming from: police and public officials. The company did nothing about the woman-hating, racism, and all-round mayhem.

In fact, Time Warner companies have worked to lower the already low standards in the field. When BMG and Sony balked at signing the loathsome Dr. Dre, a Time Warner-affiliated company, Interscope, was there to sign him. When David Geffen, to his credit, refused to sign the out-of-control Geto Boys (who sing lyrically about slitting women's throats and cutting off their breasts), a Time Warner label picked them up. It helps to have a fat checkbook and no standards.

Last week Time Warner bought another chunk of Interscope, the hottest record company around, and now owns 50 percent. This is the cultural equivalent of owning half of the world's mustard-gas factories. One Interscope talent, Nine Inch Nails, seems to specialize in meditations on self-loathing, sexual obsession, torture, suicide, and dismemberment. Another huge seller, Dr. Dre, is author of the immortal line: "Rat-a-tat and a tat like that/ Never hesitate to put a nigga on his back," which author Nathan McCall says is "Plain and simple...a boastful call for black men to kill each other."

Time Warner puts out a lot of benign or harmless music, too. But it makes huge profits by bombarding the young with destructive messages. The company and its president-CEO Gerald Levin, commonly try to wrap themselves in the flag, pointing piously to the First Amendment and artistic freedom.

But as the *New Republic* pointed out during the Ice-T uproar, "the contents of American culture cannot be hidden behind the freedom of American culture." There is more to say about the convulsions of the culture than just to point out that singers can sing whatever they wish, and companies can sell whatever they wish.

We are living through a cultural collapse, and major corporations are presiding over that collapse and grabbing everything they can on the way down. Time Inc. was a respectable and socially responsible company only seven or eight years ago. Now it's an anything-goes corporation that refuses to look at any of the larger social implications of what it is selling. Along the way, the company has compromised its own magazines, which are hardly in a position to report honestly on what Time Warner is doing to the culture. It's a mess, and it ought to come up in an organized way at every stockholders' meeting.

THE PRIVATE PARTS OF DON IMUS

I thought President Clinton should have walked out on Don Imus' performance at the Radio and TV Correspondents' dinner, maybe first getting Newt Gingrich to go with him. By staying put, frozen smile in place, the president probably got the politics of it right. A walk-out could have changed the subject—making Clinton's behavior and not Imus' the issue. We might all be talking about Clinton's thin skin instead of Imus' ghastly jokes.

Still it's hard to imagine other recent presidents putting up with a speech like this. Clinton still doesn't grasp the symbolic importance of the presidency, and hasn't really tried to draw an important line against awful behavior since his Sister Souljah speech.

The obvious comeback to this is that we shouldn't make too much of a roast that got out of hand. Well, yes. Imus didn't intend to have this sort of impact. He meant to be humorous. This was his version of David Letterman at the Oscars, a man trying to be funny outside the carefully controlled environment where his humor flourishes naturally. On the radio, unseen and in command, he can be hilarious. Trying to do it while sweating in a tux at a head table is apparently something else.

But there's also an argument here about civil discourse. Lenny Bruce, who invented Imus' form of anarchic humor, said far stronger things, but he said them in clubs, not at formal Washington dinners with C-Span coverage. He made some awful jokes about Eleanor Roosevelt, but he didn't discuss her private parts or copulatory habits at a big banquet. Imus' performance amounted to a claim that all barriers are down, that you can say anything anywhere about anybody and the

Washington elite will just chuckle along as our degraded political discourse moves to yet another new low.

The degraded-discourse argument hovers over Imus' radio show too, mostly because he is both a sophisticated political interviewer and a comedian arrested at the level of penis jokes and towel-snapping insults.

The political regulars who go on his show at lot, including Tim Russert, Bob Dole, Bill Bradley, Dan Rather, and Jeff Greenfield, like to talk about the high-minded Imus, the one who is bringing fresh political concern to an alienated audience of young listeners who pay no attention to *Meet the Press* or *Nightline*. Naturally, they wish to separate themselves from the low-minded Imus, the one who makes the racial wisecracks and broadcasts "The First Lady Is a Tramp," a song about Hillary Clinton complete with references to her urinary habits and menstrual cycle.

Jeff Greenfield says this is like being an important novelist excerpted in *Playboy*. You wish to be judged by your brilliant writing, not by your proximity to the centerfold mammaries. But it does raise the question of what Greenfield is doing when he goes on Imus: is he helping improve our politics, or is he helping debase them by legitimizing a shock-jock fixated on Richard Nixon's penis and Hillary Clinton's menstrual cycle?

This is a particularly acute question for Bob Dole and Joseph Lieberman, who have attacked, respectively, Hollywood cultural pollution and trash TV. Both regularly go on Imus, where they are surrounded by material quite similar to the stuff they complain about. In Washington, a city increasingly mesmerized by Imus, this is simply a power question. Being on his show can raise your profile, sell your book, and maybe even get you elected. Imus loves Dole. How can Dole reject him now?

I admit to some ambivalence about Imus. He is very funny, well-informed, doesn't take himself seriously, encourages guests to punch back. As radio humorists and shock-jocks go, he is far more serious and useful than Howard Stern, broader and less partisan than Rush Limbaugh.

Yet there's a clear trivializing aspect to Imus's demand that his polls and reporters be crisp, quick, and entertaining. Massachusetts Governor William Weld, denounced as a "dud" by Imus after an insufficiently sprightly performance, now goes on the show with a bunch of one-liners and jokes. "It's embarrassing what the politicians do" to curry favor with Imus, says Dan Payne, media consultant for Weld's senate opponent, John Kerry.

And there's definitely a nasty streak in there. One of Imus' less lovable traits is his habit of alternately praising and abusing guests.

Writing in *Esquire*, Martha Sherrill calls this an interviewing style of "two kisses, then a slap; two slaps, then a kiss." It keep guests off balance and pathetically eager to please.

People who criticize his show get slapped over and over. One critic who wrote a negative column in the *Washington Post* was called a "homo" and a "Jew" and attacked for weeks on the air. Emily Rooney of Fox Television made one anti-Imus remark on CNN and says Imus pummeled her for three weeks as "a cow" and someone "getting into the liquor cabinet."

Now Imus is abusing Cokie Roberts for boycotting the show over his speech. This kind of overkill looks a lot like an enforcement policy to keep other potential critics in line. I would like to hear Imus' many Washington regulars say what they think about this.

SELLING THE CHILD-WOMAN

Kate Moss is in the news again, this time for getting tied up and shot to death in a music video. Actually, the murder isn't shown on the video. She is seen beautifully dressed, dead, and bound to a chair while Johnny Cash warbles his recording of "Delia's Gone."

Moss is the emaciated supermodel whose vacant stare, unsmiling lips, and frequently nude 105-pound body are on endless public display these days, mostly in Calvin Klein ads.

Her wan and breastless "New Waif" look irritates many women, mostly because it seems to glorify anorexia. Her ads have been targeted by a Boston-based group called Boycott Anorexic Marketing. In some cities, anti-starvation graffiti appears often on Kate Moss outdoor ads, usually "Feed Me," or "Give me a cheeseburger." Sometimes the skull of a skeleton is drawn over her face.

"To many people, she represents a skeleton and death anyway," said Barbara Lippert, a columnist for *Adweek*. Lippert thinks that getting tied up and gunned down by Johnny Cash can be viewed as a logical extension of the ghostly victim theme pushed so hard in some of Moss' work. In many ads, the naked Moss looks as if she has been abused, or is about to be.

Moss is a very troubling figure, and a prime indicator of our degraded popular culture. She is the modern female as blank, fragile, stick figure. Her pictures are full of strange allusions, many of them perverse. In a report last month on the new glamorizing of heroin use, the *New York Times* mentioned that "some social critics see an allusion to hard drugs" in Moss's dead-eyed, hollow-cheeked look.

Here and there, her photos show fleeting references to masturbation (fingering her breasts under her bra), bestiality (posing nude with a large dog), incest (under a towel, apparently nude, being hugged by her brother), and violence (one Obsession ad shows her bare-breasted, with blackened or bruised eyes, holding her hand over her mouth and looking upset).

None of this is unusual in the fashion world. What makes these themes explosive is her very young look. She has just turned twenty, but as she said a year or so ago, "I look 12." This propels many of her photos into the category of child sex, or child porn.

In her ads, Moss often looks like a vulnerable and compliant child, stripped for sexual use. "The message of these pictures is that she is very young and very available," said Linnea Smith, a North Carolina psychiatrist and anti-porn crusader. Other commentators have noted the theme of Moss as a slightly soiled and exploitable street urchin. *Harper's Bazaar* said she looks "like a kid from a latter-day Fagin's gang."

The naked child, staring vacantly and helplessly at the camera is a staple of child pornography. One of Moss's photos shows her cringing nude in the corner of a huge sofa, with legs locked and arms pressed to her breasts, as if bracing for an impending sexual assault.

A more familiar shot of Moss shows her lying nude on her stomach on a sofa, legs parted, looking up pliantly at the camera as if to say, "Is this what you want me to do?" In the picture, she appears to be about 10 or 12 years old, slightly fearful, and unusually androgynous, thus appealing to pedophiles of all persuasions. A cropped version of this photo appears in outdoor Calvin Klein ads, on buses and phone booths.

With little resistance, Calvin Klein has placed images that sexualize children on the streets where they register with adults and children alike. "You can't turn the dial to escape it," said Linnea Smith. "What are we supposed to do, run for a bus with our eyes covered?" Well, no. A good rule is that those who want soft-core should be able to get it, but those who don't should be able to avoid it. Under current arrangements, they can't.

The usual interpretation of no-frills nymphets like Kate Moss is that they represent a reaction to the busty Amazonian models of the 1980s, and express the bleak, anti-glamour, anti-status spirit of the 1990s. Calvin Klein says they represent a return to a more sensitive, more fragile beauty.

Could be. But they also represent the old game of taboo-breaking. Six years ago, Klein was quoted in *Vogue* as saying that in his ads "I've done everything I could do in a provocative sense without being arrested." But scrounging around for taboos to break in the age of Oprah is a hard business. Sexualizing children may be the final frontier.

Then, too, there is the personal input of Calvin Klein to consider. In *Obsession*, the new biography of the designer by Steven Gaines and Sharon Churcher, he is portrayed as a sexually ambiguous figure. Klein eroticizes both sexes in his ads, but the males are portrayed in a straightforward way—lots of writhing and crotch-grabbing, but no death masks, bruised eyes, anorexia or child exploitation hovering around the edges. That seems to show up only in his women.

His clothes are nice, but in advertising he's a perverse force. The child-sexuality theme alone is enough to make magazines and billboard companies think twice about the stuff they are pumping into the culture. And consumers should consider letting a boycott come between them and their Calvins.

Decadence, the Corporate Way

Calvin Klein is at it again, this time with a series of bus and magazine ads showing young teens posed in what look like opening scenes from a porn movie. In one photo, a girl is shown lying down with her skirt hiked up, exposing her panties. In another tacky crotch shot, a curly-haired boy gazes out at us, as if scanning desperately for any nearby member of the North American Man/Boy Love Association.

These are creepy pictures, and like Calvin models going back twenty years, nobody looks capable of ever having an actual relationship. Sex is rather blankly offered here as a commodity by and for the bombed-out and the hopelessly numb. Some of the teens look coaxed into posing. Others seem like they're wearily going through the motions for a customer. It's not just in our face and totally inappropriate on buses. It's decadent.

This is about what we have come to expect from Calvin, our most relentlessly tasteless tastemaker. Why does he bother with this tawdriness? Don Nathan, a spokesman for Calvin Klein, told the *Washington Post*: the target audience is made up of a generation that's independent and media-savvy. They're "people who do only what they want to do." The *Post* reporter, Robin Givhan, summed up his analysis: "Hence the rule-breaking attitude of the ads."

It's interesting to focus on rule-breaking, rather than the more obvious themes of sex, numbness, and the sensibility of a cheap porno film shot quickly in a motel or basement rec room. But in fact the rule-breaking theme is nearly always more potent in ads today than the sexual themes that draw far more attention.

It works like this: advertisers are focusing more and more on the emerging market of "people who do only what they want to do," that is, people who yearn to be completely free of all restraint, expectations, and responsibilities. This is a familiar Sixties product now tinged with Nineties pessimism. So a socially subversive pro-impulse, anti-rules, and anti-restraint message is casually being built into more and more campaigns, often with the help of hired psychologists and focus groups.

The modern classics in this effort are Nike's "Just do it!" (act on impulse, don't analyze or inhibit yourself) and Burger King's "Sometimes you gotta break the rules." These were very successful campaigns and their power can be measured by the number of imitators. A jeweler, Best, picked up the break-the-rules theme and so did Don Q rum ("When you have a passion for living, nothing is merely accepted. Nothing is taboo...Break all the rules"). Another rum, Bacardi Black,("The taste of the Night,") promises to take the drinker to a boozy evening universe where it seems that anything goes ("Some people embrace the night because rules of the day do not apply.")

A Nieman Marcus ad says: "Relax. No rules here." Even a shoe ad can promise a world without norms or rules (Our shoe "conforms to your foot so you don't have to conform to anything"—Easy Spirit shoes). A batch of ads concentrates on changing the rules or the glamour of crossing lines (Isuzu's campaign making fun of the imperious and bald teacher who tells children "Stay within the lines. The lines are our friends.") Others strum the theme that the only real rule is self-preoccupation. These are so common that they regularly go by without raising eyebrows. ("Peel off inhibitions. Find your own road"—Saab, "Your own rhythm"—Drum tobacco products, "We are all hedonists and we want what feels good. That's what makes us human"—Nike).

Another group focuses on getting rid of boundaries. ("Living without boundaries"—Ralph Lauren's Safari, "Your world should know no boundaries"—Merrill Lynch, "It's not trespassing when you cross your own boundaries"—Johnny Walker Scotch). While there is an obvious healthy side to the no-boundary theme—the computer world, for instance, has no real boundaries—the idea plays to the classic infantile wish for an infinite self, free of all restraint. At its worst the no-boundaries theme shows up in narcissistic personality disorders as the inability to know where the self ends and others begin ("I don't know where I end and you begin"—Calvin Klein's perfume Eternity).

The point here is that while everyone is aghast over blatant sex, violent movies, and gangster rap, the ordinary commercial messages of corporate America are probably playing a more subversive role.

The drumbeat of rule-breaking slogans has a devastating effect. Our commercial culture and the advertising industry are not just at war with traditional values. They are at war too with the possibility that new common values will emerge from the current social chaos.

By pushing self-obsession, narcissism, and contempt for all rules, they strike at the sense of connectedness that any society needs to cohere, and to care about its common problems and least fortunate members. It's time to call the corporations and ad agencies on this. They are busy financing our social meltdown.

PART SEVEN

SOCIETY AND SOCIAL BEHAVIOR

THANK YOU FOR NOT SMOKING

Addiction theory was one of the grander social mistakes of the 1970s and 1980s. Every conceivable hard-to-shake habit was declared to be an addiction and therefore beyond the control of the newly defined and helplessly passive addict.

Womanizers were revealed to be "sex addicts," and gamblers, joggers, daredevils, and deadbeats were all labeled addicts as well. Romance as an alleged addiction sold many thousands of self-help books. The novelist Erica Jong said some women are addicted to behaving like babies. Actress Valerie Bertinelli announced she was addicted to her husband.

Chaka, a notorious graffiti sprayer who defaced 10,000 signs, walls, and other surfaces in California, grasped the spirit of the age and explained that his behavior was "no different than an alcoholic."

Alcoholism shed its aura of moral fault and moved from addiction to disease. Those of us who thought that heavy drinking often took place to escape or relieve conflict were told we had it backwards: the conflict and stress are mostly a consequence of the drinking, not the cause. A specialist who treats alcoholics said, "If we thought that yesterday's alcoholic was haunted by internal conflict, we know that today's is primarily haunted by his liver." Drinkers were victims of their own livers.

But this is the Nineties and some of the fever has passed. Many addictions have quietly been downgraded to habits and choices, and alcoholism may be in the process of being downgraded from disease to addiction. At a recent Harvard Medical School conference on addictions, the conventional view of alcoholism as a disease under the control of biological factors was attacked in a way that would have been inconceivable a few years back. As reported by Alison Bass in the *Boston Globe*, some specialists now say that "while biology certainly plays a role in addiction...it isn't the whole or even most of the story."

Various speakers made these points: the psychological, behavioral, and social factors involved in choices to drink or take drugs have to be taken into account. ("Once we can find out what needs the drinking satisfies, then we can eventually help people find something to replace it with.") Emphasizing the medical causes and consequences of drinking undermines therapy by giving drinkers the impression that they don't have to (or can't) take personal responsibility for their behavior and recovery. No one doubts that long-term drinking causes changes in brain chemistry that makes it very hard for people to stop cold turkey, but they are more likely to stop if therapists explore why people drink and push them to take charge of their lives.

James Prochaska of the University of Rhode Island's Cander Prevention Research Center said "The disease model is predicated on the idea that alcoholism is something that happens to you and it puts us into a passive-reactive mode that doesn't help us prevent or solve the problem."

This discussion has some obvious echoes in the debates about smoking. There is no longer any doubt that nicotine is physically addictive. But nobody seems to notice that smoking has been just as narrowly medicalized as drinking. The anti-smoking forces have the tobacco companies on the run for many reasons, but one is that they have succeeded in medicalizing a problem that is just as much behavioral and psychological as it is medical.

There's no mystery about why this is so. The argument over health effects has been the trump card. Seminars, conference, and grants have all been dominated by medical people and technicians, most of whom seem to be absolutely certain that a cigarette is nothing more than a nicotine delivery system.

But people don't smoke just for nicotine. They smoke for a great array of non-chemical reasons, from depression and peer pressure to a courting of danger, or a belief that smoking equals liberation. Or because lighting up has become embedded in day-to-day life as a ritual, a way of punctuating a phone call, the end of a meal, the start of a difficult project.

By pruning away all the meanings behind smoking, earnest anti-smoking people leave this field to the tobacco companies. The result is that cigarette ads are rich with psychological come-ons, and most anti-tobacco ads just shriek about health dangers, which everybody knows about and which are often part of the allure.

The passivity and poor results that Prochaska notes among drinkers who are told that alcoholism "is something that happens to you" also shows up among smokers. In a forthcoming academic paper recommending aggressive anti-smoking campaigns, he says that how-to-stop-smoking clinics have little impact in the United States: when HMOs offer free clinics, only 1 percent of subscribers who smoke take advantage of the offer.

There are lots of reasons for this. Stopping is hard and many smokers are demoralized. But stupid social theories play a role, too. Addiction theory is a formula for no-fault, no-improvement misery. It tells us we are not in charge of our own lives, and that nobody should expect us to be. Should we be surprised that a theory like this has social effects?

Doing the Disorder Rag

News reports say that "road rage" is on the brink of being certified as an official mental disorder by the American Psychiatric Association. Until now, most of us have assumed that drivers who cut us off and give us the finger are just irate swine. But no, they appear to be suffering from a mental disorder, just like schizophrenics.

Brand new diseases, including a lot of implausible ones, are an old story for the psychiatrists and their professional bible, the *Diagnostic and Statistical Manual of Mental Disorders*. The DSM has been revised six times, usually with a few old diseases thrown out and a large number of new ones tossed in. Among those added were caffeine-induced anxiety disorder, inhalant abuse, and telephone scatologia (making heavy-breathing sexual phone calls). Now a boom is under way for "internet addiction disorder" (IAD). In June, Cincinnati police arrested a woman accused of neglecting her children because of IAD. Huffy people on the internet suggest that the DSM might invent another illness as well: television viewing addiction (TVA). Possible criteria for a grave disorder: five sitcoms or four football games in a single day.

It's easy enough to make fun of all this, but there's a serious problem here. The DSM is converting nearly all of life's stresses and bad habits into mental disorders. Almost everything we feel or do is listed somewhere in the DSM as an indicator of some dread disorder. This has the effect of creating and trying to enforce social values on the basis of scientific evidence that most people in the field admit is rather weak and unconvincing. In their new book, *Making Us Crazy*, Herb

Kutchins and Stuart Kirk point out that these psychiatric criteria include the inability to quit smoking, thinking a lot about a former lover, holding a grudge, having a hangover, and feeling apprehensive about giving a speech. No one criterion labels you as a psychiatric case, but the language of DSM makes it impossible to tell the normal from the disordered.

According to DSM-IV, one problem alone—general anxiety disorder—will afflict 5 percent of the population, or 12 million people, at some point in their lifetime. "The pharmaceutical companies—the makers of Prozac, Xanax, and the beta blockers for stage fright love those numbers," say Kutchens and Kirk. And GAD is only one of the 374 official disorders which the psychiatrists say hit half of all Americans.

Worse, the psychiatrists are busy broadening definitions and lowering thresholds so that much of the other half will be listed as disordered too. The clearest current example is attention deficit hyperactivity disorder, a diagnosis which now descends on many perfectly healthy small boys who bother school officials by misbehaving in class. ADHD cases have nearly doubled in five years.

The growth market can be seen in all the new talk about "shadow syndromes," or mild versions of serious ailments that many psychiatrists insist must be treated. Currently five of nine criteria may have to be met before a disorder is diagnosed. A "shadow syndrome" may drop that to two of nine, thus creating many more sufferers. Something like the "shadow syndromes" is listed in the back of DSM-IV as worthy of study, i.e., here are the new diseases of tomorrow. They too include light versions of serious disorders. Some "shadowy" ailments may be real, but most appear to be the result of product differentiation by successful entrepreneurs. New disorders do for therapists what the litigation boom did for lawyers.

Pharmaceutical companies have a stake in this too. PRIME-MD, a simple one-page questionnaire used to screen for psychiatric problems, was funded by Pfizer, Inc. In a recent study of a thousand patients, PRIME-MD turned up 287 people with identifiable problems. A sympathetic newspaper report said: "In about half of these cases, doctors had failed to diagnose the problems on a previous visit. "Another way of saying this is that a screening test funded by a drug company managed to double the number of people with psychiatric difficulties, many of whom will therefore be needing regular pills.

The psychiatrists are free to declare as many people disordered as they wish. But the effort and the concepts behind it are seeping deep into the culture, reinforcing the victim industry and teaching us to look for psychiatric answers to social and personal problems. It's much easier to sedate an alleged ADHD youngster with Ritalin than to do something about the environmental or family problems that might better explain his behavior.

Financially, we are seeing a shift in resources, away from very disturbed patients and toward the worried well, who are adequately covered by insurance and much easier to deal with. An effort under way in Congress to gain "parity" between physical and mental illness would seal this shift and probably break the bank as well. If only half of the growing number of psychiatric disorders are paid for just like real physical illness, the cost would be in the vicinity of $75 billion, according to the *New York Times*. But we know that this is an effort to cover lots of imaginary disorders as well as the real ones. Do we really want to do this?

May the Feel Be with You

Tarzan and his ape-mother appeared on *Good Morning, America* last week in a scene from the new Disney animated movie, *Tarzan*. The ape was warmly lecturing the boy. "Now forget what you see," she said. "What do you feel?" "My heart," replies Tarzan. He feels her heart too and they hug.

Tarzan is said to be a very good movie, and isolated scenes watched while brushing one's teeth at 8 a.m. probably shouldn't be overanalyzed. Still, I think the lovable step-ape made a big mistake here. Listening to your heart is important, particularly in a Disney movie, but little Tarzan wouldn't last two days in the jungle if he forgot what he saw and merely consulted his feelings. More likely the movie would end abruptly as Tarzan became a snack for some emotionally underdeveloped but visually alert predator who lacked a feelings-oriented adviser.

Tarzan is hardly the only fictional hero placed in needless jeopardy by the feelings culture, Hollywood division. It happens to Jedi knights, too, in one *Star Wars* picture after another. In fact, this is one of nagging problems about being a Jedi, which is otherwise a very good job. You have to be able to fight deadly duels blindfolded and drop important bombs without looking because, in times of crisis, feelings are way more important than eyesight, facts, reason, technology, common sense, and computerized bombsights.

In the original *Star Wars* movie, Obi-Wan Kenobi sternly tells Luke Skywalker, "Stretch out with your feelings," "Let go your conscious self and act on instinct" and finally, "Let go, Luke!" This last piece of advice comes when Skywalker is foolishly trying to destroy the evil Death Star by using a computer instead of his feelings to hit a target the size of a grapefruit while flying 300 miles per hour at an altitude of 20 feet. Luckily Luke has the wit to turn off his mind and his computer, so there are no remaining obstacles to successful bombing.

The same sort of keen advice about the power of feeling is dispensed in the new *Star Wars* movie, *The Phantom Menace*. Obi-Wan Kenobi is in this movie, too, but this time the sage advice on the folly of thinking comes from an older Jedi master, Obi-Jee-Wye-En (I hope I have that name right), played by Liam Neeson.

Nine-year-old Anakin Skywalker is about to risk his life in a 300-mile-per-hour race of pods, or space chariots. So the Jedi knight naturally thinks this is a good time to offer the child useful advice about feelings. "Feel, don't think!" barks the master, who must have been drilled in the dangers of common sense and rational thought by some other Master Feeler back in the year 3049, when he was tiny himself and listening to a Hollywood Jedi seemed perfectly normal. Young Anakin wins the race, so maybe the advice to avoid thinking at all costs served him well. On the other hand, the child grows up to be Darth Vader, so maybe not.

In the forthcoming *Episode 2* of the continuing Star Wars saga, a dramatic debate takes place among galaxy historians. They argue over where the Jedi got their odd philosophy of celebrating every feeling as a precious trump card and struggling to stamp out every trace of actual thought. Most of these scholars will conclude that it came from a brief blip in American popular culture in the emotionally fertile period of 1990 to 2010, when the United States decided to stretch out with its feelings, just as Obi-Wan shrewdly suggested when they put him in the first *Star Wars* movie.

This was the period in which America was busy switching to a feelings-centered morality. Since the self was more important than society, values created by the self (feelings) took precedence over any social or traditional values, which are the encrusted remains of other people's feelings and biases.

The language of "Me Decade" pop therapy, not shaken off until the late 2020s, played a role, too. If we are open to experience, wrote the famous therapist Carl Rogers, "doing what feels right proves to be a competent and trustworthy guide to behavior which is truly satisfying."

Galaxy scholars found that thinking, on the other hand, fell into disrepute. It was an abstract, culture-bound, Western activity. Undemocratic, too, since it privileged people who could do it over people who couldn't. In contrast, anyone can produce feelings, and because they all are personal and self-created, they can't be challenged, like old-fashioned arguments used to be.

So more and more laws and behavioral codes were written in the language of feelings and insensitivity. Politicians felt everybody's pain. With thinking gone, colleges turned into summer camps, heavy on entertainment, pop culture, and consumer satisfaction. A small remnant of pro-thinking students was left alone so that someone would produce the great Death Stars that could be blown up, and the computerized bombsights that could be turned off. Everybody else, even the cartoon apes, came out in favor of feeling over thinking. But it didn't last very long and even the Jedi became disillusioned. All this takes place in episode 2, A *Disturbance in the Farce: The Rational Mind Strikes Back.*

MY SOBBING VALENTINE

Mill Valley, Ca. (AP)—In a dramatic televised experiment, a hard-nosed Malibu car dealer today became the first man in California to get in touch with his feelings.

The startling and risky Valentine's Day test, watched by enthralled millions across the state, was immediately hailed by former governor Jerry Brown as "an historic milestone in the exploration of inner space."

"What a ride, "exclaimed Bobby Babble, 34, as he emerged from his cramped and windowless capsule at 11:32 A.M., ending a grueling six-minute experiment in which he was deliberately exposed to strong emotional material. The material had been gathered from female donors and carefully stored for months under antiseptic conditions. It is believed to be the first scientific experiment showing that males can handle emotions, and may one day even develop their own.

A surprised team of medical experts reported that Babble was "supernormal," and appeared to retain all of his masculine functions. Aside from some brief vomiting, he displayed none of the troubling side effects which scientists had predicted would accompany any male attempt to feel actual emotions, among them a much higher speaking voice and the disappearance of facial hair.

His face wreathed in a broad smile, the weary Babble called for a copy of *The Bridges of Madison County*, and quipped "I'm A-OK. I'm up front, fully centered, and touching some really deep chords." Some experts believe that these phrases will ultimately be translated, while others think they are just meaningless words triggered by the random firing of neurons in the brain of a male under extraordinary stress.

Proud Californians from Yorba Linda to Eureka exulted in the stunning achievement. "It was horrible, listening to that countdown, not knowing what would happen," exclaimed Marge Metuchen, 54. "He risked everything, didn't he? He's a hero and a credit to his sex."

"He did it for all of us; God knows why," gulped Gus Grizzle during a break in all-star wrestling mania. Men's theorist Robert Bly, interviewed while embracing a gorgeous redwood near Yosemite, predicted that by the year 2100, male emotions "might be as common as table salt." Tammy Taylor, a Long Beach cosmetologist, said, "This sort of thing would be quite a small step for womankind; but it's definitely a giant step for mankind."

Many women suggested that the Babble experiment may point the way toward a new type of relationship, marked by two-way communication between the sexes. "Two people feeling in one household," cried Myrna Bellwether, 29, of Barstow. "What a concept!" Yet many women around the state called for caution. "Men having feelings has always been theoretically possible, of course," conceded feminist theoretician Twyla Tompkins. "But let's not jump to conclusions. We have to go over the data carefully."

Several churchmen and moralists have raised questions about the propriety of subjecting a normal male to such experimental pressures. A storm of ethical protests arose last fall after a controversial experiment at the State Feeling Center, located in a heart-shaped building on the campus of the University of California at Santa Cruz. In the test, a high-testosterone male was told he would watch Monday Night Football, but he was actually locked into a room with his eyes taped open in front of a made-for-TV movie starring Valerie Bertinelli. His condition is reported as stable.

A spokesperson for the California Inner Space Program (CISP) revealed that Babble had experienced stress only when CISP leaders asked him to hold onto an emotion for as long as a minute. During this period, described by the spokesperson as "a rocky ride...truly harrowing," Babble suffered disorientation and briefly groped toward the escape hatch.

Unlike the chimp used in the last Valentine's Day experiment, Babble was at the controls of his capsule, able to touch various dials and levers which correct for panic, irony, distancing, sports talk, previous engagements, subject-changing humor, and other indicators of male stress.

As launch time approached, rehearsals were staged using two-second bursts of actual feelings under realistic conditions in a centrifuge in Santa Barbara. Although no announcement has been made about which feelings were used in the final experiment, they were said to include joy, surprise, and empathy. A source said the agency was afraid to expose Babble to more than seven seconds of empathy, for fear of risking permanent psychic damage and jeopardizing his career in auto sales.

Instead, CISP strategists are said to have exposed Babble to higher and higher doses of sadness. A highly placed source said, "All the best women are looking for Nineties guys who can cry when they need to. Babble is a bachelor. After all he's been through, the least we could do is give him an edge in the sobbing department."

Babble's normality was established two months ago in a standard psychological test: while viewing photos of mangled accident victims, his face showed no response at all. Since the experiment, he has been writing letters to the Menendez brothers, attempting to share their pain.

LIFE AMONG THE CYBERFOLK

Dressed in cowboy clothes, John Perry Barlow is either ambling or moseying across the stage, telling the techies they must secede from the United States and become citizens of cyberspace. "We may have to declare cyberspace sovereign," he says. "They do not know very much about our country." This is certainly true in my case. I hadn't even heard about the secession plans.

I am in Monterey at TED 6, the sixth edition of Richard Saul Wurman's cutting-edge conference on Technology, Entertainment and Design. Wurman, a remarkably warm and talented character, seems to know all 800 people here by name, and treats the crowd as one oversize family.

But despite all the bonhomie, the electronic people can't help treating the print people as if they were pitiful time-travelers from the

Pleistocene. They talk about books, magazines, and newspapers the way nuclear warriors talk about the slingshot and the club.

Paul Saffo, director of the Institute for the Future, said that print is "hair-triggered on the edge of oblivion." His only problem with that is that he thinks print is dying too fast—there will be a "media gap" because the electronic media aren't yet ready to take over entirely.

It's an article of faith here that computer technology and the rise of the Internet are the most discombobulating events since the discovery of fire.

This "nothing-will-ever-be the-same" theme has a triumphal, libertarian edge, as if the cyberfolk were finally freeing themselves from a cultural dungeon. John Perry Barlow thinks computer use is creating more political libertarians every day, and there seems to be something to the theory.

Within six months, he said, the flow of digital cash will rearrange the financial world and "taxes will become voluntary." (An overstatement, but unless governments get to monitor what takes place on the Internet, they will have no way of knowing how much money people are making or what they do with it. Hiding or laundering income will be a home project. As one conference-goer said, "It will be like having an off-shore bank for everyone.")

Like his western clothes, the word "frontier" seems to connect the psychic world of the free-wheeling Old West to the new one of libertarian hackers. In myth, at least, the denizens of the Wild West wanted to escape the entanglements and controls of citified folk, and live on their own. Barlow's version of this is simple: no interference at all from government, and no property rights—everything on the Net should be free.

This means an enormous number of political and ethical conflicts are descending upon us all at once. Most of us don't like government looking over our shoulder, or having access to private messages. But if it doesn't, how can we hold anyone responsible for libel or the destruction of a private business with a flood of false messages? If we want government to be able to wire-tap organized crime, shouldn't it have similar tools to use against cyber-criminals?

If everything can be downloaded free, as Barlow says, why would anyone write a column or a book, or go to the trouble of shooting photographs in Bosnia under dangerous conditions for no pay? Or take censorship. Is censoring the Internet even possible? As one critic says, the Internet interprets censorship as damage and routes around it.

"Technology is on the side of anarchy," says Walter Isaacson, head of new media for Time-Warner. All the rules of publishing and communications are up in the air. Are we ready for any of this?

Damn, I'm Good!

The self-esteem movement is one of the marvels of our time. It goes on and on, even though its assumptions are wrong and its basic premises have been discredited by a great deal of research. Like a monster in the last ten minutes of a horror movie, it has enough fatal wounds to stop a platoon. But it keeps stumbling on, not seeming to notice.

Will it ever expire? Apparently so. A long article last week in the *New York Times* sounded very much like an obituary. To be fair, the article contained a brief disclaimer ("Self-esteem is by no means dead"), but most of the text suggested otherwise. A subhead said "An idea whose time has come...and gone?" Since the *Times* caters to and usually speaks for the educational elite that has kept the movement afloat, we are surely entitled to detect some significance here.

One obvious factor mentioned in the *Times* is that the increasing emphasis on school standards and achievement has weakened the hold of self-esteem theory and preoccupation with feelings at the expense of actual learning. The world of how-to books and self-help books also seems to be turning away from the excesses of the 1980s and early '90s. The conception of self-esteem as a kind of commodity one can acquire by constant self-affirmation now appears to be trivial and silly.

The *Times* quotes Albert Bandura, a psychology professor at Stanford, as concluding from his research that "self-esteem affects neither personal goals nor performance." This is certainly so. The core assumption in the self-esteem movement is that children cannot learn or develop properly unless they form a positive self-image. But no study has ever demonstrated a connection between feeling good about oneself and improved performance. Some students feel terrible about themselves and become academic and social successes. Others brim with self-confidence and do awful work. *The Social Importance of Self Esteem*, a 1986 book of essays on the movement contained this line: "One of the disappointing aspects of every chapter in this volume...is how low the associations between self-esteem and its consequences are in research to date." And that book was published by true believers, as part of a effort to promote California's $750,000 program to make self-esteem an official state goal.

Since 1986, the research on self-esteem has been devastating. When psychologists Harold Stevenson and James Stiegler tested the academic skills of elementary school students in the U.S., China, Japan, and Taiwan, the Asian students outperformed the Americans, but the U.S. students felt better about themselves and their work. They had managed to combine high self-esteem with poor work. The researchers found that American schools worry more about sensitivity and how students view themselves than about actual academic performance. Instead of bringing performance up, the pop-therapeutic approach was helping to dumb down.

For more than forty years, low self-esteem has been widely cited as a serious obstacle to black success in school and the workplace. The theory is that a racist society holds blacks back by imposing a low sense of self-worth. But researchers have repeatedly found that black self-esteem is no lower than that of whites, and often quite higher. A summary of this research, published under the title *The Myth of Black Low Self-Esteem*, points out that that this consistent finding goes all the way back to the mid-1960s. A massive 1966 study by James Coleman (of the famous "Coleman Report") showed that blacks as a group had a remarkably strong sense of self-esteem, despite all the social pressures arrayed against them.

The Myth of Black Low Self-Esteem gently raises a point about public policy. "The low-self esteem argument has become a leading rationale for many state and federal initiatives in hiring and education," write the three authors of the report, Stephen Powers, David Rothman, and Stanley Rothman. The assumption that blacks were psychologically damaged by whites became a foundation stone for affirmative action programs, emphasis on black role models, and the installing of the multicultural curriculum in schools and colleges. Though arguments for these policies can be made without reference to self-esteem theory, in fact the theory was used to frame and promote them. As the three authors wrote, the policies "draw their authority, at least in part" from the theory of low black self-esteem. What happens now that the theory seems to have no validity at all?

Another argument from self-esteem theory—that low self-esteem is the cause of violence, hate crimes, and many other anti-social acts—has also been discredited. As the *Times* mentions, studies of gang members and criminals show that their self-esteem is as high as that of overachievers. Another study disproved the familiar theory that welfare mothers become pregnant to boost their self-esteem. The *Times* ends its report with a professor saying of self-esteem theory, "It will be back." This sounds like the final line of a conventional horror movie.

But at least it indicates that something scary is going or gone. Will someone please tell the schools?

WE'RE ALL NUMBER 1

The Massachusetts Youth Soccer Association has some big news. From this season on, all tournament games involving players 10 and under will have no winners or losers. Keeping score is prohibited. The idea here is to have a restful, pressure-free, no-winner, post-season tourney with no parents or coaches ruining everything by screaming hurtful advice to the players. And since there will be no losers, nobody will have to suffer the agony of defeat, along with all the negative feelings and crippled self-esteem that usually go with it.

Trophies are not allowed unless every player on every team gets one. "The non-results-oriented competition," said Dean Conway, head coach of the soccer association, will give kids "more opportunity to develop all-around soccer smartness" and will "enhance natural, intrinsic competition," although how the children will actually be competing is unclear, since nothing seems to matter and victory is not allowed.

Some children, alas, do not agree with this line of reasoning and have been keeping score in their heads as they play. One who admits doing so is Paige Beauregard, 11, of Belchertown, who said, "I'd like to know the score so I can get better." Although this is not strictly forbidden by the rules, and no penalties are planned, counting goals as if an actual game of some sort were taking placed certainly violates the spirit of the competition, so players are strongly urged to clear their minds and forget about each score as soon as it occurs.

(When news reports on this non-scorekeeping began to circulate, the association explained that it's OK to keep score informally, but not publicly. As one official explained: "In non-results-oriented tourneys, score is not kept for all to see, but only for tourney officials to view, to make sure games aren't too one-sided.")

One of the purposes here is social equality. Having winners and losers in soccer, checkers, or ping-pong clearly divides us, when we need to be drawn closer together in purposeful social cohesion. As the soccer association president, Steve Koerpers, says, "When one team wins, everyone else is a loser." That's why everybody (or nobody) gets a trophy, and all teams are equal. This idea that games should not have losers goes back to the 1960s, when progressive-minded gym teachers urged children to roll giant balls around a field so that everybody could be on the same team and avoid divisive competition.

Under non-results-oriented competition, Conway thinks applause will be doled out equally too, since there is now a "higher likelihood that parents will cheer for all the kids in the game." Equality of applause is difficult to achieve, however, since some onlookers may insist on cheering children who score most of the goals, instead of issuing the same number of cheers for stars and less competent players who fall down all the time. In that case, the next step may have to be the elimination of the goals themselves. Removing the goalie and the net may help. Players who happily dribble the ball back and forth for an hour or so might quickly forget that there is no place at the end of the field to kick the ball into.

Or perhaps the association could continue to allow scoring, but make sure that goals are distributed equally among all players, just like trophies. This could be done by giving each player credit for a goal when he or she touches the ball for the first time. Or scoresheets could simply be handed out at the start of each game, showing one goal for everybody. (One flaw in this plan is that it's hard to give everybody credit for one score when keeping score is so toxic.)

In a similar spirit, many schools have eliminated grades, which are inherently undemocratic and difficult to distribute equally with any precision, since some students always seem to ruin things by working harder and therefore doing better than others. The equal-outcome classroom, like the no-win soccer field, prepares youngsters for the world of work, where everyone is equally talented, works equally hard and is paid exactly the same amount of money. This is why so many equality-minded bosses, when you ask them for a raise, shake their heads sadly and say, "If I gave you a raise, I'd have to give everyone else a raise too."

Professional sports may wish to keep an eye on no-scoring, non-results-oriented competition. As a New York Knicks fan, I know better than most that many hoopsters are already dedicated to the ideal of non-scoring, and whole teams (the Los Angeles Clippers and Dallas Mavericks come to mind) have spent years committing themselves to non-results-oriented play. Unfortunately, however, sports pages still insist on ranking the teams by won-lost records, so that a principled avoidance of old-fashioned "results" tends to create the impression that these are just bad teams.

Personally, I am toying with the idea of a non-results-oriented column, in which all ideas (being equal) would simply be listed neutrally, and none would be harmfully pushed forward as somehow superior or potentially divisive. Any reader who cheered or booed any idea would be asked to desist in the name of idea equality. Or maybe we could all be on the same side and just push one big idea around. Watch this space for details.

Mainstreaming's "Jimmy problem"

A few professors wrote me complaining about a recent column heaping some blame on the field of sociology for helping to undermine moral and social norms. But social scientists studying deviance and stigma in fact played a crucial role in this process. It's worth taking a look at how it happened.

In the 1950s, a few sociologists began to look at society from the bottom up, focusing on outsiders and "deviants"—prostitutes, homosexuals, runaways, transvestites, drifters, winos, gamblers, addicts, beach bums and carnival workers. The studies, done from the outsiders' point of view, beamed the message that stigmatization of bad behavior and low-life activities was oppression by an intolerant majority.

Howard Becker's 1963 book, "Outsiders: Studies in the Sociology of Deviance" opened with an argument that amounted to a preview of thinking that became commonplace later in the decade. All social groups make rules and regard people who fail to live by those rules outsiders, but the person who is thus labeled an outsider may have a different view of the matter. He may not accept the rule by which he is being judged and may not regard those who judge him as either competent or legitimately entitled to do so.

Becker arrived at a view of deviance that sounds like the official voice of the cultural left in the 1990s: the labeling of people as outsiders is a political act, and "social groups create deviance by making the rules whose infraction constitutes deviance." So deviance is simply the result of arbitrary community feelings, "a kind of behavior some disapprove of and others value." The problem was no longer in the behavior, but in the labeling of the behavior as unacceptable.

Many kinds of behavior regarded as deviant in the 1950s and early 1960s seem normal and harmless enough now. But the sweeping relativism of the deviance studies explained away too much. If all deviance is merely politicized labeling, the legitimacy of community norms—any norms—is undercut. Among sex educators, for example, the concept of perversion quickly disappeared. Using the exact language of Becker, Mary Calderone of SIECUS (the Sex Information and Education Council of the United States) explained that perversion was a term used by some people to indicate behavior they disapprove of.

The same thing happened in the poverty debate. The 1971 book, *Blaming the Victim,* by Boston sociologist William Ryan provided the theory that made it impermissible to talk about chaotic behavior that often keeps people poor: poverty had nothing to do with character, striving, or any characteristics of the poor. For Ryan, poverty "is most simply and clearly understood as the lack of money." In one phrase, Ryan laid the groundwork for our current politics of victimization, and the alleged need to blame society for all social troubles.

These liberators failed to acknowledge that communities cannot function without some system of informal controls. As a more aware sociologist, Christopher Jencks, writes, communities cohere by a moral demand system in which "censoriousness and blame" are the principal tools for holding the society together. This included "blame for teenage boys who steal from their neighbors, blame for drunken men who beat up their wives, blame for young women who have babies they cannot offer a decent home, blame for young men who say a four-dollar-an-hour job is not worth the bother, blame for everyone who acts as if society owes them more than they owe society." What happened in the '60s, Jencks argued, amounted to a tearing up of the moral contract. The abandonment of the social norms and stigmas by the larger society left the inner city particularly vulnerable. Given this retreat on values, "the respectable poor" could no longer fight illegitimacy and desertion with the old fervor.

Society, parents, and various authorities could be held responsible for our ills, but what appeared to be individual immorality or bad behavior rarely turned out to be the fault of the perpetrator involved. Therapists soothed patients by liberating them from social expectations. Freedom came to mean freedom from the judgments made by others. Maintaining social norms gradually came to seem self-righteous, harsh, and judgmental.

This is the cultural disaster we have to face today, and much of it was created by the ideas of our intellectual elite. Some intellectuals, at least, are beginning to speak out for social controls. "Sooner or late our remissive elites will have to rediscover the principle of limitation," Christopher Lasch wrote in his final book, *The Revolt of the Elites.* Lasch spoke of culture as a way of life backed up by the will to condemn and punish those who defy important norms, and he saw hope in evidence that ordinary Americans still endorse "old-fashioned moralities." Moral deregulation—"It is forbidden to forbid" in the revolutionary slogan of the Sixties—cannot continue indefinitely, Lasch wrote. At some point, the strain of anything-goes morality becomes too great and society starts to coalesce again around whatever it finds necessary to discourage or forbid.

THE "NEW PRIMITIVES"

The days when body piercers could draw stares by wearing multiple earrings and a nose stud are long gone. We are now in the late baroque phase of self-penetration. Metal rings and bars hang from eyebrows, noses, nipples, lips, chins, cheeks, navels, and (for that coveted neo-Frankenstein look) from the side of the neck.

"If it sticks out, pierce it," is the motto, and so they do, with special attention to genitals. Some of the same middle-class folks who decry genital mutilation in Africa are paying to have needles driven through the scrotum, the labia, the clitoris, or the head or the shaft of the penis. Many genital piercings have their own names, such as the ampallang or the Prince Albert. (Don't ask.)

And in most cases, the body heals without damage, though some women who have had their nipples pierced report damage to the breast's milk ducts, and some men who have been Prince Albert-ed no longer urinate in quite the same way.

What is going on here? Well, the mainstreaming-of-deviancy thesis naturally springs to mind. The piercings of nipples and genitals arose in the homosexual sadomasochistic culture of the West Coast. The Gauntlet, founded in San Francisco in 1975 mostly to do master and slave piercings, now has five shops around the country that are about as controversial as Elizabeth Arden salons. Rumbling through the biker culture and punk, piercing gradually shed its outlaw image and was mass marketed to the impressionable by music videos, rock stars, and models. The Gauntlet says business has doubled every year for the past three years.

The nasty, aggressive edge of piercing is still there, but now it is coated in happy talk (it's just body decoration, like any other) and a New Age-y rationale (we are becoming more centered, reclaiming our bodies in an anti-body culture). Various new pagans, witches, and New Agers see piercing as symbolic of unspecified spiritual transformation. One way or another, as Guy Trebay writes in the *Village Voice*, "You will never find anyone on the piercing scene who thinks of what he's doing as pathological."

The yearning to irritate parents and shock the middle class seems to rank high as a motive for getting punctured repeatedly. Some ask for dramatic piercings to enhance sexual pleasure, to seem daring or fashionable, to express rage, or to forge a group identity. Some think of it as an ordeal that serves as a rite of passage, like Indian males suspended from hooks in their chests as a ritual entry to adulthood.

Piercing is part of the broader "body modification" movement, which includes tattooing, corsetry, branding, and scarring by knife. It's a sign of the times that the more bizarre expressions of this movement keep pushing into the mainstream. The current issue of *Spin* magazine features a hair-raising photo of a woman carving little rivers of blood into another woman's back. "Piercing is like toothbrushing now," one of the cutters told *Spin*. "It's why cutting is becoming popular. "One of the cutters has a bland justification for back-slicing: people want to be cut "for adornment, or as a test of endurance, or as a sacrifice toward a transformation." Later on we read that "women are reclaiming their bodies from a culture that has commodified starvation and faux sex." One cuttee says: "It creates intimacy. My scars are emotional centers, signs of a life lived."

But most of us achieve intimacy, or at least search for it, without a knife in hand. The truth seems to be that the sadomasochistic instinct is being repositioned to look spiritually high-toned. Many people have found that S&M play "is a way of opening up the body-spirit connection," the high priest of the body modification movement, Fakir Musafar, said in one interview.

Musafar, who has corseted his waist down to 19 inches and mortified his flesh with all kinds of blades, hooks, and pins, calls the mostly twentyish people in the body modification movement "the modern primitives." This is another side of the movement: the conscious attempt to repudiate Western norms and values by adopting the marks and rings of primitive cultures.

Not everyone who pierces a nipple or wears a tongue stud is buying into this, but something like a new primitivism seems to be emerging in body modification as in other areas of American life. It plugs into a wider dissatisfaction with traditional Western rationality, logic, and sexual norms, as well as anger at the impact of Western technology on the natural environment, and anger at the state of American political and social life.

Two sympathetic analysts say this about the body modification movement: "Amidst an almost universal feeling of powerlessness to "change the world," individuals are changing what they have power over: their own bodies....By giving visible expression to unknown desires and latent obsessions welling up from within, individuals can provoke change."

Probably not. Cultural crisis can't really be dealt with by letting loose our personal obsessions and marking up our bodies. But the rapid spread of this movement is yet another sign that the crisis is here.

CHORTLE WHILE YOU WORK

For years I have been a mesmerized observer of the play-and-laughter industry. This is a loose alliance of consultants, authors, and therapists who are grimly determined to make us funnier and more playful, for our own good. If you chat up any of these people, humor and playfulness will likely be scarce, but you will hear a lot of somber talk about the healing power of fun and games. As psychiatrist Lenore Terr writes in her new book, *Beyond Love and Work*, "Adult play is picking up interest and therapeutic usefulness." Play is turning out to be "a great nonmedicinal tranquilizer."

One of the missions of this movement is to make the office a merrier place. For instance, *Simple Fun for Busy People*, a new how-to book by Gary Krane, Ph.D., suggests that employees might want to spend five minutes of each work day "cackling like chickens, or meowing like kittens, or pairing off into thumb hat wrestling matches, using those office coffee sugar packets." If that doesn't sound like a sure-fire recipe for sudden unemployment, Krane has other ideas that seem just as good: why not create a secret handshake for your office, or bring in a boom box and lift employee morale by playing Afro-Haitian music or a few polkas?

To the general public, these may sound like outlandish suggestions, but those of us who keep up with the play-and-laugh business consider them fairly mainstream. Humor consultant Marianna Nunes, who works with companies to incite workplace levity, encourages people to have pillow fights. Terry Braverman, a comedian and corporate consultant, advised one CEO to use a ventriloquist's dummy whenever he had to present bad news to his board. Kathy Pasanisi, another humor consultant, recently appeared before a hundred Bausch & Lomb managers in Rochester, N.Y., wearing a huge hat shaped like a crab. "I'm feeling a bit crabby today," she quipped. "Does it show?" If you have ever been encircled by a group of clowns in hotel lobbies or on convention floors, this, too, is an idea that comes from the humor business. "Laughter and play are a way to make the workplace more human," said Matt Weinstein of Playfair, Inc., a company that helps corporations realize the health and morale benefits of fun.

The corporate world is now swarming with humor advisors who have evolved their own technical terms, including "eustress" (good stress), "psychoneuroimmunology," "humor quotients," and the peril of TS (terminal seriousness). They show up regularly at serious conferences with titles like "Humor and Stress Management: Moving From Grim and Bear it to Grin and Share It." The advisors help major corporations like AT&T and General Electric, often at the rate of $5000 per hour.

The humor biz also makes a lot of money in direct sales. CDs, tapes, and books are hawked on the Internet, along with $80 humor software called SMILE (Subjective Multidimensional Interactive Laughter Evaluation). The Humor Project of Saratoga Springs, N.Y., offers funny business cards, a set of clown's noses (just like the ones used therapeutically by Robin Williams in the movie *Patch Adams*), and a smile on a stick (held in front of one's face to simulate mirth).

The consultants are sure that humor in the office is at a low point ("In spite of a good economy, people feel unsettled," said humor advisor Tom Dondore) or perhaps approaching a high point, with more emphasis on relaxation than in the go-go 1980s or early 1990s ("They didn't take humor seriously. Now we're realizing the value," said psychologist Terry Paulson).

Like all burgeoning fields, the humor biz has evolved a number of statistics. Robert Provine, a psychologist and neurobiologist at the University of Maryland, reports that speakers who are trying to be funny laugh 46 percent more than the people they are addressing, and people laugh 30 times more often when they are in a group than when they are alone.

One statistic is controversial: the number of times a healthy person should be expected to laugh each day. Laughter Club International, which sponsored World Laughter Day on January 10, believes that we all should laugh for 15 or 20 minutes a day. Some in the field recommend one risible outburst every five minutes. This would amount to more than two hundred laughs, chortles, or chuckles per day.

Loretta Laroche of Plymouth, Mass., perhaps the best-known humor consultant (she has had three shows on PBS) once was quoted as saying that healthy people laugh one hundred to four hundred times a day. Yukking it up at this recommended peak capacity would be awesome—24 times an hour, 2,800 times a week, 146,000 times a year. Even holding it down to five seconds per laugh would still take 200 hours a year. More expansive laughers, who devoted ten seconds to each laugh, would be committing themselves to guffawing for three weeks of 17-hour days each year. This would surely break the spirit of even the most dedicated merrymakers.

Ms. Laroche disavows the estimate attributed to her. This is good news for those of us who think laughter is a response to something funny, not a timed and calculated self-therapy. Skip the three weeks of planned laughter. Resume normal life.

THOU SHALT NOT COMMAND

These are dark days for the Ten Commandments. It's not just that people go around breaking them all the time (nothing new there), but that so few of us seem able to remember what these oft-broken rules actually say.

In 1994, a survey of 1,200 people, aged fifteen to thirty-five, found that most of those polled could name no more than two Commandments, and as the essayist Cullen Murphy writes, "they weren't too happy about some of the others when they were told about them."

Surely it is time to spruce up these 3,000-year-old Commandments and render them memorable and pleasing. Murphy pursues this idea gracefully in the November issue of the *Atlantic Monthly*, noting that a British commission is considering "punctuality," "patience," and "a sense of fair play." This sounds like Monty Python satirizing the grim decency of the British upper classes.

A tireless reporter, Murphy interviewed Charlton Heston on the subject (after all, he did play Moses) and was told that up-to-date commandments might include "do your best" and "keep your promises." It's hard to imagine any organized opposition to these proposed rules, though it's fair to say that Adolph Hitler lived up to both, working tirelessly at world conquest and doing nearly everything he promised in *Mein Kampf*.

It's possible to put together a modern, pro-impulse set of commandments based on advertising slogans—"Just do it," "Just be," "Sometimes you gotta break the rules," "Peel off inhibitions. Find your own road." The National Parenting Center asked children to suggest additional commandments. Among their ideas: "No bombing for the heck of it," "Thou shalt not address people by their color," and "No grabbing."

Naturally enough, some insist that any new set of commandments should be called the Ten Tentative Suggestions. This is the age of personal autonomy, and few of us really wish to be pushed around by upstart commanders and their would-be commands.

One way out of this search for command-free commandments is simply to focus on niceness. For example, on the Internet someone has posted the Ten Commandments of Human Relations. They include "speak to people," "smile at people," "be cordial," and "be friendly." This sounds uncontroversial, but some people resent being told to smile. For example, the sociologist Arlie Hochschild, in her book *The Managed Heart*, argues that flight attendants are unfairly manipulated by their bosses when they are told to smile at customers. So we clearly need commandments more inclusive and less controversial than "Smile at people." (Is smiling another unfunded mandate?)

New Age people have been working overtime to create fresh commandments. Shirley Maclaine offers two in her book *Dancing in the Light*: "Know that you are god" and "Know that you are the universe." Since everybody is god, she might want us to retain the original First Commandment as a celebration of self.

In his book, *The Second Ten Commandments*, Orion Moshe Kopelman says the original set of ten is an outmoded unicultural guide. The first of his new multicultural, worldwide commandments is "Maximize your time spent in flow and happiness." This rule may not make a lot of sense to people in southern Sudan or Kerala, unless they keep up with theories of personal growth or have spent some time in a California beach community.

Among the other Kopelman commandments are "Act true to your inner voice and fulfill your mission," "Develop greater self-acceptance by loving yourself unconditionally," and "Base your level of relationship commitments on bottom lines—what you can't live with and can't live without." The first nine commandments are naturally about the self, but Kopelman surprises us by devoting one to other people: "Repair the world by treating others reverently and fairly..."

Another way out of the commandment dilemma is to keep the negative and bossy language of the original ten, but add some modern loopholes and explanatory matter. For instance:

- Thou shalt not steal, but creative work on your tax return is OK.

- Thou shalt not kill, except during any of the trimesters or if the Pentagon says you must.

- Thou shalt not covet thy neighbor's goods, except in the sense that our whole economic system depends on the power of envy and wanting more.

- Thou shalt not commit adultery, except if thou art unhappy or if personal fulfillment points thee toward the new secretary in thine office. (An English writer suggests no adultery "unless, of course, thou art a close relative of her majesty the Queen.")

- "Honor thy mother or mothers, including thy birth, adoptive, step-, surrogate or same-sex-partner mothers, and honor thy father, thy mother's sperm donor or her casual inseminator, current whereabouts unknown.

My friend Roger Rosenblatt, when asked to name a new Number One commandment, said he was torn betweeen "If it feels good, do it" and "Always remember to place the shower curtain inside the tub." Of course, it's possible that he was joking, but given some of the other suggested commandments, who can tell?

THE UNMAKING OF CIVIC CULTURE

One night last summer I was the substitute host on one of the popular late-night radio talk shows here in New York. For four hours, the switchboard lit up with listeners eager to talk about the two hot-button topics of the evening: domestic violence and Afrocentrism. Calls rolled in from feminists, anti-feminist women, abused women, abused men, blacks and whites discussing the fine points of ancient Egypt and the treatment of blacks by white historians. With one exception (a man who calls in regularly to disparage blacks), the callers conducted a very serious, informed debate with great civility.

Why doesn't this happen more often? On most talk radio, about 75 percent of the listeners seem to phone in just to echo what has just been said. Most of the rest seem to be patrolling for group slights, or to point out that the guest is full of beans.

So far the political discussions on the on-line computer services haven't seemed much better. Last week in the U.S. News & World Report forum on CompuServe, an exasperated woman named Julie tapped out the message that "Reading some of the threads on line is like listening to my two teens arguing over anything and everything: "Did not...Did too...Did not...Did too...MOM!!"

Many social critics have tried to explain the low level of political discussion and debate. Some think the increasingly truculent and ideological tone of American politics makes debate seem too wearing and pointless: each side knows what the other will say, so why bother going through it again and again?

In his last book, *The Revolt of the Elites and the Betrayal of Democracy*, the late Christopher Lasch blamed the rise of television debate (which puts a premium on appearance and unflappability rather than on the substance of argument) and the rise of "commercial persuasion" (an increasingly cynical electorate comes to feel manipulated by PR people, lobbyists and advertising campaigns).

Jean Bethke Elshtain, in her new book, *Democracy on Trial*, makes a related point. Technology, she says, has brought us to the brink of a politics based on instant plebiscite: with telepolling and interactive television, politicians can respond to the majority's wishes (and whims) on any subject, "so there is no need for debate with one's fellow citizens on substantive questions. All that is required is a calculus of opinion."

This is a skewed form of democracy that fits the current atomized state of American society. Politics can be based on the offhand views of mostly semi-informed individuals sitting alone in front of the TV, randomly pushing buttons. But as Elshtain says, "A compilation of opinions does not make a civic culture; such a culture emerges only from a deliberative process."

Lasch argued that a citizenry can't be informed unless it argues. He wrote that only an impassioned political argument makes the arguer look hard for evidence that will back up or tear down his position. Until we have to defend our opinions in public, he said, they remain half-formed convictions based on random impressions: "We come to know our own minds only by explaining ourselves to others."

Many critics argue that the rise of state bureaucracies, converting citizens into clients, has eliminated the local meetings which served as seedbeds of public political argument. So has the rise of politics based on litigation, which downgrades all political argument not conducted in front of a judge. This has gone hand in hand with the "rights" revolution. Once a desire is positioned as a right, by definition it can't be challenged. It's a trump card, beyond debate.

A great many of these offenses against ordinary democracy have been conducted by the left, but the right has been guilty too, chiefly of importing strongly held moral positions directly into politics as assertions rather than as matters of debate. A conviction may be personal or religious, but it has to be defended rationally against people with different principles or there is no point in discussing it at all.

The hollowing out of our civic culture has many causes that help explain the decline of political debate. A crucial one is the rise of the therapeutic ethic. Starting in the 1960s, the nation's sense of itself has been deeply influenced by the rapid spread of therapies, encounter groups, self-help, the language of self-esteem and personal growth and an array of New Age notions, some of them quasi-religions based on the primacy of the self.

This has created a vast Oprahized culture obsessed with feelings and subjective, private experiences. In some ways this culture of therapy has positioned itself as the antidote for America's fragmentation and the decline of civic culture. It pushes young people into monitoring their own psyches, and away from environments where they might learn civic and political skills. And it tends to kill any chance for political debate by framing values as mere matters of personal taste. You like vanilla. I like butter-pecan.

It's important to reverse this process. We need a lot more emphasis on public discourse and common problems, and a lot less mooning about our individual psyches.

WHEN STABILITY WAS ALL THE RAGE

It's an article of faith among many Sixties people that the 1950s were a period of great fear, oppression, and unchecked Ozzie-and-Harrietism. Now these people must all make a collective mental note to avoid reading *The Lost City*, Alan Ehrenhalt's forward-looking and non-nostalgic book about the Fifties in Chicago.

It's a tribute to Ehrenhalt that he doesn't try to make his case about what the Fifties did well by talking only about suburbs. He studies one new suburb, but also two city neighborhoods, one black, one white, in the totally segregated, graft-ridden city of Boss Richard Daley.

The Fifties, famously safe and stable, were marked by a bland, centrist Eisenhowerish politics and a yearning for peace and quiet after two grueling decades of depression and war. (Hence the easily mocked cult of domesticity.) Ehrenhalt sees Chicago life then as built around very limited choices, long-lasting relationships, and a bustling communal life that presupposed rules, authority, and a strong sense of being rooted in neighborhood.

That rootedness meant clubs, saloon life, PTAs, union meetings, Holy Name societies and in the suburbs, service organizations, little leagues, and welcome wagons. Even under the appalling Jim Crow conditions in the Bronzeville ghetto on Chicago's Southside, community life flourished around churches, clubs, newspapers, and civic groups.

All that was swept away in the 1960s. The culture of the streets, the sidewalks, and the porches was chased indoors by the arrival of television and air-conditioning. Technology and the market economy multiplied choices and helped loosen neighborhood ties. And the cultural revolution of the '60s, hostile to all rules and authority, produced the hyperindividualism and the narrow generational worship of "rights" and "choice."

Ehrenhalt doesn't think the Fifties were any kind of Golden Age. He is quick to acknowledge the gains in freedom since the 1960s, particularly for minorities and women. His message is that there's no free lunch. The breaking of the implicit bargain of the Fifties—some loss of options and freedom in return for stability, order, and lasting relationships—has come at a high cost, including far higher levels of anxiety, isolation, and alienation than the Fifties ever knew.

Where commitments were once expected to be kept, husbands now feel free to run out on wives, parents on children, businesses on employees who make the mistake of turning fifty or fifty-five, and factories on the towns built around them. Moral and social decisions are whittled down to mere choices.

The needs of an expanding capitalism and a triumphant counter-culture coalesced around a view of life as an endless series of unfettered individual and ever-changing "choices" that were nobody's business except that of the consumer-chooser, responsible only to "do his own thing." And all choices were supposed to be treated with equal respect.

Now we have unlimited choice, but live in a culture dominated by "egotism, incivility, disloyalty," Ehrenhalt writes. Sixties ideas about freedom from authority, family, and traditional norms made their own hefty contribution to the current unraveling of the culture and our stunning rates of crime, violence, illegitimacy, drug use, and family break-up that few people think we can really do much about.

Ehrenhalt thinks the pendulum can swing back, but he flirts with a deep pessimism, implying that the hostility of his fellow baby-boomers toward any form of authority has gone so deep in the culture that America may not be able to revive any sense of legitimate authority until the boomers pass from the scene. "There is no easy way to have an orderly world without somebody making the rules by which order is preserved," Ehrenhalt writes. "Every dream of community in the absence of authority will turn out to be a pipe dream in the end."

This book is part of a large wave of commentary focusing on the social crisis and what to do about it. A lot of this commentary focuses on virtue. "It is evident that we are suffering from a grievous moral disorder...moral pathology would be more accurate," writes Gertrude Himmelfarb. Others point to the steady withdrawal from the civic order. David Blankenhorn sees the decline and fragmentation of the family as "inextricably linked to the decline of other institutions in civil society"—the ominous decline in voting (down 25 percent since the early '60s), PTA membership (down 50 percent in the same period), union membership, and participation in voluntary associations.

One of the current chorus of voices makes his case in clearly economic terms. In his new book, *Trust*, Francis Fukuyama, a social scientist at the RAND Corporation, says that America simply won't be able to compete in the international economy if it's civic culture is allowed to erode—it badly needs the trust generated in moral communities of shared value. "The ability to obey communal authority," he writes, as if echoing Ehrenhalt, "is the key to the success of the society.

This current commentary shows that the old debate about whether we are in real trouble is finally over. We are, and the debate is starting to focus on what to do.

THE PRICE IS WRONG

How brilliant is Ted Turner as a executive?

Well, as head of Turner Broadcasting, he was worth $7,011,904 in salary and other compensation over five years, 1990 through 1994.

If the sale of Turner Broadcasting to Time Warner goes through, Ted Turner will apparently acquire a great deal of additional executive value. Over the next five years, he will rake in 14 times as much executive compensation from Time Warner, according to figures published in the *New York Times*, or perhaps 27 times as much, according to an independent analysis.

Mark Landler reports in the *New York Times* that Turner is being showered with stock options—an extraordinary 2.2 million Time Warner shares over five years—to go along with an annual salary of $5 million and a long-term performance incentive worth $10 million a year.

The *Times* estimates that the package is worth at least $100 million, but the analyst said that with any kind of normal performance by Time Warner stock, the total value should be listed at $193 million or more. All this is in addition to the approximately $2.6 billion in Time Warner stock he will get from the sale.

"Steve Ross lives!" was the three-word summation of the analyst, Graef Crystal, a specialist in executive compensation and adjunct professor at the University of California at Berkeley's Haas School of Business.

He was referring to the late and raffish Steve Ross, once dubbed "the Babe Ruth of executive pay" by *Fortune* magazine for his hallmark trait of assembling staggering compensation packages for himself wherever he went.

From 1973 through 1989 Ross hauled in $275 million in compensation. By contemporary standards, this isn't all that stunning, but remember that Ross's record was set mostly in the dead-ball era of executive home runs, before the whole character of the game changed.

Like Turner, Ross displayed a sudden burst of value when he arrived at Time Warner—his 10-year contract, valued at $143 million, came on top of a $193 million windfall from the merger between his Warner Communications and Time Inc.

Ross's arrival quickly eroded the restrained and non-greedy culture of Time. In his book, *To the End of Time*, Richard Clurman says that the top honchos at Time gave themselves whopping numbers of options at the time of the merger and then agreed that their suddenly paltry million-dollar salaries "would have to be massively adjusted upward to take into account the disparity compared to Ross and the other Warner executives."

This is the now familiar game of financial leap-frogging, with another round possibly about to be set off by Ted Turner's haul. Crystal predicts it: "It's an unprecedented package and it sets up the irresistible impulse to offer Gerald Levin more money."

Levin, one of the Time executives stuck in the paltry million-dollar range in the pre-Ross era, is now company CEO and is up in the $21 million range of total compensation (at least for 1993, the year detailed in *Fortune* magazine's most recent survey). This raises a burning question: if Turner is worth $20 to $38 million annually as Number Two man in an enlarged Time Warner, what does that make Levin worth now as Number One?

Each of the great benchmarks of corporate compensation has set off predictable waves of envy and leap-frogging. These would include Roberto Goizueta's package of $56 million in shares (not options) from Coca Cola in 1991, the options on more than 1.4 million Enron shares that went to Kenneth Lay in 1994, and the more than $200 million Michael Eisner made in 1993, a year in which he cashed in some of his older Disney options.

Many corporate chiefs deserve what they get. The disturbing factor is that the top tier of executives now seems to constitute a class that's able to move ahead on its own, almost independent of its true economic function. Crystal's analysis of CEO compensation in 1994 shows that the take of top CEO's went up 12 percent for the year, while the wages of their workers went up only 3 percent, and income to shareholders rose only 2 percent.

Worse, the compensation of CEOs, in relation to the average worker, grows ever higher. Crystal's numbers show that in the mid-1970s, the U.S. showed a 39-to-1 dollar ratio between a corporation's most highly compensated executive and the average worker. His recent study of 292 CEOs who have held their current job for three years or more showed the ratio at 145-to-1 in 1992, 170-to-1 in 1993, and 187-to-1 last year.

These are combustible numbers. How long can any sane society tolerate an ever widening gap between the average worker and a new, self-enriching class of ultra-wealthy managers?

"Executive compensation is utterly out of control," says Crystal. "These people never look down, to see what the average worker gets. They never look across, to see how much less their counterparts in Europe and Japan get. They never look back, to see how far they have come. They just look ahead at what other people are getting and they want more."

In an envy-driven system such as this, does anybody think reform will arrive on its own?